EYE OF THE CONDOR

a novel by

SIDNEY HARRIS

First published by AuthorHouse 05/13/04

ISBN: 1-4184-7277-8 (e-book)
ISBN: 1-4184-3754-9 (Paperback)

Library of Congress Control Number: 2003099938

This book is printed on acid free paper.

Printed in the United States of America
Bloomington, IN

Author's Note

   This historical novel is a work of fiction roughly based on actual events which occurred in Bolivia during the period of 1933-1942. To add authenticity, I have used the names of real participants in some cases, such as Juan Lechin, Colonel German Busch, Colonel David Toro, and others. The disastrous defeats of the Chaco War, the huge losses of life among the Bolivian soldiers, the subsequent military junta, the Catavi massacre, and the bloody revolution of 1942, unfortunately all took place. However, the three main characters, Carlos Obregon, Ingrid Kunnert, and Ramon Sanchez, plus most others are fictional persons. All meetings, incidents and dialogue are imaginary. Any resemblance to actual persons, living or dead, is coincidental.

Prologue

Ocampo, Bolivia

May, 1933

The condor soared effortlessly at sixteen thousand feet above sea level, held aloft by the frigid air currents under its nine-foot wingspan. It glided without movement, suspended like a weightless black cross in the pale blue sky above the long Andean valley, scanning the bleak terrain two thousand feet below. Snow capped peaks towered majestically above the giant bird on both sides. Its sharp eyes spotted a movement on the valley floor, and the condor banked slowly in a huge circle.

Carlos Obregon stopped his work, bracing his calloused brown hands on the worn handle of his wooden foot plow, the same type that his Aymara ancestors had used for over eight hundred years, and tracked the bird's path through the clear atmosphere. Although the sun was behind him, he squinted at the brightness of the high snow and the sky. He knew the condor had seen something, observing that the circles were gradually decreasing, along with the altitude, marveling at the condor's ability to spot a prey from that height. His people blessed a newborn male son by saying, "May he have the eyes of the condor, the speed of the puma, and the patience of the llama."

Carlos took his eyes off the circling bird, now almost directly above him, to look for the prey. He was not afraid for himself.

Condors preferred dead carrion, and never attacked a grown man - a newborn sheep or alpaca maybe, more likely a sick hen or a rodent. Old stories, told at nighttime in hushed, feeble voices, spoke of condors that snatched babies from their cradles, bearing them aloft to rocky crags, never to be seen again, but Carlos was skeptical. His ancestors had thought the sun was borne across the sky by a giant condor every day, and he certainly didn't believe that.

His eyes searched the plowed field and found what he was seeking some fifty yards away. A wild hare, almost invisible against the brown earth, crouched without movement in the broken sod, its long ears flattened against its furry body. The hare sensed the presence of a predator, and hoped to go undetected by remaining motionless. An unwise tactic, thought Carlos, but perhaps the hare's den is too distant to risk a run for it.

The condor was now only one hundred yards above the ground, directly over the frightened hare, and descending quickly. Suddenly the hare broke into a mad dash, flinging clods of earth in the air as it wildly changed direction, searching desperately for shelter. The condor collapsed its wings and fell like a boulder. At the last minute it spread its wings to cushion the shock, but still hit the ground with an explosion of black feathers and dust. A wild piercing scream, like that of a woman, rent the air. Carlos did not know if the scream came from the condor, or the hare, or from another world.

As the dust settled and the blurred figures regained their identity, the condor stood with his wings half-folded, the stunned hare imprisoned under one talon, its soft body quivering. Carlos saw a flash of silver and red as the giant bird gutted the animal in one stroke. Perched on top of its dying prey, the condor turned and looked directly at Carlos, fixing him with a steady gaze for what seemed an eternity. Its eyes burned red in its ugly black head, like glowing coals in a bed of charcoal. Then the bird extended its massive wings in all their splendor, and rose regally into the air, carrying the dead hare aloft.

Carlos felt no pity for the hare. It had ventured too far from home, seeking something better, and had paid with its life. But the condor's stare bothered him.

In the old days, before Catholicism, his people had worshipped the condor. It was said that from its lofty heights in the sky, the condor could see forever, even into the future. His ancestors had glorified the massive bird as the god of destiny, able to forecast events to come. This must be an omen, thought Carlos, for he had never seen a condor so close before, so aggressive, and never had one stared at him as this bird had. Ten years ago, he would have asked the *kuraka* for the meaning, but the old diviner was now dead, gone to the land of perpetual water. Perhaps Carlos' mother would know how to interpret this sign.

While he pondered this, he saw a low cloud of dust rising on the dirt road that reached his village from the west. In the distance he could make out a brown truck with high sideboards, a type he had not seen before. He decided to stop his plowing and walk into the village, even though his work was not finished. Somehow he knew that the condor, its kill, and the brown truck were connected, and that his life was about to change.

BOOK I
THE CHACO
1933—1935

Chapter 1

He picked up a clod of earth and squeezed. The dry substance crumbled easily, leaving his hand covered with a fine dust colored silver white by the moonlight. *Tierra de mierda*, he cursed, dead from lack of water, lifeless, worthless, so different from my own land. A land where you either kill or get killed.

Carlos Obregon hated the Chaco. During the dry season, the scorching daytime temperatures turned his brain soft inside his head, like thick corn liquor slowly fermenting in a clay bowl, and he walked in a dizzy stupor, slurring his speech. The ground beneath his feet felt brittle and cracked like a shattered mirror, the searing heat tricked his eyes with false images, and even breathing became a chore. When the sun was overhead, he and his comrades-in-arms could do nothing but lie motionless in their tents, naked except for their sweat-soaked underclothes, cursing the war that brought them to this barren desert, and praying the bastard, foreign Lieutenant would leave them alone. Lizards and other small animals hid from the heat by burrowing into the dry earth, emerging cautiously at night. Only the poisonous snakes remained outside during the day, lazily coiled under dry, leafless bushes, eyes alert and bodies relaxed, waiting for the careless soldier.

A virtual hell on earth, the Chaco embraced one hundred thousand square miles of flat wasteland maliciously thrown between his homeland Bolivia and its enemy Paraguay by a perverse God. Shaped in the form of a rough arrowhead, its base rested solidly in the Bolivian foothills, but its tip pointed menacingly southeast to

Asuncion, the capital and heart of Paraguay. Stunted, thorny scrub brush, an occasional small forest of dwarf hardwoods, and cactus dotted the otherwise dry plain. There was nothing of value except the stands of quebracho trees lining the Pilcomayo and Paraguay rivers on its southern and eastern borders. Like the Chaco itself, the quebracho wood was hard and unyielding, difficult to carve into furniture and reluctant to give up its resin. The only inhabitants were a scattering of semi-nomadic Guarani Indians, now augmented by thousands of soldiers. Carlos could not understand why this land was worth fighting for, much less dying for.

A full-blooded Aymara Indian, Carlos loved the high Andes, with its clear, cold air and pure mountain streams. He came from a small farming village nested in a valley off the Bolivian Altiplano, the flat high plateau enclosed by the eastern and western mountain ranges. He liked working with the soil. At home he rose willingly before dawn, eager to be in the field. He would remove his sandals when hoeing, sinking his feet and toes into the moist, dark earth, sensing its richness, savoring its fertility. Chaco soil was different - arid and barren, permeated with the stench of desiccated plants, open latrines, and death.

Like his people, Carlos was short at five feet seven inches. His forehead slanted downward into a long, prominent nose with slightly flared nostrils. His thick, straight hair, parted on the left, shown black as a raven. His eyes, as dark as his hair, tilted subtly upwards at the outer corners. When he smiled, which wasn't very often, his white teeth contrasted with smooth bronze skin. A small dark mole on the left side of his strong chin marred an otherwise clear complexion. His chest, expanded to compensate for the rarified air at high altitudes, was overdeveloped for a man his size, while the muscles in his arms and legs were hard from long hours of farming. At twenty-five, Carlos was a handsome man, with the best features of his race.

Despite the cooler night air, fine beads of sweat coated his forehead and his armpits were soaked with perspiration. It was past midnight, and he had been on sentry duty for four hours, huddled in a small pit in advance and to the right of the main Bolivian trenches. A cramp in his right calf reminded him of the restrictions on his movements, and his fingers were numb from holding his rifle at the ready position. The toes on his left foot, constrained inside the stiff army boot, had gone to sleep, but he didn't dare take off the boot for fear of scorpions in the hole.

Two nights ago there had been a full moon, and the shrinking yellow globe still gave enough light to distinguish the terrain around him. He could see, but if the enemy were out there, they were watching him, too. He didn't like being out at night. In the Andes, when the sun fell, his people hurried into their homes, closing the door against the cold and the wind. The Aymaras believed that the night belongs to the Old Ones, mystical people who lived before the sun came to the earth, when the world was in continual darkness. They died when the first light arrived, but their spirits still came out at night to work the fields under the moon. It was not natural for a living person to be outside at this time.

His fear tonight was not of the Old Ones, but of the *Macheteros de la Muerte*, silent killers who relished their work. He shivered at the thought. This select group of hardened guerillas had been attacking outposts and sowing terror in the Bolivian troops for the last month. Natives of the Chaco, recruited from the nomadic tribes, they knew the area intimately. Operating in groups of four to six, they were capable of living off the land and behind enemy lines if needed. They preferred to work in the dark, and could move as quietly as the desert lizards. Carlos had seen what happened to sentries caught asleep by the *Macheteros*.

Although each guerilla carried a standard Army rifle, they favored the weapon which gave them their name - the machete. These yard-long knives, dull on one side, razor sharp on the other, served wonderfully for killing in silence. The dull side could stun, crack a skull, or break a neck. The sharp side severed arms, legs, and throats with quiet efficiency.

Carlos knew their trademarks. The necktie cut was a favorite. They slit the victim's throat below the chin, a long clean horizontal cut, and pulled his tongue through the opening. After a few hours, the tongue, swollen by death and heat, bloated and covered with flies, resembled a grotesque red necktie. At other times the *Macheteros* disemboweled their prey, pulling out the intestines and draping them over a bush. Carlos had seen one soldier with his severed penis and testicles bulging from his mouth, his unseeing eyes wide with shock, like a roasted pig stuffed with sausage. The victims were lucky if they were dead before these rites of the machete were performed.

Fear kept him alert. It was now well past midnight, and his six-hour tour ended at two in the morning. Sleep could wait until he returned to the safety of the trenches, after his replacement arrived. Carlos had been on edge all night, turning constantly in his foxhole, looking backward as well as forward. Several times he thought he saw shadows moving, but it could have been his fear playing tricks on him. He didn't like the small bushes which provided cover for anyone moving in the darkness. Since he dared not trust his vision, he strained his ears until his head hurt, forcing a heightened sensitivity to the night sounds, but these too betrayed him, for which noises were made by the crawling animals, and which by the crawling enemy? He smelled death, an obscene dark presence, moving about and fouling the night air.

At two-fifteen he looked at his watch. Something was wrong - his replacement had not arrived. His orders commanded him to stay until relieved, but relief had not come. At two-thirty he looked again at his watch. He knew the penalty for disobeying orders, so he remained in place. By three he was certain something was wrong, and decided to move.

Leaving the protection of his foxhole, Carlos followed the path he knew his replacement would have used. If he met him, together they could cover up for his abandoning his post. His eyes were accustomed to the darkness so he could follow the winding dirt trail easily. Nevertheless he moved slowly, in a crouch, holding his rifle level in front of him, safety released, finger on the trigger. He avoided the big shrubs, even if this meant leaving the path, for the dark shadows were good places for an ambush.

The trenches were two hundred yards in the rear, and Carlos had covered half the distance when he saw the crumpled figure. The body lay partially hidden in the shadow of a shrub, but the legs were clearly visible in the moonlight. Carlos froze and listened. Nothing. He looked on all sides around him. Again nothing. He let his eyes dwell on the shadow until he could distinguish the form of the fallen soldier. He approached carefully, entering the shadow slowly. Kneeling, he recognized his replacement. The dead man lay on his back, his throat sliced open. Blood covered the front of his tunic and soaked the ground on both sides. Flies crawled on the congealed dark blood, indicating he had been dead for a while.

Carlos gagged and stepped back from the corpse. At least the man died quickly. Probably stunned first, then his throat cut. His killers didn't stay long. No trademark. So they must be creeping forward to strike again.

Carlos moved quickly now, running in a low crouch. He was twenty yards from the trenches when his friend, Ramon Sanchez, on guard duty, challenged him. After identifying himself, Carlos asked urgently in a shaky voice, "The Sergeant? I need to see him."

"What's the matter, *compadre?*"

"My replacement. Dead, killed by *Macheteros*. They must be close by."

"Jesus! Did you see them?"

"No. They were in a hurry. No trademark. Where's the Sergeant?"

"At the dugout, checking on the machine gun."

The dugout, a small, man-made cave, served as a command post, ammunition depot, and sleeping quarters for the Company Commander, Lieutenant Kunnert. The company's only machine gun was mounted in front of the dugout, protected by a roof of quebracho logs, the hardest wood in the world. From its elevated position, the gun could cover a one hundred twenty degree semi-circle, firing over the heads of the defenders and providing them protection. In turn, the machine gun was shielded from an attacking force, which would have to break through the dug-in line of infantry forty yards in front of the gun.

"Wake up the others. I'll alert the Sergeant," Carlos said. He moved off in the darkness over familiar ground.

As he neared the machine gun emplacement, Carlos stopped, waiting to be challenged. He did not want to be shot in the dark by a jittery guard. But no challenge came, only a prolonged silence. Carlos moved more cautiously now, uncertain of his legs. The gray barrel of the machine gun jutted out from the blackness of its cover like a dismembered arm. He entered the defensive trench excavated in front of the dugout, then stopped to listen for any movement. He carried his rifle pointing forward at waist level, and moved slowly.

He tripped and fell. The noise of his fall exploded in the silence. Sweat broke out all over his face. He cursed under his breath, tried to stand, but found himself on top of an irregular shape. A body lay below him, face down and still warm. He groped for the shoulder with shaking hands and turned the corpse on its side. The Sergeant's lifeless eyes stared at him. From the awkward angle of his head, Carlos guessed the neck was broken.

Carlos regained his footing. A complete silence had returned. He moved slowly down the trench. This time he saw the body of the machine gunner before falling over it. His throat had been cut.

Carlos reached the closed wooden door which led into the dugout. Quietly, he applied pressure to the door, but it would not budge, locked from the inside. He tapped gently, not wanting to make a loud noise. No reply. He knocked more firmly, and called, "Lieutenant." A groggy voice answered from inside.

"Yes, who is it?"

"Corporal Obregon, Sir." He fought to control his voice.

He heard a rustling inside the dugout. Someone was moving.

"Stand back from the door where I can see you. Do you understand?"

"Yes, Sir."

The pale rays of a flashlight glowed through the cracks in the wooden door as Carlos moved backwards. The door swung open, and the light focused on his face, blinding him momentarily. When his vision returned, he made out the Lieutenant in his underwear, flashlight in his left hand, and a Luger pistol in his right hand pointed at Carlos' chest.

"What do you want, Corporal?"

"The enemy, Sir. They're about to attack."

Chapter 2

Only three and a half months before, Carlos had been plowing, turning the dark earth in preparation for planting, when the truck came to his village. Not that trucks were unusual - sometimes two or three trucks came to Ocampo the same week, even though the small pueblo was at the end of the valley and the last stop on the rutted, dirt road.

He picked up his worn poncho from the ground, along with his *chuno*, a woven wool cap, pointed at the top, with earflaps that tied under the chin. He didn't need them right now, but when the sun went down the temperature dropped quickly in the mountains. He slipped on his sandals, whose soles were made from pieces of old rubber tires, and fastened them to his feet by looping their thick leather straps around his bare ankles. He brushed the dirt from his dark wool pants, which ended just below his knees, exposing the dusty calves of his legs.

The walk into town took him thirty minutes, not a long walk for a young, healthy man. He followed a well worn dirt path which descended slightly, skirting several fields owned by Don Simon, fields waiting to be planted with potatoes or quinoa. Carlos was lucky. His family had their own plot of land, purchased with money sent by his father from the tin mines. Carlos did the heavy plowing, but the whole family helped with the harvest, working on their knees with crude knives to dig up the ripe tubers, or alternating with the scythe to cut the mature, brown grain.

They ate potatoes every day. His mother, Maria, prepared biscuits, porridge, soup, and puddings from the quinoa grain. The guinea pigs which his sister Segundina raised in the back yard, and the money his father sent, provided the essentials of life. Carlos smiled at his good fortune. Most other villagers spent their lives working for Don Simon, a miserly patron who paid poor wages.

Carlos walked slowly. He did not like to be hurried. As a farmer, he used the sun as his timepiece, the seasons as his calendar. For as long as he could remember, his life revolved around the crops. As a baby, his mother had carried him on her back, wrapped in a cotton cloth and held firm by a twisted wool shawl tied over her shoulders, while she worked the earth. When he became heavier, she placed him on the ground, swaddled in wool, while she did the harvesting.

By the time he was six, he was helping his mother, using his small hands to bury seed potatoes in the upturned earth, scattering grain through tiny fingers, assuming more and more responsibility as he grew. His father, who had left for the mines before Carlos was born, returned only one week a year, normally during the Christmas season. Carlos learned from his mother and from his neighbors never to plant when the moon is full or the sun has a halo. He knew that animals in heat and pregnant women, or women with the curse, should not be allowed into the field when dew is on the ground, for they brought plant disease. He could recognize the black spots on young potatoes which signaled a threatened crop, and knew to sprinkle ashes on the plants and place *muna* branches between them to contain the blight.

Despite the demands of the land, Carlos had managed to attend the local monastery school where Dominican monks had taught him to read, write, and pray. The fathers suspended lessons during planting and harvesting, for all the young Indians in Ocampo worked in the fields. Carlos was persistent, remaining in school when his classmates dropped out, and he was proud of his ability to read and write Spanish, even though he couldn't afford the newspaper from La Paz. He didn't even own a radio. He had no need for news from the outside; he knew his country was at war, but the fighting was somewhere far away, in a place called the Chaco.

A group of curious men had gathered around the brown truck by the time Carlos arrived at the town square. Unlike other trucks Carlos had seen, this one was all straight angles, flat metal joined together in the most graceless way. A bumper of heavy steel bars jutted out menacingly two feet in front of the truck itself, and a round winch encircled with dark metal cable perched in the center of the bumper. The broad hinged windshield opened outward, where it rested horizontally, a flat plane reflecting the afternoon sun. Slatted wooden sideboards enclosed the truck bed, empty except for two rough benches bolted to the sides, facing each other.

The villagers were talking with six enlisted men, young Indians dressed in wrinkled khaki uniforms with rifles slung nonchalantly over their shoulders. Carlos approached the group and listened.

"All men between seventeen and twenty-five," one of the young soldiers was saying. "The Lieutenant is with the Mayor now, making a list."

Carlos knew this included him, for he had turned twenty-five during the spring.

"How long will they be gone?" asked one of the older villagers.

"For as long as the war lasts," the young soldier responded, acting as spokesman and enjoying the chance to display his knowledge. "The war should have ended with a quick victory according to the politicians, but we have been fighting for over a year now."

"Why do they need our young men?" another villager asked. "They are not soldiers."

"The Army needs all the young men in Bolivia now," the soldier replied.

"Does that mean that we are losing?" the old man pressed on.

The young soldier looked at his companions, not wishing to say anything that might bring punishment upon him. "It means that the war is more difficult to win than the government thought," he responded.

"When will the men have to leave?" Carlos asked, interrupting the conversation.

15

"Tomorrow morning," answered the spokesman. The villagers looked at each other in silent shock, for planting had not yet begun.

"And will there be no exceptions?" Carlos questioned.

"We are at war," the young soldier replied, "and all must serve." He looked kindly at Carlos, as if understanding his plight.

Carlos left the group at the square and walked slowly home, his mind in turmoil, confused by the possibility of leaving Ocampo. He rarely left his village. Twice he had gone to a nearby town to sell the excess of an abundant potato crop. Recently he had traveled to the same town, at his mother's request, to see a matchmaker. He was happy here, tending his field, caring for his mother and sister, chewing coca with his friends on the fiesta days.

When he arrived home, he pushed back the wooden door and parted the ragged hanging cloth that kept the cold air out. Maria looked at him questioningly, for he never returned from the field before dusk, but she said nothing. Carlos was so disoriented he forgot to ask her about the condor he had seen earlier, the huge bird that had stared at him so long. He squatted in one corner of the room, his back resting against the mud wall, and closed his eyes. Two wrinkles crossed his forehead.

In the late afternoon a young mestizo officer came to his home, escorted by two of the Indian soldiers. The officer was about thirty years old, with dark, pomaded hair and a round, smooth face. His soft belly protruded over a shiny brown leather military belt, and his cold eyes were the same color as the belt, reflecting neither warmth nor sympathy.

"Lieutenant Roberto Gutierrez," he announced, opening the door without knocking. "Are you Carlos Obregon?"

Carlos rose and nodded.

The officer's chest puffed up like a little rooster. "Under the authority vested in me by President Salamanca, Commander-in-Chief of the Bolivian military, I inform you that you are hereby inducted into the Bolivian Army, and will report to the village square tomorrow morning at sunrise, for transport to the Chaco." He said it without feeling, as if he had done it a hundred times before, was tired of repeating himself, and wished to get it out quickly.

"*Patron*," began Carlos, using the term employed by the Indians when speaking to a superior, "my father is a miner at Catavi. My mother and sister are alone except for me. If I leave, who will work the field and provide food?"

The Lieutenant was clearly irritated by this waste of time. He looked at Maria and Segundina, who avoided his eyes and stared at the floor. "They must adapt. The young girl is strong enough. They can ask their neighbors for help."

"I am the only man in the family," Carlos repeated.

The Lieutenant was now annoyed. "Who cares? Your name is on the list and you must serve."

"But *Patron*," Carlos pleaded, "be reasonable. They may starve without me," indicating his mother and sister who remained silent in the background. The two young soldiers behind the Lieutenant looked on sympathetically.

The Lieutenant took a deep breath and shouted in Carlos' face, "Tomorrow morning! At sunrise! In the square! If not, we will come for you." He wheeled and strode out, pushing the two soldiers aside. They glanced at Carlos guiltily before hastening after the officer.

Carlos remained standing in the same place a long time. The women continued to look at the floor, and the silence became unbearable.

Later Carlos left the house without speaking, and went to seek advice from Father Augustin, the Dominican monk who had taught him at the local monastery school. Father Augustin was in his sixties, a thin, white haired man whose frail body was swallowed up by his black robes. Carlos had a special relationship with this servant of God who had been responsible for his education, and who had replaced his real father in times of crisis.

"*Padrecito*," Carlos began, "the soldiers have arrived. They will take all the young men for the war."

"I know, my son. I saw the truck pass."

"What shall I do, Padre? My mother and sister depend on me."

The old priest was silent at first, but then answered in a resigned voice, "You must go, Carlos."

"And if I go, Padre, must I also kill other men? You have taught me that killing is a sin, that I can lose my soul to *Huari* if I kill."

Father Augustin ignored this reference to the Aymara god of the underworld. Most of the Indians practiced a form of folk Catholicism, identifying their former local deities with Christian figures such as Satan. Four hundred years had passed since the first missionaries arrived in Bolivia, yet the Aymaras still clung to many of their ancient beliefs. Some of these old beliefs had been incorporated into their new Christianity, but others existed at a different level, contradicting the teaching of Jesus. He wondered if any European would ever understand the mind of an Indian.

When he first arrived in Ocampo thirty-seven years ago, a young priest fresh out of the seminary, Father Augustin did his best to teach the pure doctrine of his church, the message of the one true God. But despite his efforts, the Aymaras clung to their old deities. On the feast day of the Holy Mother, when Her elaborately dressed statue was carried from home to home, supporting roles were played by the condor, the puma, and the monkey, costumed dancers who followed her progress. A handful of parrot's feathers invoked more reverence than the wooden crucifix which graced the altar of the chapel. Before he was summoned to administer the last rites, other older and more mysterious rituals were performed on the dying, rituals calling forth gods who lived in the mountains and in the streams, gods who existed long before the Spaniards came, perhaps even before God's own Son walked the earth.

Father Augustin had given up his fight long ago against these heathen practices. He no longer lay awake at night, doubting his own efficacy, cursing his parishioners who practiced their double religion behind his back, and crying because his hatred was unworthy of one of God's representatives on earth. The fight had sapped his strength, leaving him exhausted and doubting.

He knew that Carlos was nervous and had used the name *Huari* without realizing it. He had posed a difficult question, and Father Augustin studied the protruding veins on the back of his left hand, rubbing the age spots with his right thumb. "The times are different now, my Son. There is a war."

"Are the Paraguayans evil men, Padre?" The young man searched for signs in the face of the man who represented God, as though his aged features would reveal the answer. Elderly men possessed more knowledge than the young.

"There is a war, Carlos. You must go and you must fight. If the time arrives, you must also kill."

"I don't want to go, Padre." Carlos' voice was emotional, strained.

Father Augustin looked into the eyes of the young man he had educated. He remembered the hopes he had for this boy who had worked so hard and learned so well. Although he had tried to disguise his feelings, Father Augustin had always favored Carlos, who was more intelligent than the other students, more sensitive, and more intense in his desire to learn. He had taught Carlos since he was six, heard his confessions since he was twelve. Now Carlos was twenty-five, and according to his confessions, still celibate. Father Augustin always thought Carlos would be a good candidate for the priesthood, although he knew his family depended on him and he could not be spared from the field. Now this young man was going to war, to be lost forever to the Almighty.

"*Padrecito, por favor,*" Carlos pleaded, "hide me here in the monastery. The soldiers will not think to look here. This is holy ground."

Father Augustin studied the anguished eyes, his heart moved by the despair within, and replied slowly, "You may hide here, in one of the vacant cells. But," his own eyes saddened, "if the soldiers come and ask for you, I cannot lie. I must tell them you are here and surrender you to them."

"Why, Padre?"

"Because it is my duty. I must obey the rules of my Order and the laws of the country."

Carlos dropped his eyes to the floor and mumbled, "I will come tonight, after dark, when no one will see me." He rose and left.

The following morning Lieutenant Gutierrez appeared at Carlos' home at eight fifteen, one hour after sunrise. Four enlisted men, rifles slung over their shoulders, accompanied him. Without knocking they pushed their way into the house, where the five men with their weapons filled the small room. Maria was sitting in front of the fire, and rose to meet them.

"Where is your son?" the Lieutenant demanded.

Maria spoke in a low voice to the earth floor, "I don't know."

"Don't lie to me, *Vieja*. Tell me where he is." He moved toward her, raising his right hand menacingly.

"I don't know," Maria whispered, her voice barely audible.

The Lieutenant drew back his hand as if to strike, and then saw Segundina standing in the door of the storage room, her youthful face distorted by fear. She was still dressed in the white cotton shift she had slept in. "Don't hit her! Please," she cried.

Lieutenant Gutierrez lowered his hand and studied the young girl, tears running down her smooth brown cheeks.

"Bring her to me," he ordered, pointing at the sixteen-year old. Two of the soldiers approached the girl, grabbed her by her upper arms and led her to the Lieutenant, who examined her more closely.

"If you won't tell us where your son is, *Vieja*, then maybe we will take your daughter instead. All five of us. Right here. In your home."

To emphasize his threat, he placed his hand on Segundina's right breast, already well formed despite her youth, and squeezed it roughly. He continued to fondle it as he looked at the mother. Segundina trembled in the soldiers' arms, too frightened to move, her legs weak with fear. The soldiers moved uneasily, studying the girl with widening eyes. The Lieutenant slipped his hand inside her shift and pushed it off her shoulder, exposing her breast fully. A wide brown areola encircled the erect nipple. The soldiers moved nervously, shifting their weight, and stared at the exposed breast. Maria looked at the ground in shame.

"This is your last chance, Woman." The Lieutenant moved his hand down between Segundina's legs and squeezed. Segundina felt his rough fingers searching through the thin cloth of her shift, probing and squeezing, for her most intimate parts. She began sobbing.

"Enough," said Maria, who was also weeping, but silently. "He is at the monastery. With Father Augustin."

The Lieutenant removed his hand. Beads of sweat ran down the foreheads of the four soldiers even though it was cold inside the room. Segundina's knees gave out from under her, and the two soldiers struggled to hold her up.

"Let her go," the Lieutenant ordered, and the girl collapsed on the floor, pulling her legs to her chest, her face buried in the dirt.

The Lieutenant turned and walked through the still open door. "Let's go," he shouted over his shoulder. The soldiers left slowly, breathing heavily, reluctant to take their eyes off the prostrate girl.

When they arrived at the monastery, the search party stopped outside the main gate in respect for the sanctuary. Lieutenant Gutierrez asked for Father Augustin and demanded that Carlos be brought to him. The elderly priest summoned Carlos from the cell where he had spent the night. As Carlos passed his former teacher, he stopped and looked accusingly at him. Father Augustin returned his gaze with moist eyes, sorrow written on his face, and raised his right hand in a blessing. "May God be with you, my son."

The moment Carlos passed through the monastery gate, two soldiers seized him. Lieutenant Gutierrez approached, a sneer on his lips, his nostrils flared. "So this is the coward who is afraid to fight for his country?" He sucked in his stomach, expanded his chest, and spat into Carlos' face.

Carlos lowered his head and the wet spittle ran down his nose, across his lips, and to his chin. Bile rose inside of him, acid filled his mouth. "My mother and sister," he mumbled in explanation.

"Fuck your mother and sister," the Lieutenant shouted in his face. "Straighten your back like a soldier. Hold your head up."

The officer walked behind Carlos, planted one knee in the center of his spine, and jerked Carlos' shoulders back with his two hands. An intense pain shot down Carlos' lower back as his neck straightened.

Carlos showed no outward emotion but his hatred for this mestizo officer was choking him. G-U-T-I-E-R-R-E-Z, he said to himself. Lieutenant Gutierrez. Someday you will pay for this.

"Take him away," the Lieutenant ordered. As Carlos turned, the officer kicked him viciously in the buttocks. Once, then again. "This is for cowards," he screamed.

"Hit him with your rifles," he ordered the soldiers, who obeyed slowly and tentatively, giving Carlos short little prods.

"Harder," Gutierrez shouted, "like this!" He grabbed a rifle from one of the soldiers and rammed it into Carlos' back. Carlos grunted and clenched his teeth, determined not to cry out. He would not give this pig the satisfaction of hearing him scream.

On the way from the monastery to the plaza, the soldiers jabbed Carlos with their weapons under the encouragement of the Lieutenant, who added his own kicks as the spirit moved him. Each time he was hit, Carlos said a letter of the Lieutenant's name to himself. By the time they arrived at the square, he had spelt the complete name five times, and it would stay with him forever.

He hobbled into the square covered with bruises, barely able to stand. Too weak to climb unassisted into the waiting truck, he was thrown upwards in a heap to join the other conscripts.

Two young villagers had run away during the night. In late morning Carlos heard shots in the distance. At noon the soldiers brought a dead eighteen-year old Indian back to his parents' home, dropping the lifeless body outside their door. By early afternoon the soldiers found the other missing man hiding at his grandparents' home. He, too, was marched to the plaza, suffering the same treatment as Carlos. The truck departed at dusk.

Chapter 3

The crowded truck bumped noisily down unpaved, narrow roads throughout the night, its passengers huddled together to keep warm. The six enlisted men sat in the back with the ten conscripts to prevent escape. Carlos lay crumpled on the truck bed, his back protesting each jolt of the truck. It was only the fourth time he had left Ocampo and his insecurity added to his physical discomfort. In his valley he knew each hill and mountain by name. They were his friends, an integral part of his existence, greeting him when he pushed open the door of his house in the early morning light, watching him as he labored in the field during the day, and singing to him as he walked home in the evenings. Now he was leaving these familiar places behind, forced to go against his will. He pulled his wool poncho close around him, tucked his chin into his chest, and tried to ignore the throbbing pain of his bruises.

Numbed by the cold and drowsy with sleep, he felt the truck climb and descend several times, turning constantly as it followed the sides of mountains. By sunrise the land had become more level; the truck forded a stream, and turned south. Carlos pushed himself up from the truck bed, then rose on sore legs to get his bearings. One of the soldiers shifted his rifle and looked at Carlos as if to warn him against any attempt to escape. Carlos knew that his swollen back and legs would never let him run far.

He let his eyes drift off to the landscape. They were on the Altiplano itself, enclosed by tall mountain ranges on both sides. Carlos removed his *chuno* both in awe and as a sign of respect for the

23

majestic snow capped peaks they passed, for he held a special reverence for the high mountains, which were called The Lords by his people. He started to say something to his companions but the same soldier pointed his rifle at him and motioned for Carlos to sit down. Carlos took a seat at the end of the hard wooden bench and let himself rock with the motion of the truck, willing himself to ignore the pain.

They traveled a full day and night down the long central plateau, where small, scattered clumps of wild brown grass grew on a flat plain of red earth. The cloudless sky overhead was immense, without limits, soaring forever. Carlos felt tiny and insignificant under this vast expanse of blue, framed by the glory of the Andes. Even the truck seemed to be swallowed by the immense sky and mountains. They passed herds of llamas, alpacas, sheep, cows, and an occasional homestead. The soil here was not as rich as in Ocampo, and more land was needed to support a family. The isolated houses were made of mud bricks, with attached walled enclosures for the animals. There were few people about; a solitary herder watching over a flock of llamas, or a lone farmer breaking ground with a wooden hand plow. The truck stopped only for the men to relieve themselves or to refuel, and drove through the night.

At noon of the following day Carlos could distinguish a change in his surroundings, even though they were still in the Altiplano. As they traveled further south, the land turned more barren, with even fewer houses and less agriculture. In the afternoon they passed the first of many tin mining towns, gray and unwelcoming, and Carlos thought of his father. He searched for signs that might indicate Catavi, where his father worked, but found none. All the towns appeared the same to him; unpaved streets, stores and houses of raw cement block, with no inhabitants in sight. Carlos realized then the sacrifice his father had made by giving up the beauty of Ocampo to toil in the mines.

The truck stopped at one of the mining towns, in front of a dingy general store, its fading painted sign almost illegible. The soldiers bought bread and oranges for the conscripts, their first meal since departing. Two poorly clothed Indian women hurried past with their shopping baskets, heads lowered, leaving behind an aura of poverty and sadness that remained long after they had disappeared from sight.

When nightfall came, the truck was again climbing and descending. Then Carlos sensed that the truck was descending more quickly, encountering more curves, throwing him against the other passengers. A warm, humid, and heavy atmosphere slowly replaced the crisp cold air of the Altiplano. By dawn they were in the Yungas, on the eastern slopes of the Andes, passing through small villages of reed houses, and Carlos saw banana plants for the first time. Orange and lemon groves alternated with fields of maize - crops which he had never seen in the higher altitudes. Lightly dressed Indians walked alongside the road, carrying produce in burlap sacks on their backs. Farmers working in the fields smiled and waved at the passing truck. By now the soldiers had relaxed, so Carlos and the other men waved back.

Finally, at mid-afternoon of the following day, the army vehicle reached the military base at Santa Cruz, the last town before the Chaco. The conscripts had eaten just one meal and had slept very little during four and a half days. Caked with dust from the unpaved roads, they jumped down from the truck on sore, wobbly legs. They were assigned bunks in a half-filled barracks and immediately fell asleep.

Carlos awoke at sunrise the next morning, with a gnawing hunger pain in his stomach. His chest felt heavy, as though it were collapsing inward on him.

"Having trouble breathing, *compadre?*"

Carlos rubbed his eyes and looked up into a long angular face, topped by curly black hair. The man sat on the bunk next to his, his left leg crossed over his right, bouncing with nervous energy.

"You'll get used to it. It's the lower altitude. Takes a while for your lungs and heart to adapt. More oxygen in the air here. We're only one thousand five hundred feet above sea level. You came from over twelve thousand feet."

"I have heard that the air in the lowlands is different, that Indians who come here from the Altiplano die."

"Not likely. The Army wants you alive to fight the Paraguayans."

"Who are you?" asked Carlos.

"I'm Ramon Sanchez. Private Ramon Sanchez. At your service." He stood up and executed an exaggerated military salute.

Carlos studied the soldier dressed in an ill-fitting khaki uniform of the Bolivian Army. Ramon was taller than Carlos, maybe five feet ten inches, slender, with a thin, straight nose and ready smile. His eyes were wide and playful. His well-defined features were those of a mestizo - part Indian and part Spanish - but a handsome mestizo. He appeared to be the same age as Carlos.

"I'm from La Paz. Arrived here two days ago. I sleep in the next bunk." He sat down and his leg started bouncing again.

Carlos lifted himself up on his cot and massaged the stiffness from his arms. The bruises on his back and legs were still swollen and painful. "What should I do now?" Carlos asked. "I'm starved."

"Wait. Just wait, *hombre*," Ramon replied, lounging back on his own cot. "Breakfast is at seven, but you won't enjoy it. Mush, brown bread, and coffee. Later today they'll issue you a uniform, some chocolate pots if you are lucky, because there aren't enough to go around. After that, we wait until the barracks is full before we begin our training. Probably be another two days. In the army, everything is wait, wait, and wait some more."

Carlos did not mind waiting; patience was a virtue among his people.

"I'll show you around later. We can't leave the camp, but we can walk inside the fence."

"What are chocolate pots?" Carlos asked.

Ramon laughed. "Knee boots. Army issue. They're a dirty chocolate color."

Ramon leaned forward and lowered his voice. "Look, when they issue the boots, take a pair even if they aren't your size. If they don't fit, you can trade them with someone. If not, you can sell them. I can help you with that. Understand?"

Carlos nodded.

"What size are you?"

Carlos shrugged. "I don't know."

Ramon pulled out a sheet of rough brown paper with black marks on it and laid it on the barracks' floor in front of Carlos. "Put your heel here," he ordered, indicating a long black mark at one end of the paper. Carlos placed his bare foot on the sheet.

Ramon looked at the marks on the paper and said, "You're a ten. Size ten. Okay?"

Carlos nodded again.

"Way you do it is listen to the sizes they have. Look, when you're in line, pay attention when they ask the men in front of you what their sizes are. If one of them says ten, and he doesn't get a pair, you ask for eleven. Better too big than too small."

When they finished breakfast, Carlos was issued his uniform and boots. The stiff new khaki shirt and pants felt awkward on his body, while the size ten, high-topped, brown leather boots held his feet imprisoned in a way he had never experienced before. Even with thick wool socks, the new boots chaffed his ankles and shins.

Nevertheless, he accepted Ramon's invitation to walk through the camp. Ramon kept up an incessant chatter during his tour, volunteering information without being asked. Before five minutes had passed, Carlos had learned that his guide was the son of a small store owner in La Paz. He had been taken by the Army because his father didn't have the right connections or enough money to pay off the officials, and was bitter that he had been inducted while many of his friends were still untouched.

They passed two tall, fair skinned officers lounging on the front steps of a brick mess hall, drinking coffee and talking. The officers wore dark gray wool uniforms, too heavy for the tropical climate, and high black leather boots. Ramon saluted and Carlos imitated him. Both officers ignored them and continued their conversation, speaking an unfamiliar language with a harsh guttural accent.

When they were out of hearing range, Carlos asked, "Who are they?"

"Germans," answered Ramon. "German officers. You know, from Europe." He studied Carlos to see if he understood. "There are as many of them here at Santa Cruz as Bolivian officers, maybe more. You'll see."

"Why are they here? What are German officers doing in Bolivia?" Carlos asked.

"The German Army has been training our military for twenty years now, *compadre*. They're the most professional fighters in the world. They're here to help us beat the Paraguayans. Be careful, though. They're bastards about discipline. Strict as hell."

"Where are our own officers?"

"Out in the field. You won't like them any better."

"Why not?"

"Nobody with any brains becomes a military officer in Bolivia. Most of our officers joined the Army because they couldn't do anything else, or they were packed off to the Military College at La Paz by parents who wanted them out of the way. The pay is miserable. They're like me, middle-class mestizos. But they can't get ahead, because the top ranks are all political appointees. It's who you know. Having a store is better."

"Maybe they'll get their chance now, with the war," Carlos observed.

Ramon laughed. "I doubt it. With General Kundt now heading up the Army, most of the training is handled by Germans. They'll probably get the best command assignments too. After waiting forty years for a war, our poor officers are getting fucked by the Germans." He laughed again.

"But I wouldn't worry about the officers," Ramon continued. "They don't know we exist. Our problem is with the sergeants and corporals. They're the most dangerous. These guys are all failures in civilian life, incapable of earning a living. Most of them are drunks."

"Why would they want to be in the army, then? Doesn't it have too many rules?" asked Carlos.

"Because they are stupid bastards," answered Ramon. "The army is the only place where they can feel important. They get kicked around by the officers, so they take it out on us. And remember, there is nothing lower than a private in the Bolivian Army."

"What do you mean?"

"I mean, be prepared for the worst. You lost your rights when you got here. Forget your pride, and eat shit if they tell you to eat shit. Don't ever argue with a sergeant or corporal. They're devils in dishing out punishment, unless you have something to bribe them with. How much money did you bring with you?"

Carlos looked surprised. "None," he answered, and Ramon shook his head slowly, with pity.

Carlos' past had taught him humility. He knew there were different classes in society, and his was the lowest, even in Ocampo. When he went to the general store to buy supplies, he had to wait patiently while the mestizo owner served those with mixed blood first. Even Father Augustin would interrupt his classes for young Indians to attend to the spiritual needs of Don Simon. It was a way of life. Therefore Carlos accepted Ramon's explanation of the military system with stoicism. He would keep quiet in front of officers, listen carefully, and do whatever he was told to do without complaint.

Over the next two days conscripts filled the barracks. Truckloads of farmers, herders, and day laborers from small Andean villages arrived regularly, depositing their dusty cargos of unschooled, silent, and sullen Indians. When they talked among themselves, their conversations were hushed, spoken with lowered voices. Other trucks brought workers from the tin mines, young men who appeared older than their years from having worked underground, who complained loudly and bitterly at having been taken from their jobs. Foreign workers from Chile and Argentina had been imported to replace the younger Bolivian miners for the duration of the war.

There were a few conscripts from the cities, mestizos like Ramon, whose fathers lacked the influence to keep them from serving. The conscripts who came from La Paz, the capital, were the most vociferous and the best informed regarding the war, while the Indian farmers from the Altiplano, such as Carlos, were silent and woefully ignorant.

"Why are we fighting?" Carlos asked Ramon the second day.

"Because we want the Chaco, *compadre*," Ramon answered, "and so do the Paraguayans."

"But who does it belong to?" Carlos inquired.

"Who knows? The Spaniards never drew any boundaries during Colonial times. After Independence, nobody cared. The Chaco didn't have any riches or any people. So the borders were never fixed."

This struck Carlos as strange, for each small parcel of land around Ocampo was clearly marked and owned by someone. Land was too precious to leave untended.

29

"Why does Bolivia want it now?" Carlos insisted.

"Oil, *compadre*, oil." Ramon spread his hands wide to indicate abundance. "Everyone thinks there may be a sea of oil under that barren land. Ever since Standard Oil hit their first well in the Western Chaco ten years ago, the two governments have been at each others' throats. Both our country and Paraguay fell all over themselves building garrisons in the area. *Fortines* they're called, little forts. To establish that they owned the land. Soon there were so many garrisons that they overlapped, and then the shooting began."

Carlos was impressed with Ramon's knowledge. "Are we winning?"

Ramon laughed, a short bitter laugh. "We should be, but we aren't. We've been losing ground and men since the war started over a year ago. It's in all the papers. Now President Salamanca has brought a General from Germany to run the war. General Kundt knows our soldiers because he headed the German Military Mission in Bolivia before the war. Things should change now."

Ramon did not mention that the General had been in Bolivia for six months and had already lost over three thousand men while trying unsuccessfully to break the Paraguayan lines, which was why men like Carlos and himself were being inducted into the Army. The regular Army had been weakened if not destroyed, and Bolivia needed fresh troops, troops to support a second major offensive. And the men were pouring into the Chaco. The new conscripts had two things in common: they were from the Altiplano and they knew nothing about combat. Training began on the fourth day.

Chapter 4

Luis Obregon awoke coughing and soaked with sweat for the third time. His chest felt as if it was filled with stones. He turned in his small cot, careful not to lose the rough wool blanket that served as his only cover. I am dying, he thought.

Luis had worked in the Catavi tin mines long enough to recognize the symptoms of the coughing disease. No miner escaped if he labored continuously in the underground tunnels, with their humid walls and poisoned air. If the cave-ins, the explosions, or the methane gas did not kill you first, there was always the coughing disease lying in wait. The mine devoured men like a hog eats swill, greedily but without enjoyment, always hungry for more. None of his friends who had started with him thirty years ago was still alive. Luis crossed himself in bed and thanked the Virgin Mother for protecting him this long.

Once the coughing came several times during the night, the illness progressed quickly; your body would swell; it was difficult to urinate, and the muscles faded away. The mine owners sent you home when you were unable to work the full twelve-hour shift. The coughing became worse, the chest heavier, and your body weakened, until finally you no longer had the strength to breathe. It could be two months or two years - no more. Luis didn't want to die, but he looked forward to going back to his village, Ocampo. He knew that Maria and Segundina would take good care of him.

The clear air and clean water of the Andes would slow the sickness. The warmth of their small two-room home, with the cooking fire always burning in one corner, would be a relief from the cold concrete barracks he shared with forty-six other miners. He longed to taste the hot stew of guinea pig and potatoes that his wife prepared so lovingly, adding wild herbs to draw out the flavor. He wanted to hear the laugh of his sixteen year-old daughter, so full of life and expectations, and to embrace his son, Carlos, so strong and solid. Luis had labored at the tin mine since he was fifteen. The youngest of seven children, there had been no work for him in the village. His older brothers were hired by Don Simon, the local landlord, but Luis was unable to find work. He helped his father while attending the only school in Ocampo, run by Dominican priests. The friars had taught him not only to read and write, but also every story in the Holy Book. Like his classmates, Luis loved the Little Virgin more than any other person in the Bible. She was kind and compassionate; she took care of the sick; and she watched over the crops. Luis could visualize her with dark skin, high cheekbones, and braided, black hair like that of his own mother. After eight years of study Luis left for Catavi and the tin mines.

The Catavi mine in Bolivia was the single biggest producer of tin ore in the world. Luis knew a little of its history. In 1894 a struggling young clerk in a general store, Simon Patino, discovered the tin vein in the Eastern Cordillera of the Bolivian Andes which would make him one of the ten wealthiest men on the planet. Patino himself helped dig the first tunnel in the side of the barren brown mountain named Catavi, bringing the ore out on his back. Now he lived in a manor house outside London.

Forty years later twelve main tunnels perforated the mountain. Other corridors and smaller feeder tunnels branched off the main passages, penetrating even deeper and gutting the mountain. Luis had worked in all of them at one time or another. The non-ore bearing earth, excavated to make the tunnels, spread across the lower slopes as if the mountain had vomited a brown pile of filth.

From the beginning, Luis had been different from the other miners. As a boy, he sent home one-quarter of his monthly paycheck to his parents. On one vacation in Ocampo, he married a village girl. Thereafter, he sent the money to his wife, never missing a single month. His family and friends helped him build the square mud brick building with thatched roof which served as his home. Later he had added a storeroom with the help of his son, Carlos.

Luis' family had never been without food. Using his savings, they bought a small parcel of land a mile from the village. This, in addition to the money he sent, was enough to provide for them.

Luis considered the future. When I die, he thought, my son Carlos will have to take responsibility for the family. He knows how to till the earth, how to plant, and how to harvest. He has always worked hard and loves his mother and sister. He is a good boy, like me in many ways.

Luis was proud that he was not paying interest to the company store. The rent for the cot, which he shared with a night shift worker, was deducted from his paycheck. Since he ate simply, his expenditures for food were minimal. He did not drink alcohol and he did not frequent the prostitutes like the other miners, who were broke within twenty-four hours after getting their pay. He did chew coca, for no one could work underground without it. His other indulgence was fresh milk, which he bought daily. Perhaps that was why the lung disease had been so long in coming.

At forty-six, Luis looked like a man of seventy. His once thick body had become thin, although his muscles and bones retained their strength. He walked leaning forward, bent at the waist from years of carrying heavy ore on his back, making him appear even shorter than his five feet six inches. His once jet black hair was now white and thin, his face wrinkled from strain rather than age. His eyes were dark, but kind.

The other miners loved Luis. He was the oldest working miner at Catavi, and always ready to help. Not with money, for his family needed every cent, but with advice when a miner was new, or care when one was ill. They respected his practical wisdom, which had helped many survive the grueling years underground. Luis had tended many miners with the lung disease, rubbing alcohol on their backs and helping them drink llama blood, which had restorative powers; but he had never seen one recover. He taught them how to hide their illness from the shift boss until they could no longer work.

Now his turn had come. Luis knew he would be able to work another month, maybe two, before the shift boss discovered his illness, but he wanted to spend every remaining moment with his family. He had lived longer than most, and was prepared to die if this was the Holy Mother's wish.

Besides, Catavi was in turmoil now. Luis felt uncomfortable with the changes that had taken place since the war began. One-third of his co-workers had been conscripted and sent to the Chaco, and still the owners insisted on more tin for the war effort. Agitators were among the miners, talking against the owners, the government, and the military. Last night there had been a big rally, and his friends insisted he attend. He had heard fiery speeches about organizing a union to correct injustices at the mine, and he sensed trouble.

Luis arose slowly. It was early, but he could not sleep. He put on a faded flannel shirt and worn burlap pants, then slipped on his sandals. He took an old woolen poncho from a nail on the wall, and placed it over his head. Finally he donned a woven wool cap. On his way out, he placed several coca leaves in his mouth and began chewing. Later he would add a pinch of ground limestone to help extract the cocaine. Then he would fix the wad between his gum and his right cheek, keeping it there throughout the day. The resulting numbness would lessen the pain of his work.

"Luis."

He heard his name as he went down the barracks' steps. Looking up, he saw a man in his early thirties. Squinting in the early morning light, he recognized the man as one of the speakers at the rally the previous evening.

"I'm Juan Lechin."

He was of medium build and average height, slightly taller than Luis. Although dressed casually, his garments and his hands were too clean to be a miner, his voice too clear and confident. From his light brown skin and wavy hair, Luis recognized Juan as a mestizo.

"I heard you at the rally last night," Luis said, speaking each word slowly as was his custom.

"Good. They told me you were there. That's why I came to see you." Juan spoke rapidly, with the clear diction of an ex-law student from the University of La Paz.

"Why me? I am a simple worker, not even a shift boss."

"You are the oldest worker here at Catavi, Luis. You have been here longer than any other. The workers respect you."

"Yes, I have been here longer than the others. I have been lucky." Luis remembered his coughing attacks during the night.

"Luis, we need to form a committee of workers to start organizing a union. We need your help."

"I know nothing of politics."

"This is not politics, Luis. This is a union! An organization which will represent all the miners and bargain with the owners. It's time to stop the abuses here at Catavi. You know that."

Luis lowered his voice. "I know nothing. In the past when there were troubled times like this, miners have been fired and others have disappeared. I know nothing."

"Luis, I didn't say that it would be easy. Setting up a union here will be a hard job, and dangerous for the organizers. But working conditions can't continue this way. They are inhuman." Juan paused to rub his forearm.

"How many hours a day do you work?"

"Twelve, like everyone else," Luis replied.

"In Europe and the U.S. unionized miners work only eight hours a day. They are healthier. They see more of their families, and more jobs are created. How many days of vacation do you get each year?"

"One week, like everyone else. I go home to my village and family."

"Luis, you've been working here for thirty years. My God, don't you think you deserve more than seven days a year?"

"I don't know. It is what I have always had."

"Have you seen any efforts to improve safety at the mine?" asked Juan.

"We must follow the tin veins. Sometimes they turn and come too close to another tunnel. Then there is a cave-in." Thinking of his work, Luis added some more coca leaves to the wad in his mouth.

"Luis, do you know how many workers have died from dynamite blasts, cave-ins, and gas poisoning here at Catavi in the last five years? Over two thousand men! These were workers just like you; some were your friends. And the company pays only for a wooden coffin and transport back home. That's disgusting."

The older man looked at the ground. It had always been like this.

"What if you get sick, Luis? Does the company provide a doctor or give you medicine?"

"Nothing," Luis murmured.

"And the company store, Luis? How many miners owe more interest than they can pay, and will never pay off their debts in their lifetime?" Juan was intense now, leaning forward and coming closer.

"Most of them," replied Luis.

"Then wake up! We can change all this. As individuals we are weak, but as a union, we will be strong. We can force the owners to change."

"You are not a miner," Luis interjected.

"No, I'm not. But I'm one of you. I'm a lawyer from La Paz who doesn't want to see Bolivian workers treated like animals."

"Are you a socialist?" Luis asked, for he had heard the speakers use this word last night.

"Yes, I am. Do you know what that means?"

"No."

Juan explained to Luis the meaning of socialism. He used simple language, and tried to limit the concepts. He omitted the more advanced ideas, such as state ownership of industry, for he didn't want to confuse the older man. He stressed that socialists represented the workers, and were determined that they would be paid fairly and be given good working conditions. He talked for a quarter hour.

Luis reflected silently for several minutes. Neither man spoke. Then Luis blurted out another question which had troubled him.

"Are you an atheist?"

Juan laughed. "Of course not. They told you that, didn't they? Atheists, Antichrists, Masons, Devil-Worshippers. These are just some of the names they use. Don't believe them. I say confession once a week and will be married by a priest when I find the right woman. Trust me."

After another pause, Juan continued, "Luis, we need you on the organizing committee. Your presence will help us. The men respect you. Some four hundred miners will probably follow you alone. With the other members and our help, the committee will be able to persuade at least half the work force to join the union. The first meeting is tonight at 8:00 p.m. at the Salazar home. Will you come?"

"I don't know," Luis replied. "I must think about it."

"Don't fail us. Be there!"

Juan shook hands and left as the first rays of sun appeared over the mountains to the east. Luis could hear the stirrings of his co-workers in the barracks. His mind returned to the peace of his village and the warmth of his home. He had been away too long, and he was dying.

The day shift was over. Luis had worked his branch tunnel alone as always, first breaking apart the bigger rocks with his pick, then gathering the ore into a burlap sack. The ore sack had three straps, two which passed over his shoulders, and one which crossed his forehead. The ceiling in the feeder tunnel was low, so he crawled the first part, and then walked doubled over for thirty-five yards until he reached the main tunnel and the ore carts. It was work which destroyed men, but he was accustomed to it. The coca numbed his body, helping him to resist the heat and the fatigue, and ignore the gnawing hunger pain in his stomach. During the day he fought off the urge to cough until he returned to the feeder tunnel, then suffocated the noise with his burlap bag, so the shift boss could not hear him.

He was exhausted when he took the mine elevator to the surface. As the wire cage lift disgorged its dirty occupants, the second shift pushed in to take their places. Walking away from the mine opening, Luis felt a hand on his left elbow. It was his shift boss.

"Franco wants to see you."

"Why?" asked Luis.

The boss didn't answer, but led him toward the rough wooden one-room building where the shift supervisor had his office. Luis knew Franco and didn't like him. Franco was a young Indian who had risen quickly in the mining company. His large size and brute force had attracted the attention of the owners. He worked in the branch tunnels for only two years before becoming a shift boss. As a shift boss, he drove the other miners mercilessly to increase their daily ore output. He was said to have broken one man's leg, and killed another. There were rumors of other deaths caused by Franco. He reported people in his crew immediately when he suspected the lung disease. At the age of thirty he had been made Supervisor of the day shift at tunnel #6, where Luis now worked. He was rumored to have a network of informers among the mine workers.

When they entered the Supervisor's office, the shift boss left Luis in front of the wooden table which served as Franco's desk. He stepped back out of the light given by a single overhead lamp, blocking the only door. Franco was seated on a wooden stool. There were no papers on the desk. A lone rusty metal file cabinet decorated the corner of the room.

"*Ola, Viejo*," said Franco. He didn't rise or extend his hand.

Luis did not reply. His Indian ancestry and his experience had taught him to remain quiet in front of authority. His head was lowered, but he could see Franco's oily face. His eyes are small, thought Luis, like those of a pig.

"I understand that you attended the rally last night." It was a statement, not a question. Luis remained silent.

"You have been talking with Juan Lechin, too. We know. We know everything."

Luis shifted his weight, but still did not speak.

"We don't like Lechin and his socialist agitators. They are trouble." Franco hesitated, then went on, "Besides, they are atheists; they spit on our Holy Mother. They would undress her and rape her if they could."

Luis was shocked by this image and crossed himself. He raised his head slightly, and mumbled, "Perhaps that is not true."

Franco sprang from his seat, "Don't argue with me, Old Man. We know what they are." He came around the table and stood in front of Luis, towering over him.

Luis fell silent again. The man at the door had not moved or spoken.

"Do you want to keep your job here at Catavi, *Viejo*?" Franco asked.

"Yes," mumbled Luis.

"Do you want to be killed, *Viejo*? I know how to make that happen. Would you like a pick in the back of your skull when you are bent over collecting ore? Or would you prefer to drown slowly with your face pressed into the mud on the mine floor? Would you like any of these, *Viejo*?"

"No," replied Luis softly.

38

"Then you must stop all contact with these anarchists, these rabble rousers. You will not attend the meeting at the Salazar house tonight. You see, we know everything. Do you understand? You will not attend."

Luis hesitated, then murmured, "I don't know."

Franco reacted like a wild animal. His powerful fist smashed first into Luis' stomach, bowing him over. Then Franco hit Luis in the face to straighten him up. When he kicked Luis in the groin, the older man collapsed on the floor in pain.

"You Old Bastard! That's the wrong answer. You will not go to the meeting, do you understand?" To emphasize his point, Franco kicked the old man viciously in the head. Luis lay curled on the wooden floor, moaning. His mouth was full of blood. Two teeth were missing. His head felt as if a heavy rock pressed down on it.

"Enough. I have work to do. But understand, you *Hijo de Puta*, you set foot in the Salazar house tonight and you are dead." Franco turned to the shift boss, "Pick him up and throw him out."

The shift boss left his position at the door, grabbed Luis under both arms, and lifted him to his feet. The boss then dragged Luis through the door and down the three wooden steps of the office. He laid the old miner on the barren ground next to a water faucet at the side of the building. There was no one around. The first shift had left and the night shift was in the mine.

"Pay attention, Luis. Franco means what he said." The shift boss left him there.

Luis lay on the cold ground for a long time. His groin ached and pain coursed through his body with the slightest movement. The blood in his mouth became sticky sweet, and he felt he might vomit. He managed to spit two broken teeth out on the ground, and felt another loose tooth next to the missing ones.

As he lay there, he thought of Ocampo, of Maria, Segundina, and Carlos. He thought of the early morning sun rising over the Andes, and the warmth it brought by midday. He remembered his wedding, and the heat of his wife under the blankets. How beautiful little Segundina had been when she was born, falling into the midwife's hands like a wet flower, ready to blossom. What a good boy Carlos is, tending the crops, taking his father's place all these

39

years. I am a lucky man. My life has been blessed by the Little Virgin.

Luis thought of the Blessed Mother, and how she looked after all her children in this world, just as she had taken care of the Christ Child. Slowly her image became clear before him. He could see the soft folds of her robe, then her kind brown eyes. She smiled at him. Luis felt the warmth of her smile, and he smiled back. They loved and understood one another. Then he asked her a question.

Hesitantly he rose to one knee. He knelt next to the faucet and washed his mouth, spitting a mixture of blood and water onto the hard ground. He splashed more water on his face and repeated this until he felt capable of standing. The pain was still there. His testicles were swollen and burned as if they were on fire. When he tried to walk, pain shot up his left side.

Luis limped slowly, tentatively at first, then with more determination. As he moved, his back straightened. He lifted his eyes to make sure of the direction. He was on his way to the Salazar house.

Chapter 5

Lieutenant Manfred Kunnert stood erect, shoulders back, chin up, looking down his aristocratic nose as his first class of Bolivian conscripts filed into the classroom. Studying the men, his heart sank. The new soldiers shuffled through the door one by one, dragging their feet and moving listlessly. An overweight Sergeant shouted at them, yanked them by their arms, pushed them, but they could not seem to understand his simple order to take a seat on the rough wooden benches. Instead they milled around with blank expressions, like cattle in an unfamiliar pasture.

Immaculate in his own tailored uniform, Manfred was shocked by their ill-fitting clothes: tunics too big, pants that either lapped over their boots or left their ankles exposed, and silly round leather-brimmed caps. In other circumstances, he might have laughed, even roared. One-fourth of the recruits still wore sandals, revealing dirt-caked feet. An odor of unwashed bodies flooded into the room along with the men, intensifying as the room filled. Manfred fought back the urge to cover his nose, and set his jaw more rigid. After what seemed an inexcusable waste of time to Manfred, the conscripts finally found their seats.

The perspiring Sergeant stopped his shouting, turned to Manfred and saluted. "Ready, Sir."

Manfred studied the rows of brown, impassive faces before him, searching for some sign of emotion, of enthusiasm, of curiosity, a spark of some kind, but found nothing. A bulge in the cheek of almost every man indicated that he was chewing coca. Filthy habit, Manfred thought. No wonder they're lethargic.

He strode to the front row, took a deep breath, clasped his hands behind his back, and announced in a strong voice, "I'm Lieutenant Kunnert, and I will be your classroom instructor here at Santa Cruz." He paused to let that sink in, then continued, "How many of you men have ever served in the army? Raise your hands if you have prior military experience."

No hands came up. Manfred looked at the Sergeant who shrugged his shoulders.

"How many of you can read or write?" Manfred continued.

Again no hands appeared. Manfred looked at the Sergeant, who stepped forward and shouted threateningly, "How many of you can read or write? Get your hands up."

Slowly a few hands rose, scattered throughout the classroom.

"Those of you who can only sign your name, put your hands back down," shouted the Sergeant.

Immediately half of the raised hands dropped. The Sergeant made a quick count, and turned to the Lieutenant.

"Looks like three men, Sir," he stated proudly.

"Thank you, Sergeant," replied Manfred, turning his back to the class and facing the chalkboard. Good God, he thought, how did I let myself get talked into this? There is no way I can possibly make this group of pathetic, illiterate Indians into an efficient, aggressive combat unit. This is the most unrealistic task I have ever been assigned. To keep his emotions under control, he picked up a piece of chalk and printed large letters on the chalkboard, fully aware that only three men at best would understand them, while his mind reviewed the circumstances that had led him to Bolivia.

Manfred had been trained to hide his feelings, no matter how strong. Uncontrolled emotions were a sign of weakness in his family. The oldest son of titled landowners, a Baron in his own right, he knew that appearances were important. The Kunnerts of Mecklenburg were well known and admired, a solid family that had produced some of Germany's best leaders. As the eldest son, he was expected to serve in the German military as a career officer, the same as his Uncle Gerhard and many other Kunnerts over the past two centuries. The younger brothers oversaw the land, became politicians, lawyers, or clergymen. The oldest sons became officers - good officers.

This suited Manfred well, for he was a tall, muscular blond who had shown his aggressive nature even as a child. He loved the strict discipline of officer training in Germany with its channeled violence. He excelled in dueling and was an outstanding competitive horseman. The pageantry of flags, the glitter of polished brass buttons, and the strident marches of military bands, had excited him since he was a boy. The military was in his blood and he loved it.

Now thirty-two, he had been too young to participate in World War I, although his officer training started before the war ended. Like the other young officers in his class, he was convinced that Germany had been tricked into accepting an early armistice, and he had wanted passionately for the conflict to continue. He fantasized a different outcome to the war if only he had been able to lead his own German troops into battle.

Much to his disappointment, Manfred received his commission as a second lieutenant after the armistice was signed. Instead of commanding men in battle, his initial work was administrative. His Uncle Gerhard, now a Colonel, requested that Manfred be assigned to his staff in Berlin. For the next three years Manfred handled requests for pensions from war widows, indemnification for crippled veterans, and support for orphaned military children. It was frustrating and tedious work, grinding salt into the wound of Germany's defeat.

In 1926, Manfred received a training assignment at the Augsburg base, west of Munich. Working with young German volunteers who were untainted by the last war, he began to enjoy his career once again. The young men shared his goal of a reborn German Army, one that would embody the strength and glory of Bismarck's Germany and erase the humiliation of the last conflict. Enthused once more, he tackled his new assignment with vigor, working hard to ensure that his units displayed the best discipline and most polish of any at the camp.

At the same time Manfred renewed his efforts to master fencing and riding. He proved a quick, agile opponent who excelled in the epee. He bought one of the best three year old jumpers in Bavaria, riding her every day until he became a well known competitor in military events and the local horse shows. He exercised his body the same way he exercised his horse, until every muscle was firm. When he socialized with the other officers, he drank with moderation. He enjoyed a good cigar after dinner, but only once a week.

In the spring of 1926, Manfred met his future wife at the Kempten horse show, where Ingrid was participating in the dressage event. Her young, blond beauty drew the attention of every male at the show. Manfred cajoled an introduction from a mutual friend, and from the first encounter he knew this relationship would be special. They were both attractive, athletic, and shared a devotion to horses. The charm and sophistication of Manfred, eight years her senior, overwhelmed the eighteen year old Ingrid. His chiseled features, strong chin, and straight nose, set off by his officer's uniform and his dominant personality, made him the most attractive man she had ever met. They married six months later at a wedding attended by the nobility and wealthy from all Germany.

The year after his marriage, Manfred was promoted to First Lieutenant. Two years later, Ingrid presented him with a son. His fencing and riding reached new heights and brought well deserved attention to this young officer who represented a new Germany.

Then in December, 1931, just when Manfred was basking in contentment with his life and career, he received a surprise visit at the base from his Uncle Gerhard, now with the Army General Staff in Berlin.

"Uncle, what a pleasure! What brings you to Augsburg?" Manfred rose and extended his hand.

"Routine business," replied Gerhard, enveloping Manfred's hand with both of his, "plus the chance to see my favorite nephew. You look well." Gerhard settled into a comfortable leather chair and smoothed his mustache with his fingers.

"Thank you. I feel wonderful. Did you hear that I won the Post jumping contest two weeks ago? My horse was superb, her best performance ever."

"Of course I know." Gerhard beamed his approval. "Your parents keep me informed, and I have friends here at the base. But I didn't come to congratulate you. I have an offer that could help your career."

"Always looking after me, aren't you? Tell me, I'm interested," responded Manfred, smiling.

"General Hans Kundt has requested that you be assigned to the Bolivian War College at La Paz."

Manfred sat down quickly behind his desk, taken completely by surprise. As he considered the idea, wrinkles appeared on his forehead.

"I thought General Kundt was living here in Germany."

"He is," answered Gerhard, "but he still takes a very active interest in everything that happens in Bolivia. You know that he was in charge of the German Military Mission in Bolivia four different times from 1911 to 1930?"

Manfred nodded. He knew General Kundt by reputation - a hardened veteran who had distinguished himself in the last war, and who had spent many years in South America before and after the conflict.

"Well, Kundt thinks that war between Bolivia and Paraguay over the Chaco territory is inevitable. Bolivia is a bigger country with more money and more arms, so they expect a quick victory. They want all the Chaco territory, and in particular a port on the Paraguay River. But they need to get their military prepared. That's why the German Mission is so important."

Manfred had heard much of this before. Germany had several military missions abroad despite their defeat in the last war. "Why me?" he asked, still shocked by the idea.

"Because you have an excellent reputation for training soldiers," Gerhard answered, "and because I recommended you to the General."

"You recommended me for Bolivia?" Manfred asked, raising his eyebrows.

"Yes, I did. If a war breaks out, there is a good chance you will get a command assignment if you are there. Until you get some combat experience, you won't be respected as an officer in the German military, no matter how good you are at riding and fencing. Remember that most of our senior officers fought in the last war, and they are the ones who will decide your future."

Manfred considered this and found his uncle's argument made sense. Besides, he liked the idea of combat experience.

Gerhard continued. "There is another reason I want you out of Germany at this time."

Manfred looked at him questioningly.

"Have you heard of Adolf Hitler, the young radical politician?"

"Of course," answered Manfred. "There are rumors that he may be the next Chancellor. Most of Germany supports him."

"His party, the Nazis, is actively trying to infiltrate the military. Already, officers at the General Staff are beginning to take sides. I'm afraid that the military will become politicized. You are either with Hitler or against him. If a young officer chooses the wrong side, it could be the end of his career. In Bolivia you would be safe. By the time you return, the political situation here will be resolved."

Everything Uncle Gerhard said made sense to Manfred. Maybe he should accept an assignment to Bolivia. But he knew so little about the country. A thought came to him. "Uncle, what if Bolivia loses the war with Paraguay?"

"Don't be silly," laughed Gerhard. "Paraguay is nothing. A backwater country with two or three million people, and no army to speak of. Bolivia has three times their population. With Germany providing assistance, Bolivia will enjoy a crushing victory."

After his conversation with Gerhard, events moved at a lightning pace for the young officer. On February 27, 1932, First Lieutenant Manfred Kunnert departed Hamburg on a combination cargo-passenger ship for South America, leaving his wife and young son behind. He arrived in Callao, Peru, in April, 1932, and took a train to La Paz. Reporting to his Commanding Officer, he found a flurry of activity at the War College, and immersed himself in the Spanish language.

Three months later hostilities began. Manfred worked overtime training the new Bolivian officers. Then General Kundt was recalled to Bolivia and immediately decided that he needed more German officers at the front. In April 1933 Manfred was posted to the Army training camp at Santa Cruz, on the western edge of the Chaco, with orders to train his own company. Now he had his men, eighty unwashed, illiterate Indians, and he wondered if he hadn't made a mistake in coming to Bolivia.

Chapter 6

When training began, time passed quickly for Carlos. Each day started at five in the morning with one hour of calisthenics. Accustomed to hard work, Carlos found that the muscles he now used were different. At home he seldom walked far in the high altitudes, but here he was forced to march for miles every day. For the first four days, every part of his body ached, but the pain lessened and finally disappeared as he adapted to the new routine.

After a breakfast of coarse bread and weak coffee, he learned to use the basic fighting weapon of the infantry, the Mauser Model 98 8 millimeter rifle. Perfected during the Great War by the Germans, the rifle had been bought by the Bolivians as war surplus. The bolt action weapon had a wooden stock that reached almost to the end of the barrel, which made it long and heavy, but sturdy and accurate. Carlos learned to take the gun apart, to reassemble it, to keep it clean and oiled, and to adjust the sights. On the second week he went to the firing range where he was issued ammunition, and began to shoot at wooden targets shaped like men.

Carlos liked the Mauser from the beginning. He was comfortable with its weight of fifteen pounds, which kept the weapon steady as he fired the five cartridges in the magazine. He learned to hold the rifle tightly against his right shoulder to lessen the recoil, to close his left eye and hold his breath as he squeezed the trigger smoothly. He liked the sharp click of the metal cartridge clip as he pushed it down into the receiver, and the clack of the bolt as it settled into its forward position, ready to fire. The smooth, wooden stock felt good, almost sensuous, nestled against his right cheek.

At first, his aim was erratic. He scattered bullets everywhere, seldom hitting the wooden silhouette. Then he put a face on the flat board, imagining in his mind that the blank target was Lieutenant Gutierrez, the pudgy officer who had spat in his face and dragged him from Ocampo. His aim became steadier, and by the second day he hit the target six times. Soon he could hit the chest regularly, then the head. Each time he saw the board splinter, he visualized the body of Lieutenant Gutierrez bursting apart as his bullet exploded within it. Satisfied with his progress, the instructors concentrated on the slower learners.

Having a rifle in his hands gave Carlos a sense of power, even if the weapon belonged to the Army. In his village, only the police and Don Simon, the wealthy landowner, possessed rifles. A few farmers owned dilapidated shotguns, but they were old, ineffective weapons suitable only for scaring birds, more dangerous to the owner than to the target. The Mauser was different; it represented the power to control, to wound, to kill if necessary. Carlos had never possessed such power before, and he was surprised by how much he liked the feeling. Maybe, he thought, it is only a desire to take revenge on Gutierrez. Or maybe it is more. Maybe a desire to take revenge on all those who had oppressed him and his people.

He spent afternoons in the classroom learning military discipline and basic tactics. Unaccustomed to classrooms, the other men struggled with the simplest lessons. Even the different military ranks caused problems. It was easy to remember Sergeant, since there was one in the barracks. They could remember Lieutenant, since the blond German officer was their instructor, but ranks such as Major, Colonel, and General were confusing to the Indians.

Lieutenant Kunnert taught the basic military tactics of 1932, founded upon the lessons learned in the last war. Trench warfare was still in vogue, with well dug-in troops protected by solid fortifications plus barbed wire. The firepower of the machine gun provided the best defense. Only massive frontal attacks using thousands of troops could be expected to break through enemy lines. Tanks were being improved, but were not widely employed. The airplane served mainly for gathering information on enemy fortifications and troop movements.

The German officer spoke in broken Spanish which made learning even more difficult. The impassive brown faces surrounding Carlos registered no emotion or understanding. Carlos noted the growing frustration of the foreign lieutenant and watched him abandon the chalkboard to rely more and more on repetition.

At the beginning of the second week, the Lieutenant started asking questions of the group regarding the lessons. The only answer was, "I don't know," followed by a hesitant, "Sir." The conscripts looked away when the officer's eyes roamed the room. Carlos felt sorry for the young blond officer who was making little progress. Then he felt the Lieutenant's eyes upon him.

"You! What is the smallest combat unit in an army?"

Carlos hesitated before answering, deciding whether or not to commit himself. It would be easy to feign ignorance. The officer approached and stood directly in front of him.

"A squad, Sir."

"How many men in a squad?" Lieutenant Kunnert shot back.

"Normally six to twelve men, Sir."

Carlos saw the look of relief in the officer's face. After the class, the Lieutenant signaled for Carlos to stay.

"Your name, soldier?"

"Private Carlos Obregon, Sir."

"You're the only one in the class who is learning anything. How do you explain this?"

Carlos hesitated once more, debating how much he wished to help the foreigner. "You teach in Spanish, Sir. Most of the men don't speak Spanish very well."

Lieutenant Kunnert's jaw dropped open. "You mean they don't understand what I have been saying?"

"No, Sir. They understand only Aymara or Quechua."

"But you understand me."

"Yes, Sir."

"Why?"

"I studied Spanish with the Dominican fathers for ten years," Carlos explained.

"What race are you?"

"Aymara. But I also speak some Quechua."

"Why didn't these other men go to school?" Manfred inquired.

"There are few schools outside of the big cities in Bolivia, and Indians have no time for studying. These men have worked in the fields or helped their families since they were six years old or younger."

"And you?"

"I was fortunate. The Dominicans have a monastery near my village, with a free school for boys. My father is a miner, and he sends money home. Therefore I was able to study, except for the time of planting and harvesting."

"There must be others in this group who understand Spanish besides you."

"There are, Sir, but if they are Indian they won't answer you, even if they know the answer."

"Why? Are they afraid of me?"

"No, Sir, they are not afraid, but they don't trust you. Our people do not speak freely with others from outside our village or our race. If you were a Bolivian mestizo officer, or a wealthy landowner, it would be the same."

"My God! How do you communicate?"

"We talk among ourselves, although not very much." Carlos had said as much as he wanted to say to this blond foreigner. The Lieutenant would have to know the history of the Aymaras to understand why they didn't talk to outsiders, Carlos thought.

He would need to know that when the Spaniards came, at the time of the conquest, they took all our possessions: our land, our women, our animals. They made slaves of many of our people. If an Indian protested, he was tortured or killed. Since Independence, the Spaniards have been replaced by the mestizos, who treated us just as badly or worse. They have cheated us when buying our products or selling us goods. They have tricked us out of the little land which remained in our hands. When they want to talk with us, we know that it is for their advantage, another trick. Therefore we remain silent. The Lieutenant is no different, another outsider looking for something to take.

"But you at least answered my question," said Manfred, breaking into Carlos' thoughts.

"Yes, Sir. I like to learn. The Fathers taught me how."

"Good. Work hard and learn well, and perhaps we can get you a promotion at the end of training. In the meantime, you can help me explain things to these other men. You can translate my instructions into Aymara or Quechua. Would you be willing to do that?"

"Yes, Sir."

"It's settled then. We'll start tomorrow. Maybe I can finally get through to these men. Until then, you are dismissed."

Carlos saluted and left.

At the beginning of the fourth week the men separated into smaller groups for specialized training. Some learned to shoot mortars, others to string and recover protective barbed wire, others to plant land mines. Carlos was taught to use the new Vickers Berthier machine gun because of his success with the Mauser rifle. The Vickers air-cooled 303 caliber machine gun, recently arrived from England, was the most effective weapon in the Bolivian Army. Spitting out five hundred rounds a minute, it could discourage the most well-organized attack. Most of the defects had been eliminated after the war, making it a reliable weapon.

Carlos learned to squeeze off short bursts of fire so the gun would not overheat. He learned to quickly insert and discard the banana-shaped clips that held thirty rounds of ammunition. His love for the Mauser was replaced by an adoration of the Vickers. He watched in awe as his machine gun tore apart the wooden targets, shredding them into splinters. If the Mauser represented power, the Vickers meant complete domination, total control.

The days ended with forced marches of an hour or longer, followed by a shower, an early supper, and bed. Carlos and most of the other conscripts had never used a shower before. Indoor plumbing was unknown in their homes. Few of the conscripts could write, so Carlos and Ramon wrote letters home for the illiterate. Their complaints were the same: I am lonely; I miss my village; I feel tired in the lower altitude. Most men wrote to their mothers, who would need to enlist the village priests to read their sad notes.

After six weeks, the training ended abruptly. New conscripts had arrived, and space was needed for them. Carlos' group was baptized B Company, assigned to the Eighteenth Infantry Battalion, and Lieutenant Kunnert was designated Company Commander. He promptly promoted Carlos to Corporal.

Some men were still unable to hit the wooden targets; others could not distinguish between a Major and a Colonel; and one-fourth were still without boots. Although they had been told that Paraguay was the enemy, most didn't know where Paraguay was located, or why they were fighting.

On July, 1933, one month into the dry season, Carlos and B Company moved out in early morning. Seven trucks, containing eighty-two men in all, left Santa Cruz, traveling south over gently rolling grassland and passing through occasional woods. In addition to their uniforms, each soldier had been issued a rifle, a blanket, and a mosquito net before his departure.

As the foothills of the Andes gradually disappeared to their right, the troops stopped talking, knowing that they were going farther and farther away from their homes. Then the trucks turned east, and entered the Chaco itself. The land flattened and the hills were lost in the distance. For as far as Carlos could see, there were no trees, no villages, nothing but dry wasteland dotted with scattered clumps of cactus. He had never seen so many varieties of cactus. Dull green shapes with threatening yellow thorns claimed a meager existence in the heat and drought. Low prickly cacti completely blanketed some areas, rendering these impassable.

Carlos saw no mountains, no streams, no animals, just a baked desolate terrain that went on for as far as the eye could see. God must have decided to punish this land, he thought, and also those who covet it.

The convoy traveled over unpaved roads that had been scraped flat by bulldozers during the previous two years as Bolivia prepared for the conflict; roads which ran for miles in a straight line through the dry plain. As more and more traffic passed, the surface crumbled and became rutted. The trucks made slow progress as the tires sank into the loose sand and had to be dug out.

The heat became unbearable. Water transported in old oil barrels quickly turned warm and stagnant. The convoy halted several times to cool overheated motors, change dust-clogged carburetors, and repair blown out tires. The first night they bivouacked by the side of the road, spreading their wool blankets out on the ground, under the stars. For eight hours, they had seen only barren landscape on the way, no other trucks, no soldiers, no inhabitants. Yet this was the land they would fight for.

Despite his mosquito net, Carlos had trouble sleeping because of sharp bites on his exposed face and arms throughout the night. He awoke with a start at dawn and discovered a large red army ant on his forearm, with its jaws locked firmly in his skin. Carlos crushed the ant and the body broke off, leaving the head and jaws still embedded in his flesh. Later the bite began to swell and itch.

On the second day the convoy entered a road with heavy traffic. Trucks rumbled past, returning west, loaded with wounded. Under the canvas covers of the passing vehicles, Carlos saw soldiers lying flat on the truck beds or braced against the sides, crowded against one another, their once white bandages now a light brown from the dust, or dark red from blood. Since the road was narrow, it was often necessary for the convoy to pull off to the side to let the hurt soldiers pass. The wounded men looked gaunt and weary, and passed the fresh troops in silence. As the day continued, the number of ambulance trucks increased, and the men began to whisper among themselves. At dusk, they arrived at a crossroads where a field hospital had been set up, and made their own camp.

After supper, Carlos and Ramon walked over to the hospital, hoping to find something to put on Carlos' bite, which was now red and swollen. The medical facility was nothing more than a large tent, open on all four sides, and illuminated by oil lamps hanging from wooden supports. The wounded lay on blood soaked straw mats, swathed in dust coated bandages. Their moaning and cries blended together in a low, constant hum, like wind blowing through a hole in a boulder. An odor of disinfectant, dried blood, urine, and feces hung entrapped under the tarp covering.

In one corner of the tent, sheets had been draped to form a makeshift room. As the two men approached, they heard a wild, agonizing scream from behind the sheets.

"Jesus," Ramon exclaimed, stopping at the edge of the tent. "What was that?"

"Look," Carlos said, pointing toward the hanging sheets.

Illuminated by a lamp inside the operating room, the shadow of a doctor played upon the sheet. In his hand he held a surgical saw, which the reflection magnified to twice its real size.

"Shit!" Ramon spat on the ground. "Do they cut off limbs with nothing for pain? Holy Christ!"

Before Carlos could reply, a man in a blood-splattered apron pushed back a corner of the sheet and came out of the room. He carried the bottom half of a bloody leg, which he unceremoniously dropped into an open oil barrel, then walked to a table near them and retrieved some bottles.

Noticing Carlos and Ramon, he asked crossly, "What are you doing here?"

Carlos rolled up his shirt sleeve and pointed to the infected bite. The doctor glanced at it quickly and shrugged. "That's nothing. Soak a cloth in kerosene and wrap it around your arm."

"Where do we get the kerosene?" Ramon asked.

"Under the table there," the officer said, pointing. "Then get back to your unit before I report you to your commanding officer."

"Okay! Okay! We're going," Ramon said.

Carlos found a rag and poured some kerosene on it. He wrapped it carefully around his arm, covering the infected area, and Ramon helped him tie it. Then they left, happy to get away from the putrid smell.

On their way back, they found a wounded soldier, his arm in a sling, sitting by himself away from the hospital tent. He was so still and so quiet that they almost tripped over him in the dark.

"Sorry, *compadre*, we didn't see you," Ramon said in Spanish.

The Indian looked up but said nothing.

"Where do you come from?" Carlos asked in Aymara, squatting down beside the sitting man.

The soldier looked at Carlos and recognized another of his race. "From the front at Nanawa," he answered.

"What is happening there?" Carlos asked.

"A disaster! The German General is crazy. He has ordered a second attack against the enemy fort. He throws us against the Paraguayan machine guns. Again and again. Like sheep to be slaughtered, while he sits safely behind the lines."

"How did you get hurt?" Carlos asked.

"I was in the attack on the first day. Our Lieutenant got lost on the way. When we arrived, the battle had already begun. We tried to charge the enemy machine guns, stepping over the soldiers already fallen, but many of us died, and we could not gain ground. Our canons started shelling the Paraguayans to break their defenses. When they stopped, we charged again. We fought like savages, hand-to-hand, with bayonets and knives. Then our canons began again." The soldier dropped his head. "I don't know why. They were shelling their own troops. It was insane."

Carlos and Ramon looked at each other. After a pause, the soldier resumed his story.

"When the shelling stopped, we had taken the first trench of the enemy, but at what price? Arms and legs hung from trees, blown there by the big guns. *Pilas* and our soldiers, dead side by side, some of them locked together, still struggling when they died."

"What are *Pilas*?" Carlos asked softly.

"*Pilas*. *Patas Peladas*. The barefoot ones. The Paraguayans. They fight without shoes. And they are brave."

He paused to rub his eyes with his good hand, and continued, "There were so many dead that we stacked the bodies together, in piles, one on top of the other, and soaked them with kerosene. It was all right when the kerosene was burning, but when it ran out, the half-burned bodies were still there, tangled and smoldering. The stench was terrible. I will never forget that sight or that smell. When new *Pilas* arrived, we fled and left the bodies there. All for nothing."

"What happened to your arm, *compadre*?" asked Ramon.

Instead of answering, the soldier pulled back the sling, and extended his left arm. Where his hand had been, there was now a stub, wrapped in a dirty white bandage. "The war is over for me. I am going home. You should do the same. Get out of here before you get killed. This is not our war."

"We've just arrived," Carlos said. "How can we leave?"

"Many of our soldiers have run away and crossed the border into Argentina. They are helped there by the Bolivian Communists, who are against the war."

"We don't know the Chaco," answered Ramon. "We would get lost if we tried to desert."

"Then shoot yourself the first time you are in combat. In the leg or in the arm. They will put you in a truck and take you to a hospital. It is better than being killed."

Carlos would have liked to ask the wounded soldier if he had shot himself, following his own advice, but Carlos knew that this would not be correct. Losing one's hand was a high price to pay. "Thank you, my friend," responded Carlos. "Thank you for your words."

Carlos and Ramon stood up and walked back to their camp. Neither man spoke. That night Carlos prayed that Company B would not be sent to Nanawa and slept fitfully, dreaming of tangled bodies burning in flames.

In the morning the convoy passed some of the small Bolivian garrisons built before the war. Although there were still only two or three crude sheds at each, they were surrounded by tents. The *fortins* now served as staging areas for the troops, and wells had been dug to provide water. The traffic returning from the front increased, and Carlos' convoy stopped for long stretches of time, parked off the road, watching the wounded pass. Abandoned trucks, no longer capable of being repaired, littered the roadside.

In mid-afternoon, the convoy turned left off the main road, and the oncoming traffic decreased. Carlos surmised correctly that they were no longer headed for Nanawa, but were going somewhere farther north. He made the sign of the cross on his chest and nodded his head in relief.

For the first time he saw small woods, with dry brittle trees scattered in clumps. That night they met up with other companies of the Eighteenth Infantry. It had taken four days to reach the front.

Manfred studied the bleak terrain, dotted with scrub brush, with the eye of the professional soldier that he was, taking in the slight rises and falls in elevation. His unit, B Company, had been assigned the task of protecting the right flank of the Battalion, which was headquartered at *Pozo Favorita*. He laughed to himself at the name, Favorite Well, for the one small well which had originally marked the spot was now dry and abandoned, the fence posts of a crude corral were on the ground, and all that remained of a small hut were the rotting boards. Consequently all water and food had to be trucked in. Nevertheless, General Kundt hat decided that the location was strategic for his offensive, and if the General had determined this, Manfred would do his part. Better yet, he would do more than his part. Appalled by the disorganization he had seen so far, Manfred decided to show the Bolivians what a German officer could accomplish.

First he ordered the construction of trenches needed to defend his part of the line. He took great care that they followed strictly the models he had studied in Germany, measuring and measuring again the trench depth, with allowances made for the shorter height of the Bolivian troops. He checked and rechecked each angle of fire. He ordered his men to fill sandbags to protect the firing positions, and to dig reinforced caves for protection from shelling. If all was not perfect, he ordered it redone. He realized that the men were becoming increasingly angry and sullen as they dug, filled in, and dug again, laboring in scorching heat, but chose to ignore this.

When the trenches were finished, Manfred ordered barbed wire strung in rolls in front of the first trench. He positioned mortar emplacements twenty yards in back of the front line, so the weapons would be protected. Since his company had only one machine gun, he placed this another twenty yards behind on a raised knoll, protected by a semi-circular trench surrounding a dugout. He ordered the dugout to be roofed with quebracho logs covered with packed earth, and used this as his command post and quarters.

When he had finished, he stood back to admire his defensive emplacements. They would draw praise anywhere in Europe, and made the crumbling trenches of the Bolivian commanders look like the work of amateurs. His were real fortifications, designed to hold the enemy at bay forever.

It was Manfred's soldiers that worried him. A listless bunch, they showed no enthusiasm for their country or their cause. No wonder Pizarro had conquered the Inca nation with only two hundred men, he thought. One battalion of Germans could defeat the whole Bolivian Army.

Manfred ordered intensive combat drills for his men, hoping to get them in shape before they met the enemy, but this only made the situation worse. The troops resisted repeating the same exercises over and over in the heat, finding more ingenuous excuses each day. Manfred reacted by threatening to hold back their daily ration of coca leaves, reasoning this must be the cause of their apathy. Fortunately, the Sergeant, fearing a mutiny, persuaded him not to act.

The oppressive heat continued without mercy. Meat arrived rotten. Water had to be rationed; showers were forbidden; rifles became too hot to pick up. Some men tried to remove their shirts when on duty, but Manfred would not allow it, punishing those who disobeyed.

Thorny bushes and cactus surrounded much of the area where the soldiers were bivouacked, and the sharp spines tore at both clothes and skin indifferently. The wounds then became infected from scratching, and festered for weeks. So many of the men wrapped their legs with rags soaked in disinfectant that the whole company seemed to be plagued with elephantiasis. Dysentery spread throughout the company with epidemic force.

Then the rats appeared - slick gray creatures which simply showed up one day, and then multiplied into thousands. Manfred couldn't understand where the big rodents were coming from. The barren land didn't seem capable of supporting them. He knew what they wanted: food. Whenever rations were left unprotected, the rats would carry them off. Each day they became more aggressive. At night they entered the tents and crawled over the men in search of nourishment. Several soldiers were bitten, and the bites quickly became infected. No matter how many rats the soldiers killed, there were always more. Finally he ordered the men to share part of their rations with the rats, leaving food outside their tents, hoping to appease them in this way.

As their living conditions deteriorated, the men turned their anger toward the foreign lieutenant, and although the Indians were passive by nature, Manfred could see the hatred in their eyes. Soldiers faked sickness in order to be transferred to the rear, and the first desertions occurred. Two men walked off during the night and disappeared forever. Never in his career had a German soldier deserted from one of Manfred's units, and he reported the missing men with a deep sense of frustration.

All this time the enemy remained quiet. Manfred knew the Paraguayan troops were somewhere to the east, close by, but he didn't know where. In the beginning he tried sending out scouting patrols, but with bad results. The first patrol was ambushed and suffered two casualties. The second patrol never returned, four men lost. After that, the patrols he sent covered only familiar territory and returned without useful information. He stopped sending patrols.

Then the *Macheteros* began harassing his outposts. A sentry would be lost on the left flank one night, on the right flank the next. The mutilations destroyed the already low morale of his troops. He had lost nine men in two months, with no known enemy casualties.

Fearing his own men, Manfred slept alone, locking the door of the dugout each night. He was even suspicious of his own orderly, insisting that his food be tasted before he would eat. Therefore, when Carlos knocked after midnight, he opened the door carefully, with a Luger in his right hand.

Chapter 7

"Why do you think the enemy is about to attack, Corporal?" Manfred asked, lowering his pistol.

"The *Macheteros*," Carlos blurted out. "They're behind our lines, Sir. They killed my replacement on his way to relieve me. They killed the Sergeant and the gunner here in this trench. I think the Paraguayans wanted to silence the machine gun before attacking."

"Have you warned the troops?" Manfred asked, an urgency in his voice as he slipped on his pants.

"Yes, Sir. Private Sanchez is waking them now."

"Is the machine gun damaged?" The urgency had turned to concern. Manfred hastily buttoned his shirt.

"I don't know, Sir."

"Then check it out. And calm down. I'll scout around the dugout to make sure the *Macheteros* are gone. Be quick." Manfred pulled on his leather boots, picked up his pistol again, and walked out into the darkness.

Carlos hurried to the machine gun emplacement and dragged the dead gunner out of the way. His eyes darted from side to side, forcing themselves to penetrate the black corners where the *Macheteros* might still be hiding. Then, steeling himself, he inspected the gun methodically, starting from back to front. He worked the action by pulling back on the bolt and letting it fly forward three times; he checked the barrel to see if it was clear and not bent; he cleaned the sights with his thumb and forefinger; and he swung the gun on its tripod. There was no apparent damage.

Manfred returned and stood beside him. "No sign of the *Macheteros* now. Can you see any activity in front of us?"

Dawn was breaking, and the rising sun was coming up into Carlos' eyes.

"No, Sir."

An incoming shell shattered the early morning silence. Carlos jerked involuntarily, shocked by the explosion which left his ears ringing. A second shell followed, this one much closer. The blast deadened his eardrums. The earth trembled. Dirt flew into the air, peppering the roof of the gun emplacement. A small crater marked the spot where the shell had landed. Dark smoke from the explosives floated past the dugout bearing an acrid odor.

Carlos shook his head. His ears were still ringing. He had not heard the low "whump" which he associated with a mortar being launched, only a soft whistle announcing each shell's approach.

"They're using cannon, Sir."

"No. Stokes Brandt mortars," Manfred said calmly. "Their distance and high trajectory makes them sound like light cannon. Not very accurate, which is good for us, but they pack a lot of explosive." Carlos missed most of what Manfred said, focusing instead on the sound of each incoming shell. The delay between the low whistle and the blast was a lifetime. Not knowing where the next mortar would land was terrifying, so the explosion itself came almost as a relief.

The Paraguayans concentrated their fire on the front line of Bolivian defenders, blowing gaps in the barbed wire. One of the mortar shells landed in the front trench itself. Screams of anguish and pain mixed in with the blasts of the mortars.

Carlos' knees were shaking, his hands sweaty. He could imagine what his friends were feeling in the front line. Nothing in their training had prepared them for this.

"Is the machine gun usable, Corporal Obregon?" Manfred asked.

"I think so, Sir," answered Carlos, trying to keep his voice from breaking.

"Then man it, and fire when I tell you."

Carlos sat cross-legged behind the gun, inserted a new ammunition clip, and released the safety. He lined up the sights so that he would be firing over the heads of the defenders, about a hundred yards range. The mortar rounds kept coming. One landed close by with a deafening burst, lifting him from his seat. Then Carlos saw figures in the distance, outlined by the sun at their backs. Hundreds of Paraguayan troops charged the front line, shouting and taunting the Bolivians as they advanced.

"*Andinos*," Carlos heard them shout. "we are coming for you. *Fuera del Chaco*! *Viva Paraguay*!"

As Carlos watched, men scrambled out of the defensive trenches, first one, then another, then several. What started as a trickle turned into a flood. Bolivian soldiers shocked by the mortars and panicked by the enemy cries, poured from the front trench and ran for the rear, abandoning the defenses on which they had worked for months.

Manfred stared at the fleeing troops retreating toward the machine gun. His visions of glory, victory, and promotion disintegrated as more men joined the flight. All his life he had dreamed of the day when he would have his own combat command, when he could show that German officers were the best in the world, and that he, Manfred Kunnert, was the best of the Germans. Now his men were running from the enemy without firing a shot. Abandoning trenches which had been laid out so meticulously.

"Shoot those cowardly bastards!" Manfred shouted, waving his clenched fist at Carlos.

"They're our men, Sir," Carlos shouted back, looking at Manfred's contorted face.

"I don't care. Fire, you Son-of-a-Bitch, or I'll have you court-marshaled."

Carlos didn't move. He couldn't pull the trigger on his own friends.

"Get out of my way!" Manfred yelled, kicking Carlos to one side, and manning the machine gun himself. Carlos fell sprawling on the trench floor, stunned by the blow.

By now forty men were out of the trenches, running toward the safety of the machine gun. Manfred lowered the gun and fired a raking arc from left to right. Fortunately the sights had been adjusted to fire high. He cursed, and moved the barrel lowered, firing again. Four Bolivian soldiers were hit and dropped in their tracks. The rest fell to the ground seeking cover.

"Get back to the trench, you Indian bastards," Manfred screamed, "or I'll kill every last one of you."

The fleeing men were now caught in no man's land, pinned down out in the open. One soldier jumped up, pointed his rifle at the Lieutenant, and fired a round. Carlos heard the sharp smack of the bullet ricochet off the hard quebracho roof above him. Manfred fired another blast from the machine gun and cut down the standing man.

"Get back, I said." Manfred's face was a bright red.

Two more soldiers jumped up and ran toward the right, hoping to avoid the machine gun. Manfred killed them both as they fled.

The Paraguayan troops kept advancing, surprised by the light resistance. Mortar shells now fell in the no man's land where the Bolivian troops were caught.

Carlos heard a clear yell above the commotion.

"Please, Lieutenant. Help us." It was the voice of Ramon.

"Get back to your positions," shouted Manfred, firing another burst in the air to emphasize his point.

"Please." It was Ramon again, pleading.

Carlos struggled to his feet and stood behind the Lieutenant. He saw the Paraguayan troops closing in, the majority of his own companions pinned down by the machine gun, and realized they would all die if he did not act. He picked up his rifle with sweaty hands, released the safety, pointed to the back of Manfred's head, and fired. His first kill of the war was his Commanding Officer.

Chapter 8

Carlos dragged the crumpled body of the Lieutenant away from the machine gun. Looking up, he saw the first Paraguayan troops breach the barbed wire and leap into the front line trench.

"Come," Carlos shouted to the prone Bolivian troops in front of him. "Keep low to avoid my fire."

He elevated the angle of fire, and turned the gun on the Paraguayans who had not yet reached the forward trench. The first burst brought down five men, but the line continued forward. He heard shouting and screams in the front trench as the enemy overpowered the remaining defenders.

Ramon was the first to reach the machine gun, followed by two others.

"Get our men organized," Carlos ordered. "Use the trench around the dugout as a defensive line. Tell them there are *Macheteros* behind us. If they continue to run, the *Macheteros* will kill them. Fighting here is their best chance."

The Bolivians arrived in small groups, crawling on their stomachs. Twenty-two survivors managed to reach the trench surrounding the dugout. Carlos positioned twelve men on the front of the semi-circle facing the enemy, the rest on the sides. Ramon hastily distributed the ammunition stored in the dugout to the defenders. In addition to rifle cartridges, he found an extra case of loose machine gun shells. Carlos stationed Ramon alongside him with instructions to keep the clips loaded.

"Can we hold them off?" Ramon asked.

"I don't know," Carlos responded. "It depends on how many they are, and their determination."

After the Paraguayans finished off the last resistance in the outer trench, they regrouped and moved forward again. This time Carlos and his men were ready for them. Carlos raked the advancing enemy with bursts of machine gun fire, cutting down the soldiers in front. His own troops supported the machine gun with rifle fire. The Paraguayan soldiers charged forward bravely, but the concentrated fire ripped huge gaps in their line. Seeing the losses, the officer in charge ordered his men back to the safety of the first trench. By this time, the machine gun barrel was red hot and Carlos feared that it would malfunction.

The Paraguayan mortar rounds began again, now aimed at the dugout. The blasts were like thunder. The explosions dug huge pits in the ground, scattering dirt over the Bolivian soldiers. One near miss collapsed part of the trench wall. Two times during the morning, the mortars stopped and the Paraguayan troops attacked. Each time Carlos and his small group of men drove the enemy back, but each surge left the remaining number of defenders diminished as the enemy inflicted his own damage.

"Carlos, we're in trouble," Ramon announced in an anxious voice.

"What is it?"

"Our ammunition is running out. The loose shells have all been used. The only shells remaining are the loaded banana clips."

Carlos examined the contents of the box by his right side. He counted twenty loaded clips, six hundred rounds in all, sufficient for about two minutes of intermittent firing.

"Have you searched the dugout?" he asked.

"Yes. There's nothing left. Even our rifle shells are finished."

Carlos frowned. "Maybe we can hold off one more attack. No more, even if I space the bursts more slowly."

Taking advantage of a lull in the mortar shelling, Carlos slid back into the open trench to examine their situation. The trench looked like a scene from hell. The wounded lay alongside the dead, and it was difficult to tell one from the other. The medic had been killed in the front trench, so the wounded lay as they fell, moaning for help. Those who could still fight stood positioned for the next attack, even though they were bleeding or exhausted. The faces of the men were black from powder and dirt, like devils risen from the bowels of the earth.

On his far left, Carlos heard the noise of another battle and saw the enemy advancing. The adjacent part of the Bolivian line had collapsed. He realized that they were in danger of being surrounded, but the enemy troops turned away from them, planning to encircle the main Bolivian force at Pozo Favorita.

"Look!" he shouted to Ramon, pointing upward and to the north. A lone tri-motor Junkers transport plane was circling Pozo Favorita less than seven hundred yards in the air, its black silhouette clearly outlined against the cloudless blue sky. From where he stood, the plane seemed like a giant condor gliding slowly over its prey. As Carlos watched, small packets tumbled from the plane, fluttering like swallows beneath an eagle. The plane circled again, and more packets filled the sky.

"What do you think it is?" Ramon asked Carlos.

"Ammunition! They must be dropping ammunition to the troops. If they would only come this way. Maybe we can get their attention."

"They are coming, Carlos. Look!" shouted Ramon.

The plane banked south and headed toward them, just as the enemy mortars began again, raining death upon the defenders. The Bolivian soldiers flattened themselves against the trench wall.

Except Carlos. He grabbed a rifle from a cowering soldier and waved it in the air. Realizing that he was too low to be seen in the trench, he scrambled up the dugout wall, slipping and sliding on the loose earth.

"Get back, Carlos! You'll be killed up there. Get back," Ramon screamed.

Carlos ignored his cry. He had to catch the pilot's attention. He jumped up and down on the dirt roof of the dugout, waving the rifle furiously. Bullets plowed up the packed earth around his feet as the enemy tried to bring down the exposed figure. A mortar shell landed twenty yards away, spewing deadly shrapnel. Carlos' men returned the rifle fire, hoping to pin down the enemy. The plane flew straight for the dugout, passed lazily overhead and continued south.

Carlos slid down the side of the dugout, back to the safety of the trench. He fell exhausted at Ramon's feet.

"Damn," he said. "They didn't see me."

The retreating airplane initiated a wide turn as Ramon watched.

"No. You're wrong, Carlos," he shouted excitedly. "They saw you. They're coming back!"

Carlos jumped to his feet and the two men hugged each other as the plane drew closer. They watched its airspeed decrease. Slowly, slowly it approached, so low that Carlos could clearly see the Bolivian markings on its wings. Then black packets, the size of rifle clips, fell from the plane, spinning end over end, tumbling crazily down from the sky. The men were cheering now, screaming their thanks to the pilot who could not possibly hear them. The packets fell in a rough swatch about forty yards wide, both inside and outside the circular trench.

Carlos was crying with joy as he grabbed a black packet from the trench floor, but a look of surprise appeared on his face as he felt the weight. It was too light to be ammunition. He ripped the packet open, and dry coca leaves spilled out, the daily ration of coca for the Bolivian soldiers. The airplane wagged its wings in a departing salute as it turned south again.

"Bastards," cursed Carlos. "Dirty bastards! We need ammunition and they send coca. This is the way our officers help us." He collapsed against the trench wall.

The incoming mortar rounds had been silent since the plane returned. Ramon looked over the edge of the trench, expecting to see the Paraguayans on the attack, but there was no movement in front of them. To the left he could see enemy soldiers streaming forward through the break in the line, but they were moving north, away from the dugout.

"Carlos," he said, speaking to the dazed figure on the trench floor, "maybe they think it was ammunition."

In the late afternoon the enemy in front of them pulled back, joining other troops on the left. Evidently Carlos' small pocket of defenders was no longer of importance. Carlos asked Ramon to count the number of survivors. Of the original eighty soldiers of B Company, nine able men and four wounded were still alive.

After the disorder and noise of battle, the night was strangely quiet. They took turns sleeping, so that two-thirds of the men were always on alert. When dawn broke the next day, the enemy had disappeared. Dark clouds of smoke rose from the area of Pozo Favorita. Something was burning, but Carlos didn't even want to think of what it might be.

Carlos looked at the chaos around him. The smell of decaying flesh permeated the air. The Lieutenant's body lay on the floor of the trench, his blond hair matted with blood and dirt. Any of the men could see that the officer had been shot from behind at close range.

Carlos bent over the dead Lieutenant and retrieved his billfold. He took out the Bolivian money but left the German Marks. As he went through the brown leather wallet, he found two pictures. One was a family scene of the Lieutenant, an attractive blond woman, and a small boy, standing in a lovely garden surrounded by flowers; all were smiling broadly. The second picture was of the same woman alone, wearing a solid color one-piece bathing suit, lying on her side on a raft surrounded by water. The peaceful idyllic scene, with such abundant water, was so incongruous in his current situation, that Carlos studied it for a long time. Besides, she was the most beautiful woman Carlos had ever seen. The inscription on the back read, "Bodensee, 1927." On impulse, Carlos removed the photo of the woman and stuck it inside his shirt. He put the billfold back in the corpse's pocket.

"Ramon, let's get started. We've got to bury these bodies," Carlos said.

Ramon looked around him. The battlefield was littered with dead. "We don't have the men for that, Carlos."

"We can use the trenches. They won't be needed anymore. Separate the Paraguayan from the Bolivian dead, and lay them in two groups in the front trench. Then cover them with sandbags and dirt."

"What should I do with the Lieutenant's body?" asked Ramon, looking at the wound, then back at Carlos.

"Put it at the bottom. Cover it with Paraguayan bodies," Carlos replied.

"What about his things?"

"Leave everything on him. As of now, the Lieutenant is officially missing in action."

Ramon raised one eyebrow, then turned to comply with his orders.

Carlos watched as the men worked. The survivors stole the boots, money, and anything of value from the dead of both sides before burying them, but he said nothing. The deceased had no use for valuables where they were going.

As Ramon was supervising the Lieutenant's burial, he noticed the cadaver wore a chain with a heavy gold medallion around the neck, evidently a family crest, and of obvious value. Ignoring Carlos' orders, Ramon removed the medallion and slipped it into his pocket.

At three in the afternoon Carlos saw a trail of dust in the west. A convoy of three trucks and a command car approached at high speed. As it drew closer, Carlos recognized their Bolivian markings. The command car jerked to a halt, and a tall, lanky Major emerged from the passenger side. He walked confidently over to Carlos.

"I'm Major Busch. Who is in charge here?" The name may have been German, but the man was definitely a mestizo.

"I am, Sir. Corporal Carlos Obregon of B Company. At your orders." Carlos saluted.

"Where is Lieutenant Kunnert, Corporal?" the Major asked.

"Missing in action, Sir. He may have been captured or killed. The Sergeant was killed yesterday morning, Sir, by *Macheteros*," Carlos volunteered, lowering his hand.

"When did the Lieutenant go missing?"

"Yesterday morning, Sir, just before the attack began."

"You mean he just disappeared? Into thin air?"

Carlos looked the major straight in the eyes. "Yes, Sir."

"Good riddance. We don't need those German bastards. But who organized the defense here?"

"I did, Sir."

The Major took a long look at the stocky Indian in front of him. "Well, *Carlitos*," he said finally, using the diminutive as a sign of friendliness, "you did a good job. The rest of our line on the left collapsed; the Eighteenth Infantry was overrun and no longer exists. The enemy has captured Pozo Favorita. How many men do you have?"

"Nine able and four wounded, Sir. We buried the dead in the trenches, both ours and theirs."

"Well done. Yours is the only unit that held the line. The others are either dead or prisoners. Get your men together, round up all the usable weapons and ammunition, and we'll take you out of here."

"Yes, Sir," Carlos replied, liking this young Major.

"By the way, *Carlitos*, you are now Sergeant Carlos Obregon. Congratulations!"

Chapter 9

Luis arose slowly, for the lung disease was advancing rapidly.
Coughing racked his body every night, leaving him exhausted in the
morning. His lungs seemed to be filled with cement and he could no
longer take deep breaths, only short, wheezing gasps, insufficient to
restore his energy after the sleepless nights. His already lean frame
was now emaciated. Several of his friends had noticed his condition,
averting their eyes to his pain, so it would not be long before the
supervisors would become aware and send him home.

The organizing was going well. Hundreds of miners had
joined the union in spite of the threat of dismissal, and the company
could not afford to discharge them for the war effort demanded full
production. Some of the younger leaders had been singled out and
sent to the front in an attempt to break the organizing effort, but many
of the new union members were too old to fight, like Luis himself.
As Juan Lechin had anticipated, the undecided men came to Luis for
advice, and many joined only because of him.

Luis dressed methodically, layering his garments carefully so
that they would protect him from the dampness of the tunnel. He had
lost his appetite and chose to forego breakfast that morning, even
though he knew not eating was a mistake. He placed the first new
coca leaves of the morning into his mouth, and began chewing. The
pain in his chest eased.

The sky was still dark when he reached the mine. He lined up
with the other workers, gray figures who materialized out of the early
morning darkness, men without voices. The underground elevator

arrived protesting with sharp metallic grunts, and vomited the miners of the night shift, their faces black with dirt, their bodies exhausted. Luis' line shuffled forward like a chain gang, the row of heads dimly framed by the rising sun, prisoners on their way to the permanent night of the mine.

The mine elevator descended noisily downward, scraping against its steel support frame. Luis watched the earth walls turn black as the night, then even darker than night, as the metal prison continued its downward voyage. He closed his eyes and listened to the eerie, rasping sounds of metal on metal. He felt a lurch as the cage ground to a halt.

The miners filed out one by one into the main tunnel, passing in front of the life-sized, bright red statue of *Huari*, god of the underworld, protector and killer at the same time, whom they had nicknamed *Tio*, uncle. *Huari* grinned down upon them with large, white, enameled wooden teeth, flashing under the string of light bulbs above his bald head, from which jutted two curved horns. Painted thick black eyebrows arched sharply over two fierce glass eyes and ran together at the top of a large hooked nose. Completely naked, his bloated belly protruded out over an enormous erect penis, which thrust itself into the miners' faces and explained his leering grin.

Luis took two coca leaves from the bag around his waist and placed them in a box at the base of the statue. His offering would protect him from cave-ins, poisonous gasses, and explosions, provided *Huari* was in a good mood. It was a ritual Luis performed each day when entering the mine, the same as all the other miners, who were superstitious to a man. Those miners who had no coca to offer, massaged the giant phallus with their hands, another way to ask protection. Over the years the bright red paint had been rubbed off the obscene shaft by thousands of rough hands, leaving a smooth surface of brown wood. Today Luis did both, for he felt weak and insecure, and had a strange foreboding when entering the mine.

The workers split into smaller groups, dividing to enter the feeder tunnels, separating again to work the branch tunnels, until at last Luis remained alone with his pick and ore sack. His sense of foreboding increased. The distance between the tunnel lights seemed to be farther than usual. His own head lamp gave only a dim glow, accentuating the shadows within the small area where he worked in solitude.

It is time for me to quit, he thought, time to go home. I am sick and weak, my mind plays tricks with me. My eyes no longer see in the darkness of the mine.

He tried to think of his family as he chipped away against the face of ore, which fell in chunks into the mud on the mine floor. In his mind he removed himself from the dark humid bowels of the earth, and sat instead alongside a small, fast rushing stream in Ocampo, where the sun bathed him with its warmth. He could feel the heat enter his aging body, lubricating the aching joints. He felt his rigid chest loosen as the warmth dissolved the clogged capillaries within, and his breathing became more regular. The sweet clear air which entered his lungs was like honey, refreshing him, soothing him. In the distance he saw his family, Maria, Carlos, Segundina, all together, walking toward him, laughing and smiling.

Lost in his imagination, Luis did not hear the steps behind him.

"The time has come, *Viejo*. I warned you."

He recognized the husky voice of Franco and turned as best he could in the cramped tunnel. The glow from his miner's lamp distorted the cruel features looming over him. The red skin and the evil eyes could have been *Huari* himself. Frightened, Luis swung his pick at the figure, which stepped back with a laugh. The motion carried Luis sideways. Two strong arms seized his shoulders and pushed him forward. He fell on the mine floor and Franco was on top of him, a knee pressed into his back, the weight of the larger man holding him down. Luis struggled to lift his face from the mud, but two strong hands gripped his head like a vise, pressing his face deeper and deeper into the black muck. He gasped for oxygen, sucking mud into his nostrils and mouth. His diseased lungs, which had little capacity for air, now received none. His body jerked with involuntary spasms as his life left him. His struggles ceased, and he saw his family again, closer now, hurrying to meet him. He reached out to touch them and died.

"Good news, Sergeant," Lieutenant Estevez said, looking up from the dispatch he was reading.

Carlos raised his head to listen to the young mestizo lieutenant from Sucre, his new Commanding Officer.

"We're finally moving out after all these months. We're going to Carandaiti. We'll be absorbed into A Company of the 7th Division. That's the division commanded by Colonel David Toro. I've heard he's good."

Carlos didn't share the enthusiasm of the recently arrived, smooth-faced officer. For four months, while he and his men were recuperating at a base camp two hundred miles to the rear, he had heard only bad news from the front. Two Bolivian divisions, almost one third of the Army, had been destroyed at Campo Via in the Paraguayan encirclement from which he had barely escaped. As a result, the German General, Hans Kundt, had been sacked and replaced by General Enrique Penaranda, a Bolivian career officer.

But even General Penaranda hadn't made much of a difference. The main body of the Bolivian troops was still retreating to Ballivian, a small trading post on the Pilcomayo River bordering Argentina, abandoning great expanses of the Chaco to the enemy. Theoretically, General Penaranda would build a second army to replace the one destroyed, but Carlos had little faith in the optimistic reports.

"When will we be leaving, Sir?" Carlos asked.

"Immediately. As soon as we can get some transportation. Put in a requisition for four trucks." The Lieutenant picked up a cigarette from his desk and lit it.

Carlos smiled to himself. They weren't going anywhere for a while, not in the middle of the rainy season.

Torrential rains now flooded the flat plains, creating riverbeds where none existed. In the sea of mud, movement had become a nightmare for men and vehicles. Heavy army boots were sucked into the quagmires, leaving the soldiers barefoot or in muddy socks. Trucks sunk to their axles and stopped, their motors whining pitifully until the engine blocks cracked.

"Yes, Sir. I'll make a requisition for your signature."

Carlos returned to the paper in front of him. He didn't dislike Lieutenant Estevez. In fact, he liked him. The young officer, who had volunteered during an attack of patriotism only six months ago, had no military experience and relied heavily upon Carlos to help him

with the troops. At times, the officer would give his orders in
Spanish, and Carlos would translate these into Aymara or Quechua,
elaborating or omitting as he considered best. At other times, the
officer would simply tell Carlos what he wanted, and Carlos would do
the rest.

"Another thing, Sergeant." The Lieutenant turned his thin
frame to face Carlos.

"Yes, Sir."

Remember that you recommended Private Ramon Sanchez be
promoted to Corporal?"

"Yes, Sir."

"Well, the orders have come through."

"That's good news."

"Would you like to tell him, or shall I? I know you two are
very close."

"I'd be happy to do it, Sir. He'll be very pleased. Thank you
for requesting the promotion."

"No problem. Here are the papers. He can pick up his stripes
from Supply, if they have any. Everything seems to be in short
supply these days."

The Lieutenant ground out his cigarette in an open tin can.
"I'll be glad to get moving. All this rain is driving me crazy."

Two days later, as they were lying in their field tent, listening
to the rain which had not stopped for three weeks, Ramon asked,
"*Compadre*, what are you going to do when this is over?"

"The rain?" Carlos replied.

"No. The war. What are you going to do after the war?"

Carlos was watching a slowly widening wet spot in the upper
corner of the tent where drops of water had formed and fell
methodically on the corner of his blanket. "I haven't thought about it.
Go home, I guess."

"What will you do there?"

"What I've always done. Work in the field. Raise potatoes
and quinoa."

"How could you do that, after all you've been through?"

"I like working with the land," answered Carlos. He used his foot to push his blanket to one side, away from the falling drops. "Besides, somebody has to look after my mother and sister."

"You won't be happy. The war has changed you. It's changed us all."

The talking stopped as both of them reflected on Ramon's last statement.

After a while, when Carlos had assumed the conversation was over, Ramon asked, "What about women? Are there any good lays in Ocampo?"

Carlos continued to stare at the wet spot, and didn't answer.

"*Mierda*! You're a virgin," Ramon roared, loud enough for anyone outside the tent to hear. Carlos wanted to strangle him.

"Ha, ha," Ramon sat up laughing, as if it was the funniest thing he had ever heard. "I should have known. There's no women in Ocampo, at least not any willing to go to bed without marriage."

Carlos nodded his head.

"Well, we can fix that. You come with me to La Paz. Doctor Sanchez will have you cured within the first hour." He kept giggling.

"It's not funny," said Carlos, frowning.

Ramon calmed down, suppressing his mirth. "Hey, I didn't mean anything. But seriously, you can't go back to that village. You'll end up marrying a cousin or something and working in a field for the rest of your life. You're too smart for that."

He leaned toward Carlos. "You may not know it, but you're a natural leader. The men who were with you at Pozo Favorita worship you. Christ, you saved their lives. The story has gotten around. Haven't you seen how the other soldiers respect you?"

"I love the land," countered Carlos. "Anyway, the thing I most want after this war is to be alive."

On that somber reflection the conversation died out, but it left Carlos doubting. He was not the same person who had left Ocampo ten months earlier. He had killed, knowingly taking the life of Lieutenant Kunnert and a multitude of Paraguayan soldiers. He had acted to save others and in self-defense, but he had killed nonetheless. Would God forgive him? He would go to Father Augustin and request absolution as soon as he returned to Ocampo.

Chapter 10

Carlos squinted down the sights of his Mauser rifle, and blinked at the sun's reflection on the metal barrel. Only a few months earlier, he had been wading through mud. Now he lay prone in the dust, the heat of the parched ground rising through his khakis into his body. The Chaco is like that, he thought, six months of drought followed by six months of floods. Twelve months of hell.

He wiped the sweat from his eyes and sighted again. The glare from the metal water tank forced him to move his vision to the left, where a wooden windmill signaled the presence of a water well. On the top of the windmill, a white propeller rotated lazily, almost stopped, then moved again.

I wonder how much water that pump is pulling out of the ground, he thought. Or how much is in that tank? God, I'd love some of it right now. He moistened his dry lips with his tongue and let his eyes drift to the other six windmills, spaced intermittently behind the one closest to him, with two small shacks in the middle. Seven wells in all, all good producers according to the Lieutenant. No wonder we want Yrandague back.

He heard a movement on his right, but kept his rifle fixed on the water tank. Shots rang out in the distance.

Ramon crawled up beside him, using his elbows to propel himself forward.

"How many do you think they are?"

"Don't know," Carlos answered. "Not more than five or six. The tank isn't that big, and there's no place else to hide."

Ramon shaded his eyes to take in the small outpost before them. "They haven't moved for the last half hour. Not since the first skirmish."

"Not much anywhere they can go," Carlos said. "The 7th Division must be behind them by now, and we've got them pinned down from here." He shifted his aim to the opposite side of the tank. I'd put a few bullets through the tank itself if water wasn't so precious."

"Sooner or later they have to come out."

"They may be waiting for nightfall, hoping to slip away when it's dark."

Ramon looked at his watch. "Won't be dark for another five hours. We'll be baked by then."

"Take two men and see if you can circle them on the right. That way we can flush them out. Stay low or you'll get your butt shot off."

"Okay. Give me some time though. I can't move very fast on my elbows. I'll fire a shot when I get into position." Ramon edged backwards through the dust.

Carlos wiped the sweat from his brow a second time and studied the water tank. Can't be much better for them, he thought. Huddled against the hot metal of that tank, knowing they'll be shot the moment they move.

He settled in to wait. Patience was a virtue in this war. If you didn't want to get yourself killed, you learned to take your time. He turned his head to look back at the other six men of his squad, all prone in the dust like himself. He made a motion with his hand, signaling them to stay where they were. Then he fixed his sights on the water tank once again. After a long time, he heard a shot from his right and surmised that Ramon was in place. He nodded to the men, alerting them to be ready.

A white object appeared over the rim of the tank. He wiped the sweat from his eyes and recognized a handkerchief knotted around a rifle barrel. The improvised flag moved from side to side. Carlos motioned to his men not to fire.

An arm followed the flag, then a head. Finally the soldier stood up, holding the rifle in the air with one arm, the other raised over his head. Seconds later, a second soldier appeared alongside the first, then another, and then a fourth man. All of them had their hands raised.

"Come out from behind the tank," Carlos shouted.

The soldier with the flag said something to his companions, then stepped into the open. He walked a few feet toward Carlos and stopped. The others slowly followed him. They formed a row in front of the tank.

Carlos rose and motioned to his squad to follow him. He approached the group slowly, his rifle ready. This was the first time he had seen enemy soldiers up close, the first time he had taken prisoners.

He examined the group carefully. All four were short, wiry men, thin from their long campaigns. Their olive drab uniforms were loose and tattered, their shirts worn outside their pants. They wore floppy cloth hats of the same color to protect them from the sun, but their faces were as dark brown as the quebracho. Three of them were barefoot.

Carlos walked up to the first soldier and took the rifle from his hand. The Paraguayan seemed embarrassed to relinquish it.

The rifle was a Mauser of the same model that Carlos used.

"Where did you get this?" Carlos asked.

"Captured," the man answered. He looked at Carlos with brown, penetrating eyes. "Your rifles are better than ours."

Ramon approached from behind the Paraguayans with his two men.

"Are there any more of you?" Carlos asked.

"No," the Paraguayan soldier replied. "The others slipped away. They are somewhere in the brush."

"Did you poison the wells?"

"Why would we do that? Water is just as precious for us."

"*Bien*," Carlos said. "Sit down. We won't hurt you. We'll wait here for our lieutenant."

Carlos ordered his men to stand guard over the prisoners and walked over to the open water tank. It was full. He reached in and tasted the water, which was warm but refreshing.

Ramon came up beside him. "Those prisoners aren't any better equipped than we are. They look like they haven't eaten in a week. I don't understand why they always seem to beat us."

Carlos splashed water on his face, then turned to his friend. "They win because they believe this land is theirs."

Two hours later Lieutenant Estevez came up to where Carlos held the prisoners. He looked at the four Paraguayans sitting on the ground and smiled.

"Well done, Sergeant. Looks as if you captured a few." He walked around the group, inspecting them, and then returned to Carlos. "Most of the enemy got away. We thought we had them surrounded, but they just disappeared into the brush. Amazing. Some of the 7th Division is chasing them now.

He extended his arms toward the windmills. "But at least Yrandague is ours. With these wells, we can push forward into the Northern Chaco, following Colonel Toro's strategy. Our next objective is Picuiba." He slapped his hand with his fist. "Then, by God, who knows? We could mount an offensive to take us all the way to the Paraguay River. After that, Paraguay would collapse. The Chaco would be ours."

Carlos remained silent. He didn't share the optimism of the Lieutenant.

"Things are looking better in the south, too," Lieutenant Estevez continued. "We've received reports that Major Busch led a successful counterattack at Canada Esperanza. You said you knew him."

"Yes, Sir," Carlos replied. "I do."

"Well, he's been promoted to Lieutenant Colonel. Looks like he's making a reputation for himself."

"I'm happy to hear that, Sir."

"Let's take the prisoners back to Division Headquarters. The officers will want to interrogate them."

"Yes, Sir." Carlos motioned to the Paraguayans to stand up. As he rose, the leader caught Carlos' eye. He looked at him as if they understood one another, and then Carlos thought he detected a hint of a smile on the prisoner's lips.

Picuiba feel into Bolivian hands as easily as the Lieutenant had predicted.

Almost too easily, Carlos thought.

Then the Bolivian offensive bogged down. Lack of trucks, not enough troops, something held up any further advance. In early November the Paraguayan Army retaliated with a series of small exploratory attacks, forcing the Bolivians to fix their defensive positions. At Picuiba, Carlos could now see enemy patrols moving in the distance.

Later that month Lieutenant Estevez entered the company headquarters tent with a long face. He sat down heavily in his camp chair and stared at the tent wall.

"Something wrong, Sir?" Carlos asked.

"A tragedy," the Lieutenant replied. He picked up a cigarette and lit it. "Seven thousand of our men have surrendered at Canada El Carmen in the south. With all their artillery and supplies. The Command Center at Ballivian has collapsed."

The Lieutenant hung his head. "There are rumors that the officers at Ballivian abandoned their troops and fled across the Pilcomayo River into Argentina. Most of the new conscripts just threw away their weapons and ran. *Macheteros* are reported to be slaughtering any soldiers separated from their units. It's a complete disaster."

Carlos watched the officer snuff out the cigarette he had just begun, then pick up a new one and light it.

"It's happened before, Sir. The Paraguayans are good at encirclement. It's their most successful tactic."

"But Colonel Toro didn't tell us anything. He kept assuring us that our offensive was going well on both fronts. He's still talking about making a dash for the Paraguay River."

"How did you find out, then?"

"A staff officer from General Penaranda's headquarters was at our meeting this morning. He brought the news. But Colonel Toro must have known about it before. It happened more that a week ago. He deliberately kept us in the dark."

"Don't take it personally, Sir. Stranger things have happened in this war."

Two weeks later, at the beginning of December, Carlos noticed something disturbing. The water distributed that day was warm and stagnant. He knew that trucks brought fresh water every day from the seven wells at Yrandague. At first he speculated that the water trucks had broken down, which was not unusual. The following day the water was still warm and stagnant, and was rationed for the first time. The rumor mill, always active among the conscripts, said that there were too many new arrivals at the camp.

Lieutenant Estevez was gone all morning at a meeting of the officers. At noon he returned with instructions that water usage was to be severely restricted. No more washing or shaving. Water was to be used only for drinking and cooking.

On the third day when Lieutenant Estevez returned from his morning meeting, he took Carlos aside.

"Sergeant Obregon, I want you to set apart one barrel of water today and hide it. Hide it anywhere you want, but do it well. Don't tell anybody and use your most trusted men. Do you understand?"

"Yes, Sir," replied Carlos, thinking this was uncharacteristic of the Lieutenant, who was a fair and honest officer. Nevertheless, he did as he was told.

On the fifth day there was no water distribution and the troops began to grumble, for they were thirsty. With the temperature hovering at 104 degrees Fahrenheit, dehydration occurred quickly. The end of the dry season was approaching, but the rains had not yet begun. The ground remained parched and dusty, emanating an oppressive heat which blurred the vision and exhausted the body. Carlos could taste the dust in his mouth.

Lieutenant Estevez returned from his daily briefing with a long face. He had Carlos assemble A Company and marched them through the dust to the center of the camp, where Carlos counted eighteen trucks parked in a disorderly row. Several cannons were scattered around the trucks.

"Maybe they're taking us out," Ramon whispered in his ear.

Before Carlos could answer, Lieutenant Estevez gave the order. "Sergeant, have your men load the artillery onto the trucks. Begin with this one."

Carlos looked around and saw other troops wheeling cannons toward the trucks, cannons which were being withdrawn from the front lines. He realized then that a full scale retreat was in progress.

The cannons, although light artillery, were heavy and awkward to position on the waiting vehicles. Using two wooden planks as ramps, the soldiers had to push each cannon up the steep incline, taking care that the metal wheels remained on the planks. The men used ropes to pull the heavy carriages up into the truck bed and to keep the wheels aligned. Carlos remained below, helping his men push, while Ramon and five others pulled with all their might from above. Each truck could accommodate four cannons, which had to be maneuvered in place.

The heat was intense and the men were sweating profusely before the first cannon was positioned, blocked by chucks so it would not shift within the moving truck. More artillery kept arriving and filled the center of the camp. Other soldiers joined in to speed the loading. Soon the troops had discarded their shirts and dark stains of perspiration appeared between their legs and around their buttocks. Rivulets of sweat ran down Carlos' face, blurring his vision, as he pushed yet another cannon up the ramp. His men had filled one truck and were loading the second. Each gun seemed heavier than the last, and the men were near exhaustion from the heat and the work, when Carlos heard a yell.

"Hurry up, you lazy bastards! Get those guns loaded!"

Carlos recognized the voice, a voice that caused him to freeze in place, his shoulder wedged against the gun carriage. Sweat ran down his forehead and blinded him.

"I said hurry up, not slow down." Carlos felt the sharp sting of a baton against his leg. It was him, he was sure. Gutierrez! The bastard officer who had come for him at Ocampo.

Carlos sunk his shoulder into the carriage and shoved with all his might, his strength multiplied by his rage. The wheels resisted and he cursed in desperation. He pushed harder. He felt the cannon reach the bed of the truck and roll forward, pulled by the ropes, releasing the pressure upon him. He spun around, wiping the sweat from his eyes, trying desperately to clear his vision. He saw the short figure of Lieutenant Gutierrez, a body and face forever engraved in his mind, walking away in the direction of the other trucks.

Carlos looked around quickly for his rifle, stacked in a pyramid with the others twenty yards away. He ran to the stacked weapons and seized the first gun his hands touched, jerking it from the pile. The other rifles fell in a noisy clatter. He wiped his eyes again, jammed the bolt backward and then forward to insert a shell, and raised the gun in the direction of the departing officer, who vanished behind a truck before he had time to aim. He remained frozen, his mouth open, gasping for breath, his heart pounding in his chest, the rifle still raised.

"What's the matter, Sergeant? Something wrong?" The calm voice of Lieutenant Estevez brought him back to his senses.

Carlos lowered the rifle and tried to calm his breathing. "Nothing, Sir," he replied between heavy breaths. "Nothing," he repeated.

The Lieutenant looked at Carlos questioningly. "Maybe you'd better get back to work," he suggested.

"Yes, Sir," Carlos answered. He stacked the fallen rifles once again, taking care to leave his own weapon on the outside.

The rest of the day Carlos kept an eye out for Gutierrez as he and his troops continued to load artillery onto the trucks. By mid-afternoon the work was finished and Carlos slung his loaded rifle over his shoulder. Large numbers of officers assembled near the vehicles, but he couldn't spot Gutierrez. Now that the cannons were loaded, the officers scrambled on board the trucks, occupying the space between the guns. The higher ranking officers commandeered the cabs.

Carlos stared at the lieutenants, captains, and majors pushing and shoving to find a place on the trucks, while ordering off the enlisted men who had done the loading. Then the engines started, one after another, like a squadron of airplanes preparing for flight, and the trucks rumbled off to the north, scattering dust over the exhausted soldiers.

"What the hell?" Ramon said.

"They're going," Carlos answered. "The officers are leaving."

"Cowards!" Ramon shouted at the departing trucks. "*Hijos de Putas!*" The troops picked up the cry.

Carlos was about to join in when he looked to his left and saw Lieutenant Estevez standing in the dust watching the trucks depart, a sad smile on his face. Carlos had not sighted Lieutenant Gutierrez again, but he was sure the fat bastard was on one of the trucks. His smoldering hatred had been ignited again, but he could wait. He knew the time would come when he could settle the score.

Most of the troops found themselves without an officer in command, wandering about aimlessly, trying to decide what to do. Some of the soldiers walked after the trucks, uncertain of their destination. Others joined the few units that still had an officer in command. Wild rumors circulated among those who remained: a massive enemy force was bearing down upon them; the war was over; *Macheteros* had been seen behind the lines.

The next day, December 6, there was still no water. Canteens were empty and the troops ate a dry breakfast without coffee. When Lieutenant Estevez returned at mid-morning, he took Carlos aside a second time.

"Sergeant Obregon, I want to discuss something with you. What I say is strictly confidential."

"Yes, Sir," Carlos replied.

"Our Army is surrounded, Sergeant. The Paraguayans have captured Yrendague and cut off our water supply. That is why most of the officers fled with the artillery yesterday, to escape the trap. Now we are completely encircled, even to the west, toward our homeland."

Carlos nodded that he understood. The worst fears of the troops were true.

The Lieutenant continued, "The few remaining officers here at Picuiba have decided to surrender. Otherwise our troops will die of thirst."

Carlos saw perspiration on the Lieutenant's upper lip.

"Sir, why didn't you leave with the other officers?"

"I couldn't abandon my men, Sergeant." He wiped his forehead with the back of his hand. "Maybe I made a mistake."

"But Sir, there are thousands of troops here. Why don't we fight?"

"There are too many of us, Sergeant. Over twelve thousand. That's the problem. These men consume enormous quantities of water and they will die without it. Even with the surrender, I don't know how many can be saved." The Lieutenant paused, and Carlos thought he saw his eyes moisten.

"The surrender is planned for tomorrow, December 7. I don't want to surrender, Sergeant. I don't want to spend the next few years

86

in a Paraguayan P.O.W. camp...if we survive. I want to go home. I'm from the Altiplano, like you. I don't want to die in the Chaco."

Carlos thought the Lieutenant was close to breaking down, but the officer pulled himself together and continued.

"I want your help, Sergeant, but only on a voluntary basis. I think a small group of us, say ten men, might be able to get through the enemy lines at night and make our way to the Andes. It won't be easy to slip by undetected. We would be risking our lives."

Carlos considered the proposal. It was a desperate move, but he trusted the Lieutenant. He had hated the Chaco from the first time he saw the land. The idea of spending years as a prisoner here was unthinkable.

The drone of a Curtis pursuit airplane interrupted his thoughts. The Bolivian biplane passed overhead and Carlos presumed it was doing reconnaissance. However, as they both looked up, leaflets floated down through the clear sky, spinning in the air like gyrating white doves. Several landed nearby, and both men picked up a copy. They read:

"To the officers of the 7th Division,

You must resist the enemy advance at all cost. No consideration must be given to the fatigue of the troops. It is necessary to exert them to the utmost of their possibilities. One or two days of effort and sacrifice will not annihilate them. The enemy troops give us more than a sufficient example in this respect, demonstrating to us that it is possible to live even months without almost any means. Yesterday they made a raid of nearly forty kilometers advancing by path and on foot in order to attack Yrendague with the utmost audacity and energy.

Col. David Toro"

As Carlos finished reading, he realized the irony of the message which must have been written several days previously. Most of the Bolivian officers had already fled with the artillery, abandoning their men to the enemy. The remaining officers had decided to surrender. And on top of this, their own senior commander, Colonel

Toro, safely headquartered at Carandaiti, over one hundred miles in the rear, was praising the enemy troops for their willingness to sacrifice.

Carlos crumpled his leaflet and threw it to the ground in disgust.

"I'm willing to try, Sir."

"Good. Sergeant, I know your men respect you. Pick nine you trust the most. Have them clean and oil their weapons and issue each a full canteen of water from the hidden barrel. Tell them to drink their fill from the barrel before leaving. I want to move out at ten tonight."

"Yes, Sir." Carlos saluted and left. For some reason he didn't feel afraid. Then he realized why — he was going home.

Chapter 11

The men assembled at 9:45 p.m. under a dark, moonless sky.
Carlos had selected Ramon and eight of the veterans with him at Pozo
Favorita. With the exception of Ramon, he told them only that they
were going on patrol that night. He told Ramon the truth, and his
friend volunteered without hesitation. Ramon, too, wanted out of the
Chaco.

At ten they departed the camp, leaving behind their blankets
and mosquito nets. When challenged by the sentry, Lieutenant
Estevez identified himself and said they were on a scouting mission.
They walked straight north into the desert instead of west toward the
Andes, calculating that the enemy would expect any breakout
attempts to be in the latter direction. Avoiding the dirt road used by
the trucks that had departed the previous day, they moved across
broken terrain. Ramon went ahead as a scout, followed by Carlos and
one man. The Lieutenant and six others formed the main body. One
soldier trailed thirty yards behind as a rearguard.

The march started well. They moved quietly but steadily
forward, alert for trouble and weapons ready. As their eyes adjusted
to the dark, they took care to avoid stepping on fallen branches or
loose rocks, and maintained complete silence. The heat had lessened
since midday, but the night was still warm and without a breeze.
Carlos could feel the sweat beginning to form on his body.

After two miles, Ramon spotted a Paraguayan campfire to
their left, so they veered farther east from their original path, farther
still from their final destination. The brush was more dense there,

with an occasional shriveled tree. Ramon followed the bottom of dry gullies whenever he could find them, the other men snaking behind him.

By three o'clock in the morning Carlos estimated that they had covered twelve miles. Every muscle in his legs ached. He could smell the acrid odor of his own sweat, which had by now soaked his underwear and socks.

Since the first sighting, they had not seen any more enemy encampments. The Lieutenant didn't know whether they were through the Paraguayan lines or not, but decided that the men needed a short rest, so they stopped in a small depression surrounded by scrub brush. Carlos posted four guards, one at each of the compass points, and the remaining men stretched out on the earth. A few opened their canteens.

Just as Carlos sat down on the ground and let his legs relax, he heard a thud to his left and then the sound of a falling body. Dark figures appeared from nowhere. Carlos saw the silver gleam of a machete blade above the Lieutenant.

"Behind you, Sir!" Carlos yelled.

Lieutenant Estevez wheeled and raised his left arm, drawing his pistol with his right hand. He screamed as the blade sliced deep into his upraised arm, and tumbled backward, shooting wildly as he fell. Carlos scooped up his rifle and fired at the figure over the Lieutenant. He dodged to block the blow of a machete aimed at him. The blade knocked the heavy rifle out of his hands and he tumbled backward on the ground. A black figure loomed over him.

The *Machetero* swung the machete behind his head, ready to strike again. Carlos crossed his arms to shield himself and saw the blade descend. Suddenly the figure toppled sideways at the sound of a loud explosion and the machete buried itself in the ground on his left side. Carlos looked up to see Ramon with his rifle still smoking.

Pandemonium broke out. Shouts, screams, and rifle retorts ricocheted off each other. Carlos recovered his rifle and fired at the figures wielding machetes. In two minutes it was over.

When the shooting stopped, Carlos set down his rifle and crossed his arms to control his shaking. Four *Macheteros* lay dead in the small depression. Carlos surmised they had been following his group, waiting for an opportunity to strike. Carlos had lost five men and the Lieutenant was badly wounded. The cut had gone through the flesh, breaking the bone in his left arm, which dangled at an awkward angle from the elbow. Carlos applied a tourniquet and made a rough sling from the shirt of a dead soldier.

"Let's get out of here. After all that noise, the Paraguayans know where we are," Carlos commanded.

"Leave me, Sergeant. I can't travel this way. Get out while you can." It was obvious from the Lieutenant's voice that the shock of the attack was wearing off and the pain was settling in.

"No, Sir. You stayed with us when you had the chance to leave with the other officers. We're taking you with us."

Carlos took charge, helping the Lieutenant to rise, and supporting him as he walked. They moved faster now, no longer trying to maintain silence but to distance themselves from this place of death. With only six men left, they traveled as one group.

By sunrise the survivors had covered another eight miles straight north. Carlos decided it was too risky to stop, so they kept walking, angling to the northwest. By noontime, they had left behind all trees, and the scrub brush was thinning out. They were exposed but had to keep moving.

The Lieutenant's sling was soaked with blood; he was weak and perspiring heavily, leaning more and more on Carlos. Carlos sat him down, gave him water, and checked the tourniquet. Satisfied there was nothing more to do, he picked up the Lieutenant, adjusted his weight on his shoulder, and started walking again.

When darkness came, Carlos felt more secure. They had walked all day across open country and seen no one. He knew they were well past the enemy lines. Tomorrow they would turn west, toward the Andes. They ate their dry rations, drank part of their remaining water, and fell asleep immediately.

The next morning they rose before sunrise and finished the last of their water before moving out. Lieutenant Estevez was feverish, his wound festering from the heat and dirt. He asked Carlos to leave him, but once again Carlos refused. He put the Lieutenant's good arm over his shoulder and half-carried, half-dragged him forward. They walked until noon and collapsed as a group, their tongues swollen from lack of water. The Lieutenant was pale and trembling with fever.

"Sergeant, this time it's an order. Leave me here," he murmured through dry lips. Carlos was exhausted. He knew he couldn't carry the Lieutenant any longer. Their eyes met, and each of them understood. Tears formed in the Lieutenant's eyes and coursed down his cheeks, washing away the dust in long thin lines. Carlos looked away in order not to embarrass him.

Carlos, Ramon, and the three remaining soldiers moved out again, leaving Lieutenant Estevez in the shade of a bush. After fifteen minutes they heard a pistol shot. Carlos did not look back.

When night fell they stopped again. There was no water or food, and thirst had become a gnawing obsession. They simply collapsed on the ground and slept. When Carlos awakened the next day and went to relieve himself, one of the soldiers followed him.

"Please, Sergeant."

Carlos turned to look at the man who was on his knees behind him, his empty canteen held in an outstretched hand, supplicating. At first he didn't understand what the man wanted, but then it became clear. Carlos took the canteen from the outstretched hand and urinated into it, then handed it back. The soldier gulped down the warm, yellow liquid greedily, spilling it down his chin and neck; a few drops spotted the dry earth. Too ashamed to look at Carlos, he murmured a barely audible thanks.

The sun burned like a torch. Even though they started early, by nine o'clock the heat was overpowering. The earth radiated transparent, shimmering waves, baking their nostrils until the skin cracked. By midday they were so dehydrated they no longer perspired. They walked in silence, their throats too dry to talk. One by one, they abandoned their rifles, dropping them along their path. Any thought of fighting had vanished; now they just wanted to survive. They no longer had enough liquid in their bodies to urinate, and their limbs were beginning to shrink, desiccated like plants without moisture.

In the full burning heat of the afternoon, one of the soldiers fell to his knees and rolled onto his back in the sand. Carlos recognized the man who had drunk his urine. Calling a halt, he knelt over the fallen soldier but could not find a pulse. The man's eyes were fixed in a glassy stare and his mouth gaped open. Even in death, the cadaver craved water.

Carlos stood on wobbly legs and walked away from the body. Two soldiers passed him with their bayonets unsheathed. They fell upon the corpse, slit the veins of the arms, and sucked the warm blood. Ramon, who had sat apart, looked at Carlos questioningly. Receiving no sign, he shrugged his shoulders, took out his own bayonet, and crawled to the body.

Carlos turned his back on the scene and sat on the ground. Low guttural sounds and occasional coughing came from behind him. Bowing his head, he tried to make the sign of the cross on his chest, but his right hand refused to move. He looked down on his trembling, disobedient fist, then lifted it to the sky. "Damn you! No merciful God would allow this!"

Carlos unsheathed his bayonet and returned to the dead soldier, where he cut a slit in the cadaver's upper leg. The blood was warm and sticky, sickening to swallow, but he forced himself to suck the wound despite gagging several times.

When he had satisfied his thirst, he motioned to the men to gather around him. His tongue was swollen and stained red with blood; a crimson rivulet ran down the left side of his mouth to his chin.

"I'm exhausted… from carrying the Lieutenant," he whispered through cracked lips. "You go ahead. I'll follow… more slowly. If you find help, send them for me."

"No, *compadre*," said Ramon. "We've come this far together. I stay with you. I'll walk slower, too."

The two privates nodded their agreement, stood up, and walked west. Ramon looked at Carlos, and they exchanged weak smiles. They rose slowly and followed the disappearing figures.

Carlos fell several times during the afternoon. Each time it was torture to rise and start again. But each time he forced himself up, following Ramon. Their two companions had vanished in the distance.

By nightfall they were barely moving. As he walked slowly forward, one foot after the other, Carlos lost all sense of balance. He wobbled now from side to side and had to put his hand on Ramon's shoulder to keep from falling. His boots stuck to the ground; so heavy that each step required a slow agonizing effort, draining his little remaining strength. Even standing was difficult. Carlos collapsed forward on his stomach and Ramon lay down beside him. Darkness enveloped them.

The next morning Carlos awoke late. The sun was already overhead and he could feel the heat on his back. He opened his eyes and saw Ramon, still asleep at his side. He realized that he could not rise. He felt no pain; he just could not get up. He knew he was still alive, for his breath stirred the dry dust beneath his nostrils, but he was too weak to stand. His body felt dry and brittle, strangely light, as if the slightest wind could blow him around like a leaf. But there was no wind, not even a breeze. Fucking Chaco, thought Carlos. I hate this place. Carlos decided to die and closed his eyes once again. A silent peace flowed through his body.

"Hello there, *Carlitos*. Taking a nap, are we?"

Carlos knew it was a familiar voice. He was sure that he was hallucinating, but felt strong arms grasp his shoulders and turn him over. He looked up into the face of Lt. Colonel German Busch.

Chapter 12

When Carlos awoke again, he was in a cot at a field hospital, covered by a light wool blanket. The air inside the tent felt cool and fresh, with a touch of moisture. Ramon lay in the cot beside him, already awake.

"Where are we?" Carlos asked with a weak voice.

"At Villa Montes, *compadre*. It's in the foothills of the Andes. We're getting closer to home," Ramon replied.

"How did they find us?"

"The two men who went ahead ran into one of our patrols. Lt. Colonel Busch organized a search and retraced their steps. We were lucky."

Carlos sighed. He didn't consider himself lucky; every bone in his arms and legs ached, his throat was raw, and his body drained of all energy.

Lt. Colonel Busch came to see him in mid-morning.

"*Ola, Carlitos*. How are you feeling?" the Colonel asked.

"Weak, Sir," replied Carlos.

"You're suffering from dehydration. The doctor says about a week before you can be up and about."

"Thank you for saving my life, Sir."

"*Nada*. Glad we arrived in time. Your men told me of your escape from Picuiba, the attack of the *Macheteros*, and how you helped Lieutenant Estevez. That was quite a feat."

"He was a good officer. I liked him."

"He certainly was a brave officer. I don't know of any others who tried to escape after the circle was closed. We lost over twelve thousand men at Picuiba. Think about it, Carlos, twelve thousand. Most of them surrendered, but some isolated units wandered off into the brush and died of thirst." The Colonel rubbed the back of his neck and sighed.

"Even the Paraguayans didn't have enough water to supply the prisoners, so many of our men died after giving up. Our reconnaissance planes said they saw corpses being dropped off the trucks that were taking them away. The road to the Paraguay River was littered with our dead. All their weapons and material were captured, except for the artillery. It was a major disaster."

"I'm sorry, Sir."

"Shouldn't be. You had the guts to escape, and tried to save your C.O. I've recommended you for a battlefield commission, *Carlitos*. If approved, you'll be Lieutenant Obregon. Congratulations!"

"I don't deserve it, Sir. I know nothing about being an officer."

"Don't worry. You have shown twice now that you have the leadership qualities to take charge in difficult circumstances. You can learn the rest. Besides, you're a hero for having led your men out of Picuiba. We desperately need a few Bolivian heroes right now." Colonel Busch bent over and patted Carlos on the shoulder.

"I'll send my orderly around and have you measured for an officer's uniform. It should be ready by the time you leave the hospital."

"Thank you, Sir. I don't know what to say," Carlos replied, his eyes moist.

"There's more. The medics say you need three weeks to regain your strength. Take a vacation and go see your family. I'll draw up the orders."

"That's wonderful, Sir. Where do I report when I return?"

"To me, here at Villa Montes. I want you under my command. Who knows? Maybe I'll need you to carry me out of a tough spot sometime."

"It would be an honor, Sir."

"One last thing, *Carlitos*. Before you leave, I want you to attend a meeting we are having eight days from now. It's a group of officers interested in improving our country. We call ourselves the Marshal Santa Cruz Lodge."

The meeting took place on the evening of December 19, 1934, at the headquarters of Colonel David Toro, the officer who had commanded the destroyed 7th Division. Carlos wondered how the Colonel could remain in the Army after such a debacle. Colonel Toro had sent his men into a trap and failed to rescue them when the trap closed. Carlos remembered bitterly the leaflets exhorting the officers at Picuiba to fight, the leaflets signed by Toro and dropped after the officers had fled. Evidently the General Command protected their own, no matter how incompetent.

Nineteen officers, all under thirty-five years of age, crowded into the small wooden building, using folding chairs to form a rough semi-circle. Colonel Toro, the highest ranking and oldest officer, sat behind his campaign table, a tall slim man with a patrician nose and pointed ears, whose eyes wandered restlessly. Lt. Colonel Busch sat at his side, greeting each new arrival.

Carlos took a seat behind the officers at the left side since he was attending as a guest, and was still weak from his ordeal. His eyes moved around the room studying the Lodge members, when one face caught his attention. He looked again to make sure, and felt his anger rising. The oval face, the slick hair, the smooth, almost feminine skin. It was him, there was no doubt. Gutierrez! The same Gutierrez who had come for the recruits at Ocampo, the one who had spit in his face, who had kicked him like a dog. Almost two years had passed but Carlos remembered every detail of that day.

The same Gutierrez whom Carlos had seen running away at Picuiba. Now he was a Captain, judging from the bars on his collar. Carlos forced himself to take his eyes off the officer for fear of drawing his attention, but the hatred inside him caused his jaw to stiffen and his skin to redden. He looked down at the floor. The time would come. Now that Carlos knew where Gutierrez was, he could wait until his strength returned.

Colonel Toro rose to his feet and opened the meeting. "Gentlemen, thank you for coming. Before we begin our discussions tonight, I would like to ask you first for a vow of secrecy. You are all aware that the Lodge is outside the normal command structure of the Bolivian Army, and is therefore illegal."

Carlos looked up with surprise.

"We are acting on our own initiative, united by our desire to improve the way the war is being conducted, introducing more dynamic leadership, like Marshal Santa Cruz himself, who gave us our independence from the Spaniards. What we discuss in these meetings must remain strictly among ourselves. If anyone ever questions you regarding the Lodge, even a superior officer, you must deny its existence. Do you all swear this?

A chorus of "I do" answered him.

"Thank you. I'll now give the floor to Lt. Colonel Busch."

Colonel Busch pushed his chair back and stood up. "Gentlemen, you all know me. I love our country and will gladly die for it if necessary. But I can't continue to serve a President I don't respect."

The officers looked at him attentively.

"I'm disgusted with President Salamanca! First he got us into this war so he could be known as the president who reclaimed the Chaco - so he could be re-elected in 1937." Busch paused to let this sink in.

"He ordered us into combat before the Army was prepared. Then, when things didn't go as well as he had expected, he called General Kundt back from Germany to show us how to win the war. You saw what happened then - the futile assaults on Nanawa, and our rout at Campo Via."

Carlos saw several officers nod their agreement.

"When our illustrious president finally realized he had made a mistake with General Kundt, he gave the command to General Penaranda, an officer who should have retired ten years ago. We have better commanders sitting here in this very room." He looked at Colonel Toro.

Toro cleared his throat and pronounced solemnly, "General Penaranda is a fine person, loyal to the army, but of the old school. He lacks the courage to be a good commander. What we need now is bold leadership."

Carlos shifted uncomfortably in his chair.

"That's why President Salamanca chose him," Busch added. "The president wants someone to take his orders, so that he himself can run the campaign from La Paz. From La Paz, goddamnit!" Busch slammed his fist on the table.

"We all know the president himself insisted that General Penaranda make a stand at Ballivian. Both Colonel Toro and I argued that he pull farther back, closer to the Andes, and the General agreed with us. But no, President Salamanca couldn't afford to give up more of the Chaco, because it would make him look bad politically. Look what happened! We lost Ballivian and another nine thousand men. That's why I'm mad. We've had enough interference from Salamanca!"

Colonel Busch sat down.

The officers were nodding and Carlos heard murmurs of agreement in the room.

A bald-headed, squat officer stood. Toro said, "Yes, Major Melendez? You have the floor."

"I agree with Colonel Busch. What we need in Bolivia is a real leader. Two years ago I was in Italy, studying at their military college, and I saw what one man can do. I tell you, Benito Mussolini has completely changed that country. Before him, everything in Italy was disorderly, unorganized, a country without direction. Now it's like another nation. The trains run on time, their hydroplanes lead the world in air transport, the military has modern weapons. Productivity of factory workers is at an all time high. Even the boys and girls are organized in Young Fascist clubs. You should see the pride they have in their country now. We could do the same thing in Bolivia if we had the right leadership."

"Thank you, Major," said Colonel Toro. "I'm sure everybody in this room agrees with your assessment. We need new leadership." He glanced around the room. Another officer stood. "Major Garza?"

"I'm mad, too. Like Colonel Busch. But I'm mad at Standard Oil. They've been screwing us since the war started. Despite their wells and their refinery at Camiri, we can never get enough gasoline. One-third of our trucks are idle for lack of fuel. We protest and protest, and they say they can't give us more. But let me tell you a secret. We've discovered that they've been pumping gasoline across

99

the border into Argentina. One of the Bolivian engineers working at Camiri told us."

"Those bastards!" Busch shouted, and several other officers echoed him.

Another officer spoke from his seat, "I've heard that the company turned over detailed terrain maps of the Chaco to the Paraguayans."

Major Garza, who was still standing, answered, "I've heard that rumor, too, but I can't confirm it. What I do know is that the gringos told us their refinery couldn't produce aviation fuel for our planes, but when we sent our own technicians, the refinery began producing it one month later. I think the oil company is on the side of the Paraguayans." He sat down.

"When the war is over, we'll take care of Mr. Rockefeller's company," Busch said, rising again, "and the mining companies, too. Patino, Hochshild, and Aramayo are making a fortune out of this war, while the country is going bankrupt. I've learned that under pressure Patino offered to loan the government money, but guess what? He wanted a higher interest rate than the foreign banks. Some patriot!"

Major Melendez spoke from his chair, "I understand that Patino owns the Schneider Creusot Arms Company in France. They're selling arms to Paraguay, supplying our enemy."

"You see what they're doing," exclaimed Busch, still on his feet and leaning forward over the table. "The politicians, Standard Oil, the mining companies - they are our real enemy! They tie our hands behind our backs, help Paraguay, while bleeding our country dry!"

Waving his fist in the air, Busch shouted, "When the war ends, we're going to make changes, and the Lodge is going to lead the way. Are you with us?"

The officers all rose in agreement. "Yes! Yes!" they cried. Even Carlos stood, although he said nothing. His anger, stronger and more profound, was focused on Captain Gutierrez.

Chapter 13

The lorry arrived at Ocampo in mid-afternoon, stopping in the small, unpaved village square. Carlos jumped down from the truck bed and thanked the driver. After being on the road four days, his new officer's uniform and boots were caked with dust, and his joints stiff and aching. An empty Army supply truck had brought him from Villa Montes to Tarija, and another one took him to Villazon. At Villazon he had used his free military transportation pass to travel north on the train. Then he had hitched rides on mining trucks and merchandise vans to reach home.

No train or bus serviced Ocampo. The small village had only three hundred twelve inhabitants, and was isolated from the rest of the world. The stone houses surrounding the dirt plaza were large, but old and shabby. Rusting iron grills covered the square windows set in peeling, whitewashed facades, leaving the impression of a town that had seen better days.

The biggest house on the plaza belonged to Don Simon. In addition, the police station, the office of the mayor, and the village church all faced the dirt square. Small merchants occupied the other buildings on the plaza, using them as both shops and living quarters. One small bar served *chicha*, the cheap white liquor made from fermented maize, which was popular with the Indians. With its four wooden tables and dilapidated chairs, this bar served as the center of what little activity existed in the village.

Carlos walked east, past the bar, enjoying the familiar surroundings. He lived in the last of a series of crude unpainted adobe houses which shrank in size as he moved away from the center, leaving more distance between them until they stood alone and isolated on the mountain slopes. Carlos was happy to be back in Ocampo and looked forward to seeing his mother and sister again. They had always been a close family and he was especially fond of his little sister, Segundina. Even his father, Luis, who took his one-week vacation during the Christmas season, might be home from the mines.

Approaching his home, Carlos frowned when he saw a black ribbon nailed to the front door. He quickened his pace and entered without knocking. His mother sat on a straw mat in front of a mud brick stove in the far corner, preparing the evening meal, her back to him. Her thin gray hair fell loosely on the black shawl covering her stooped shoulders. A large open kettle hung over the wood fire and a wisp of smoke, the same color as her hair, curled up and out through a small opening in the straw roof.

"Mama, it's me. I'm home," Carlos announced.

Maria dropped her wooden stirring spoon at the sound of his voice, and turned her head with a start. He lifted her easily, a weightless substance in his hands, and embraced her. He could feel her frail body trembling against him.

"Carlos," she sobbed, burying her face in his chest, and repeating his name over and over.

"Don't worry, Mama. It's fine. I'm okay," he tried to console her. She looked up at him with a face more wrinkled than he had remembered, a face lined with suffering and now stained with tears.

"It's your father, Carlos. He died while you were away. It was an accident at the mine. They sent his body home."

Carlos held her at arm's length.

"What type of accident, Mama?"

"They didn't say. Just an accident."

"When, Mama? When did it happen?" Carlos supported her in his arms, afraid she might fall.

"This summer, Carlos, before the harvest. I had no way to tell you. I didn't know where you were," Maria answered, still crying.

Carlos pulled her to his chest again and rocked her in his arms.

"Didn't you get any of my letters, Mama? I sent you money and told you how to reach me."

"No, nothing. Nothing at all. We thought that you might have been killed."

Carlos cursed the Army and the Postal Service. What bastards! Someone had stolen the money he had sent and thrown away the letters.

"I'm sorry, Mama. I am so sorry. I wrote several times." He held her until she stopped weeping.

"Where is Segundina, Mama? I want to see her."

"She is working at the house of Don Simon," replied Maria, looking aside.

"But Mama, you can't till the land and harvest by yourself. Segundina has always helped. It's too much for you alone."

"We no longer own the land, Carlos. When your father died, the money stopped coming. We had nothing to eat. We had to sell the land. To Don Simon."

The news hit him with the same impact as a Paraguayan bullet, wounding him internally. "But Mama," he stared at her with disbelief, "the land was everything Papa worked for."

"We had to eat," Maria said sadly.

Carlos cursed the Army and the Postal Service again. The money he sent could have saved the land.

"When will Segundina be home?" he asked.

Again Maria averted her eyes. "Perhaps after supper," she replied.

"Where is Papa buried?"

"At the cemetery."

"I want to visit his grave."

"Not now, Carlos. It will soon be dark. The Old Ones will be there. Go tomorrow."

Carlos hesitated. The trip had exhausted him.

"Sit down. The food will be ready soon."

Carlos and Maria ate in silence. She had prepared potato soup which they ate from clay bowls, using tin spoons. When they finished, Maria cleaned the bowls, but Carlos had nothing to do. He lay down on the straw mat and cured llama hides that served as his bed, intending to wait there for Segundina. Until he was twelve, he had slept in a common bed with his mother and sister, and even his father if he were home, but after that he slept apart. He yawned, covered himself with a blanket, and sleep overcame him.

The sweet, pungent smell of dried llama dung burning in an open fire awakened Carlos the next day. Opening his eyes, he saw his mother sitting in front of the mud brick stove. Steam rose from the blackened kettle hanging on a wooden crossbar. It had been this way as long as he could remember. Maria rose early, started the fire, and prepared breakfast before the other members of the family awakened. She spent most of her life in front of the stove, never letting the fire die out, tending to the kettle, adding spices and herbs from the small cubbyholes in the nearby dirt wall. Using potatoes and quinoa as the main staples, she cooked a variety of simple dishes.

When Carlos got up, he dressed in his civilian clothes, fingering his wool poncho like an old friend. He found an old pair of sandals and carefully strapped them on his bare feet, studying them with pleasure. For the first time in many months, his feet felt unrestrained, natural, free from the confinement of his stiff army boots.

Then he set off down the hill to collect wood for the fire. He returned with a bundle of small branches on his back and threw them down outside the house, alongside the pile of dried llama dung. He went inside and took a seat on the stool across the room from the fire. Breakfast consisted of boiled potatoes, which he peeled with his fingers and spiced with pepper before eating. He saw no sign of his sister.

After breakfast he walked to the cemetery on the other side of the town, pausing frequently to inhale the chilled mountain air and study the familiar mountains. Along the way he stopped at the bar to buy a paper bag full of coca leaves and some *chicha* in a used open topped tin can. The small, unkempt cemetery lay one-half mile from the village, isolated from any dwellings, for his people did not like to be close to the dead. Weeds grew among the crumbling mud markers and rotting wood crosses used as gravestones. Carlos searched until he found an unpainted wooden cross with the initials L.O. crudely carved into the horizontal stick. Flowers had been entwined on the cross, but they were now dry and crumbling, their dead petals scattered on the grave. In the corner of the cemetery, a large pile of bones lay exposed to the elements. It was the custom to dig up the graves after ten years, to provide space for the more recently deceased. The old bones were mixed together and thrown in the corner to dry and bleach.

Carlos dropped to his knees and crossed himself. He poured a small amount of *chicha* in a circle around his father's grave as an offering, taking a sip for himself when he had finished. Then he opened the paper bag, and selected three of the choicest coca leaves, ones which were green and undamaged. He laid them carefully one on top of the other, with the three points slightly spread, and held them between the thumb and forefinger of his right hand. Once this was done, he bowed his head and blew gently on the leaves in the direction of the cross, transferring the blessing of the coca leaves to his dead father.

He placed the leaves at the base of the cross for his father's spirit and rummaged in the bag for more coca, which he chewed slowly, closing his eyes so he could appreciate the taste. If the coca were sweet, this would bring him good fortune. If it were bitter, more trouble awaited him. He grimaced as a sour taste spread through his mouth.

Carlos remained at the cemetery for over an hour, drinking the rest of the *chicha* and chewing more coca, praying for his father's soul, and thinking of the man who had sacrificed himself for his family. The man who had endured the mines for so many years in order that his family could have their own plot of land. Now it was all gone. A life wasted. The coca made him even more depressed.

Since he no longer had the land to tend, Carlos wandered into town from the cemetery. He spoke to several of the merchants he knew, and then walked aimlessly around the square, still under the influence of the *chicha*. He squatted for a long time in front of Don Simon's house, hoping to see Segundina. It was an imposing house with a massive entrance door, as befitted the wealthiest patron.

Don Simon was the local landlord, the most important person in the village. He had received his lands from his deceased parents, who in turn had inherited it, for the family had owned it for several generations, a grant to one of their Spanish forebears for helping conquer the Aymaras. After attending the university in La Paz, Don Simon had returned to live in Ocampo, although he often left on long trips. A tall, thin man in his sixties, with white hair and a sharp nose, he carried himself erect as he walked or rode, his head tilted back under a felt hat, and spoke as though he were looking down on the rest of the villagers, who did not share his pure Castilian blood.

Each morning he took his mare on an early ride to inspect his extensive holdings. Local Indians worked his fields under a system in which they labored three days a week without pay on Don Simon's lands. In return Don Simon allowed them to use small, designated plots on which they could raise their own crops. Very few Indians in Ocampo owned land. Carlos could count them on the fingers of one hand, for Don Simon's family had greedily acquired plot after plot to add to their original grant.

In the afternoon Carlos went to see the field which had once belonged to his family, a simple rectangle of land, sloping gently downhill, on which he had spent so much of his life, plowing, hoeing, and harvesting. It had never been more beautiful to his eyes. He wanted to take off his sandals, pick up a hoe, feel the earth under his feet once again, but he couldn't. The land no longer belonged to him. Again that night Segundina did not come home. It was less than a mile from Don Simon's house to their home, an easy walk, so Carlos was puzzled by her absence.

The third day, on Christmas Eve, Segundina appeared after supper. Carlos was shocked by how she had matured during his absence. She was now seventeen, with a round face crowned by dark, braided hair. Her figure was also round, wide hips and big breasts, with the excess pounds that Latin men love so much. She had bright white teeth, which had radiated in a wide smile before Carlos left. Now she was serious, hesitant, afraid of her brother. Carlos recognized immediately that something was wrong and took her outside the house. Maria did not follow.

"Why don't you come home at night?" Carlos asked, his voice threatening.

"I work at the house of Don Simon," Segundina replied, looking at the ground.

"Yes, I know. But why don't you come home at night?"

"Sometimes I must rise early to prepare breakfast for Don Simon." She continued to avoid his eyes.

"You lie," Carlos said, grabbing her roughly by one arm. "It is an easy walk. Why don't you come home? Tell me."

Segundina began to cry softly. She looked like a little girl again.

"Don Simon wants me to sleep at his house," she murmured.

"Why?" insisted Carlos, squeezing her arm so strongly that it caused her pain. "Why?"

"He wants me there," Segundina said, almost inaudibly.

Suddenly it became clear to Carlos.

"He is sleeping with you."

"Yes," she whispered.

"For how long?"

"For many months now."

He relaxed his grip, looking at the crying girl with her lowered head. He felt revulsion and sorrow at the same time.

"How did it happen?"

"When I began working at his house, I noticed that he looked at me, all the time. His eyes would follow me around the house as I cleaned. After the second week, Don Simon insisted that I sleep at his home in order to prepare his morning meal. He always rises early. I was given a small room with a cot for myself." She paused and used her shawl to brush away a tear.

"One night after midnight, when I was sleeping, he came to my room. He put his hand over my mouth so that I couldn't scream when I awoke. I was terrified. I didn't know what to do. My legs couldn't move. He was on top of me with his nightgown pulled up to his waist. He lifted my shift. Then he took me. It was my first time and I bled. When he finished, he said I must keep quiet and must submit to him if I wanted to keep my job."

Carlos grabbed her by the shoulders and shook her. "*Putana*! Why didn't you tell the Mayor or the police?"

"The Mayor has lunch with Don Simon every Sunday. They are good friends. The police would never believe my word against that of Don Simon," she answered softly.

"You could have left his house," Carlos insisted.

"We need the money, Carlos."

Carlos cursed to himself. What a poor son he was! With his father dead, his mother had lost her land and his sister her honor, both to the same man.

"How often does he come to your room?"

107

"Once or twice a week," she replied. "Whenever he wants me." She had cried so much that no tears remained.

The next day Maria prepared roast guinea pig, rice, and sweet potatoes for lunch, a special Christmas feast. Carlos had no appetite and the three of them ate in silence, toying with their food, aware of the heaviness in the air. Segundina would not look Carlos in the eye.

In the afternoon Carlos went to see Father Augustin, not sure what he would say to his former teacher, but wanting to talk. So many things had happened to him since he left; so many boundaries had been crossed; so many taboos had been broken. He had killed. Not once, but many times. At first hesitantly, but later automatically, without thinking or remorse. He had cursed God in a moment of desperation. Carlos wondered if there was a way back.

When he arrived at the monastery, however, he was told that the old priest had returned to Spain to spend his remaining years there. Father Augustin had departed four months previously, leaving no messages. A young man in his thirties, a trained professor, had replaced him. Carlos left the monastery dejected, more certain than ever that he had been abandoned by the Crucified Christ. The gods of the mountains and streams, the condor and the puma, not the Christian God, now controlled his destiny.

During the following week Carlos rose early and left the house before sunrise. He was always gone three hours, returning in time for breakfast. He never said where he had gone or what he was doing. He went to the village once and made a purchase, but did not show it to his mother. In the middle of the second week, Carlos announced to Maria that he was leaving, and gave her what little money he had left.

She prepared a bag of dehydrated potatoes for his trip, potatoes which she and Segundina had harvested over a year before. They had soaked the whole potatoes in water, then spread them on the ground to dry, baking under the sun of the day and chilled by the freezes at night. After two weeks they had trod on the potatoes with their bare feet for several days, squeezing out the remaining moisture in this way. Now the *chuno* would last for several seasons. Maria selected the best for her son - small, unblemished white tubers which would expand and regain their taste when boiled in water. Then she handed him a crumpled white envelope.

"Take this with you, my son. It is a letter from Catavi. Perhaps it will be of help one day."

Carlos slipped the envelope inside his shirt and held her against him for a long time. He knew he would never see his mother again, that this part of his life was finished. Without land, Ocampo, once the center of his life, no longer had a hold on him. That same day he arranged with a local merchant to catch a ride on a delivery truck leaving for the west. After bidding farewell to Segundina in the square, he departed in the late afternoon, riding in the bed of the truck, along with tins of crackers, bolts of cloth, and cans of paint.

Six miles from Ocampo, when the truck slowed for a curve, he jumped off. He watched it disappear in the distance, then turned and retraced his route. Once he heard another truck approaching and hid on the side of the road until it passed. Before reaching Ocampo, he left the road altogether and made his way in darkness across the fields. He found the place he was seeking and lay down for the night.

At morning he was up before dawn. The spot he had chosen was in a ravine. A well worn horse trail ran down the center of the ravine for two miles. From his knapsack Carlos took the length of barbed wire that he had purchased in the village, and strung it across the path two feet above the ground, tying it to a tree on one side and around a large rock on the other. Then he hid behind the rock and waited.

At seven he heard the sound of a horse approaching at a trot. There was a loud whinny as the horse hit the wire and fell forward. Carlos heard a cry of pain. When he left his cover, he saw the horse struggling to rise, its breathing ragged, its head covered with perspiration, and its eyes wide with fear. Don Simon sat on the ground, one leg doubled under the other, holding his left arm and grimacing. He saw Carlos and looked up with relief.

"Thank God! There's someone here. I've had an accident. My arm may be broken. Give me a hand."

Carlos stood above the fallen man but didn't move. Don Simon focused on his military uniform and then on his face.

"I know you. You're Carlos Obregon. I need help, boy. Don't just stand there. Help me up."

Carlos looked down at Don Simon and smiled. He moved around behind him as though to pick him up. Instead he took Don Simon's head between his two hands and broke his neck with a sharp twist. Don Simon's body jerked and his uncontrolled bowels soiled his white pants. The offensive odor of excrement reached Carlos' nostrils as he dropped the lifeless head in the dust.

Carlos untied the barbed wire, rolled it up neatly, and placed it back in his knapsack. He cut a branch from the tree and brushed away his footprints. Before leaving, he looked again at the lifeless figure of Don Simon and the lame horse still struggling to rise. He felt neither joy nor remorse. He had done his duty.

Then he slung his knapsack over his shoulder and walked away. He had a long way to go.

Chapter 14

The crowded train rocked from side to side, throwing Carlos against the passengers on both sides of him. The hard wooden bench of the second class wagon, the jolts, and the noise would have kept him awake under other circumstances, but he had walked for sixteen hours, his feet ached, and he was exhausted. The smell of chickens, pigs, and unwashed humanity permeated the green and black railroad car like a dense fog. There were three drunks in the cabin, and one had thrown up in the aisle, adding an acrid stench to the other odors. Some passengers had lowered their windows for relief, but this let in clouds of evil smelling, dark smoke from the coal burning locomotive. Each time the train stopped, the passengers hastily threw open all the windows and leaned out, either to buy food from ambulant vendors alongside the tracks, or simply to clean their lungs.

Carlos dreamed of Father Augustin. He was kneeling before the elder priest, who was dressed in a white habit instead of his customary black robes. A huge, dark, metal crucifix, as big as a machete, hung from a golden chain on the priest's neck, swinging back and forth in front of Carlos' face. The sides of the crucifix were razor sharp, and Carlos was afraid to get too close. He asked for the Father's blessing, but when the priest bent forward and laid his hands upon Carlos' head, blood spurted from the top of his head, soaking the priest's hands and staining the pristine habit. Father Augustin grimaced with disgust, but pressed his hands harder on Carlos' head to stop the flow of blood. Instead, the pressure forced Carlos through the dirt floor, which drew him down like quicksand, down into the unknown, down into the underworld.

Father Augustin watched sadly as Carlos disappeared. As he sank into the ground, the screaming began, the screaming of men, of horses, of women. He moaned in his sleep. Then he felt the gnawing of sharp teeth on his feet and legs, the gnawing of hundreds of rats buried in the earth, eating him alive. Furry gray shapes with stained teeth and beady eyes tore at his flesh, moving up his torso, tearing him apart. He screamed, drowning out the others.

Carlos awoke with a start, still bouncing from side to side. He checked his hands and legs, expecting to see blood, and sighed with relief when he realized it had been a dream.

He took several deep breaths to control his pounding heart. The man next to him pushed against him, trying unsuccessfully to make more space. All the benches around Carlos were packed, each person crushed against his neighbor. Some passengers sat in the aisles along with their animals. Carlos stretched and pushed his neighbor off of him. It was a two day trip South to Villazon, where he would catch an Army truck going on to the Chaco.

Carlos remembered the letter his mother had given him, and took out the envelope from inside his shirt. The address was written by hand in black ink and addressed to the widow and family of Luis Obregon. He opened it and read:

Catavi, August 7, 1933

Dear Mrs. Obregon and family,

By the time you receive this, the remains of your beloved husband and father will have arrived at Ocampo. The mining company will tell you that Luis died in an underground accident. Because of the friendship and respect I felt toward Luis, I want you to know the truth: Luis was killed by the owners and died a martyr in the cause for just representation of his fellow workers.

On May 17, Luis joined the Organizing Committee of the new Catavi Union of Mine Workers. He joined despite having been beaten and having received a death threat from his Shift Supervisor. Luis was instrumental in enrolling hundreds of workers; many became members solely because of his example. At the present, more than half of the work force has associated itself with our new union, and we are confident that we will be able to force the owners to recognize us as the legitimate workers' representative any day now.

In their effort to stop our organizing success, I am sure that the owners had Luis killed. The only witness to his death was the Shift Supervisor, whom I do not trust. The owners refused to let us examine Luis' body and rejected our request for an autopsy.

I regret that the truth is so brutal, but you should know that your husband and father was a man of extraordinary courage. I was proud to consider him my friend.

If there is any way I can help you in the future, please do not hesitate to call upon your faithful servant,

Juan Lechin
President, Catavi Union of Mine Workers

The letter left Carlos confused. He knew his father as a quiet, humble man who avoided problems; perhaps Carlos had underestimated him. Even if Luis had been brave, his courage had cost him his life, and his death had resulted in the loss of their land and his sister's virginity. Was that type of sacrifice a good thing? The thought troubled Carlos during the weary traveling days that followed.

When Carlos arrived at Villa Montes, he reported to Lt. Colonel Busch, who seemed genuinely glad to see him.

"*Bienvenido, Carlitos*. How was your vacation?" asked the Colonel.

"Fine, Sir," Carlos answered, withholding the news of his father's death.

"There's been a lot of activity while you were gone. That fool President Salamanca came down here with the idea that he was going to sack General Penaranda because of the Ballivian disaster. The officers sacked Salamanca instead. We forced him to resign." Busch laughed. "He was a lousy President and an even worse Commander-in-Chief. The idiot knew nothing about fighting a war. Got what he deserved. The Vice-President, Tejada Sorzano, is now running the country, with help from the Army."

"I hadn't heard," replied Carlos.

"No, I didn't think you had. We're taking an active role in the new government. It's time we got rid of all the corrupt, drunk, politicians. Bolivia needs the strong discipline that comes from a military background. Don't you agree, *Carlitos*?"

"Yes, Sir," Carlos replied, remembering this was his new Commanding Officer.

The rainy season had arrived with Carlos, so troop movements were handicapped for the next six months. The Paraguayans had finally run up against an impenetrable wall. The Bolivians were now fighting on more familiar terrain, with their backs to the Andes. When the Bolivian troops tried to counterattack, however, their maneuvers ended badly. Both sides were stuck in strong defensive positions.

Colonel Busch named Carlos his adjutant, so Carlos worked closely with the Colonel every day. His admiration grew as he saw the decisiveness of the Colonel and his ability to inspire the troops under his command. Busch himself led one of the counterattacks and was out in front during the fighting. Carlos, who accompanied him, respected his bravery but thought the Colonel took unnecessary risks. It was as though Busch considered himself protected by some almighty power, impervious to bullets and grenades. He was always optimistic, even when the attacks failed. However, even Busch's optimism could not break the stalemate.

During his half-year at Villa Montes, Carlos attended all the secret meetings of the Marshal Santa Cruz Lodge. Since Carlos was now a lieutenant, he was accepted as a new member upon the recommendation of Busch. At first Carlos sat quietly, trying to better understand the subjects that aroused so much passion in the other members but so little in him. Being exposed to the world outside his village was a new experience.

Although he had never been to the capital, La Paz, he learned the names of the various political parties and their leaders. He heard that a once dormant party, the Socialist, was being rebuilt, and that for the first time the labor movement was showing success in its organizing efforts, despite the fact that many union militants had been sent to the Chaco. Outside of Bolivia, the talk centered on Italy and Germany, countries which were taking a leadership role in Europe and the world. Italy's strong fascist government, which based its support on organized labor, was the model that the officers of the Lodge most admired, wedding strong nationalism with the new socialist movement.

Initially, Captain Gutierrez showed no sign of recognizing Carlos as the Indian he had dragged from Ocampo. Undoubtedly, Carlos was just one of many who had suffered under Gutierrez. At times Carlos would catch the Captain studying him, a quizzical look on his face, as if he were trying to make the connection, but it was not until the third meeting that the confrontation came. Gutierrez, who was a compulsive talker, a man of words rather than action, was denouncing the lack of bravery in the Bolivian troops.

"Have you seen the numbers?" he raged. "The Paraguayans have captured over twenty thousand Bolivians, while we've captured only three thousand of the enemy. Our troops are worthless in front of the Paraguayans. Worthless! At the first sight of the enemy, the Indians throw their rifles down and their hands up. They run like rabbits instead of fighting. They are dumb brutes who let their comrades die without lifting a finger. That's why we're losing this war."

"I disagree," said Carlos. Silence fell over the room. This was the first time Carlos had entered a discussion. "The Indians are not cowards. They don't fight because they don't understand this war. The Chaco is not their land. It has no fields suitable for planting, no pastureland for animals, not even clear streams for water. Put our troops on the other side of the enemy and ask them to fight their way back to the Andes, to their own villages. Then you would see their courage."

Captain Gutierrez looked at him angrily, unhappy at being challenged by a junior officer.

"Bravo, Carlos," Colonel Busch encouraged him. "What else?"

"For the soldier in the field, his first enemy is the land itself, then come their own officers, and finally, his third enemy, the Paraguayans."

"I understand why they would hate the land, but why do they hate us?" Busch asked.

"They don't trust their officers, Sir," Carlos continued. "They see the officers sitting far back from the front lines, drinking wine and eating well, away from any danger. For many soldiers, Spanish is no easier to understand than German, yet how many officers speak Aymara or Quechua, or have even tried to learn a few words? During the defeat at Ballivian, how many officers fled to Argentina, leaving their troops to surrender to the Paraguayans? Or to be chopped to death by the *Macheteros* as they retreated? What about the officers who deserted their troops at Picuiba?"

"It was necessary to save the artillery," interrupted Captain Gutierrez. "I was there and I know." He looked at Carlos more carefully and his eyes widened in recognition.

"Most of the officers fled with the cannons and abandoned their men to die. Only the brave ones remained," insisted Carlos.

"That is an insult," shouted Captain Gutierrez, rising from his chair and unfastening the leather holster where he carried his pistol. "I know this officer," he said, pointing at Carlos. "He is an Indian who tried to avoid military service by hiding in a monastery. He is a coward and a liar."

"No, Captain. Lieutenant Obregon is not a coward. I have witnessed his heroism on two different occasions. Unfortunately, he speaks the truth. Sit down and put your gun away." It was Colonel Busch who spoke. "We have asked the poor Indians to suffer the brunt of the war and we have let them down most of the time. Now we must repay our debt. The future governments of Bolivia must incorporate the Indians into our society. They must have their own land and their self respect. We owe them that."

Captain Gutierrez took his seat sullenly and glared at Carlos across the room. Carlos sat passively, betraying no emotion, but Gutierrez had insulted him and his people. Carlos knew that one day, a day of his own choosing, he would kill Gutierrez, and the thought gave him pleasure.

In future Lodge meetings, prompted by Colonel Busch, Carlos acted as a spokesman for the highlands Indians. The other officers began to ask his opinion on how the Indians might feel about this or that subject, and listened to his replies. Since Carlos himself was a

116

full blooded Aymara, while all other members were mestizos, he was not fully accepted in the Lodge, particularly by Captain Gutierrez, who never forgave his challenge. Although the others treated him with outward respect, none of them tried to cultivate his friendship. Only Colonel Busch stood up for him and for the Indians.

Carlos was in the Colonel's office on June 14, 1935, when news of the armistice arrived on the field telephone.

"It's over," said Colonel Busch, rising from his chair. "They've beaten us. A country half our size has kicked us out of the Chaco. Fighting stops tomorrow at noon."

Carlos didn't know what to say and stood in silence in front of his Commanding Officer.

Busch chuckled. "At least we're finishing this with a bang. For the last thirty minutes before hostilities end, we are going to let go with everything we have, all up and down the line. Shell the hell out of them."

"Why?" Carlos asked.

"It's our way of showing them that the Bolivian Army is not defeated, that we can still fight."

Carlos shook his head in disbelief. One more piece of madness in an insane war.

"I'll go tell the others. Want to come?"

"No, Sir. With your permission, I'll stay here."

"Suit yourself." The Colonel strode through the door, leaving Carlos alone.

Carlos walked to the Colonel's camp table and picked up the latest casualty report from the Bolivian High Command. He knew the statistics were unreliable, mere estimates, due to the disorganization within the army.

Sixty thousand, he read. Sixty thousand Bolivian soldiers either killed or missing during three years of combat, almost all of these young Indians from the Altiplano, poor farmers like himself who had been dragged from their villages to fight in a losing war, a war they never wanted, for a barren wasteland of no value. With little training and poor leadership, they had been sent to the front, to be slaughtered like sheep. Sixty thousand Indian sheep.

Someone should pay, thought Carlos bitterly. Not only Gutierrez, but all of those responsible. Otherwise, my people will have died for nothing.

BOOK II

LA PAZ

1935—1939

Chapter 1

The bright morning sun hung over their shoulders, close enough to touch, under a pale blue sky. Its rays danced among the vivid reds, greens, blues, and oranges of the multicolored shawls worn by the Indian women, adding to the warmth created by the mass of people crowded into the plaza, and easily dispersing the early morning nip in the air. It was Sunday, market day at the top of the world, La Paz, eleven thousand feet above sea level. Carlos and Ramon pushed their way through the crowd, joking and laughing, with all the temerity of two young bulls in a herd of cows.

A Sunday morning visit to the market with Ramon had become a ritual for Carlos since he had decided to remain in the Army, and had followed Colonel Busch to La Paz two years ago. He had never regretted his decision. In the first year, Ramon served as his guide and companion, helping Carlos find a place to live, a cook, and a cleaning woman. He had taken Carlos to movie theaters, small restaurants, illegal cock fights, fortune tellers, and the Sunday market. There was nothing that Ramon did not know about the city, and he shared it all with Carlos. Even though Carlos now knew La Paz well, almost as well as his guide, the Sunday market remained his favorite place.

The market attracted peddlers, buyers, and spectators from all over the Altiplano. The size of La Paz - two hundred fifty thousand people - and its strategic location on the railroad running north-south along the central plateau of the Andes made it a natural center for farmers and merchants to bring their wares. They came by train, by

121

truck, on horses and mules, or by foot, trotting behind loaded llamas or shuffling on sandaled feet, from as far as two hundred miles. This morning, as on most Sunday mornings, the market overflowed with humanity.

Carlos had risen early, a lifelong habit he could not break, to watch the vendors converge before daylight to stake out places on the large paved square in front of the massive brown cathedral, whose twin bell towers served as beacons. The merchants spread woven woolen blankets or well worn straw mats on the rough stone pavement, creating eight poorly defined rows which ran in one direction, and four meandering aisles that crossed the rows. The rows and aisles were left free so shoppers could circulate, but movement along the corridors became slow and erratic as the plaza filled.

Ramon met him at ten. They enjoyed a strong coffee together at a little bar on the square and then joined the other shoppers, lingering occasionally to look and bargain. Now Carlos and Ramon quit pushing and let the crowd determine their pace, giving in freely to its movement, stopping when it stopped, surging forward when it moved again.

Carlos loved the color, movement, noise, and odors of the market. The peddlers, mostly Indian women like his mother and sister, wore hand woven multicolored shawls over layers of black or brown pleated skirts. Their hats and hatbands identified their villages, and were worn with pride. Brown derbies predominated, but black bowlers, straw hats, and felt fedoras, also rested at just the right angle on dark round heads.

Everywhere he looked he saw jet black hair tied in braids, slanted foreheads descending to prominent broad noses, eyes which curved upward at the outer corners, brown faces that came alive when large white teeth pushed through a wide smile. But unlike his quiet mother, these women cried out like quarreling geese, shouting their offers, negotiating prices, defending their territory.

In contrast, the outnumbered mestizo male vendors were sullen and quiet, as if they disdained the art of selling. They too sported hats - brown and black fedoras reminiscent of gangsters. Their dark, drab suits showed bare patches and loose threads, partially hidden by layers of dust accumulated from walking on dirt roads or traveling in open trucks. They were the poor relations at the wake.

Children swarmed underfoot like newborn frogs on a spring day. Babies rode on the backs of women, round bundles disguised in shawls except for black silky tufts of hair; others lay wrapped like colored cocoons on the pavement. Small figures flitted by, clothed as their parents, but half the size, their small hats barely reaching Carlos' waist. Young children watched over even younger children, while their mothers shopped or sold.

Merchandise of every shape and size lay splashed on the ground: llama and alpaca rugs, blankets, and ponchos; painted clay pottery and figurines; medicinal herbs from the jungle; oranges, bananas, and a multitude of vegetables, including over thirty varieties of potatoes; items of woven straw; cotton and wool cloth; amulets and prayer cards, to assure one of good health or a faithful lover. Slick pigs tethered to short ropes squealed noisily; ruffled chickens with glassy eyes lay prone with their feet tied; and frightened rabbits huddled together silently in wooden cages. The confusion of products washed together with a variety of aromas from food cooking over open fires, and mixed again with a mélange of Andean tunes competing with each other from a multitude of radios, like waves breaking on rocks, a glorious churning of clashing currents.

Carlos loved the chaos of the Sunday market more than anything else in La Paz. In a city of stone buildings and cobblestone streets, of mestizos and offices, it was the one place where the Indian way of life still dominated, Sunday the one day of the week when the country invaded the city, bringing with it a fresh and exuberant innocence.

Ramon stopped in front of a pretty Indian girl with color in her cheeks and big breasts pushing against a cotton blouse. She sat cross-legged on a straw mat with a pile of loose oranges in front of her. A crude hand-held scale lay by her side.

"*Ay,*" Ramon exclaimed, looking down at her bosom. "What pretty ones! Come and look, Carlos."

The girl giggled and returned his look with the same boldness. "The best ones in all the Yungas," she said proudly, holding up an orange while arching her back ever so slightly at the same time.

Ramon laughed. "And how much do they cost, *Mamacita?*" he teased.

"The price is low for the quality you get," she answered.

"Can I squeeze them first before buying?" Ramon winked at Carlos, who had been watching the exchange with amusement.

Before he heard her answer, Carlos felt a sharp blow on his shoulder and was jostled forward. He turned to yell at the offender, but saw only a pair of muscular legs hurrying away under a massive bundle of cut wood, twice the size of the man carrying it. The man's ankles were as thick and wide as his knees, and the bare, leathery soles of his feet had lost their arches long ago, the result of a lifetime of carrying oversized loads.

Carlos recognized the offender as one of the Indian laborers who worked at the market, silent figures indistinguishable from one another. They all dressed in rags, wearing dirty gray shirts without buttons, their tattered pants held up by worn cords. Their once-bright knit hats, pointed at the top, with earflaps that hung well below their ears, were now as colorless as their dull eyes. Brown cheeks bulged from the wads of coca leaves they chewed continuously as they crisscrossed the plaza, rushing forward to keep from falling. They were men, but they did the work of pack animals. They were Indians without land, who had come to the city seeking employment, and had been reduced to beasts of burden.

Watching the man disappear, Carlos was glad he had remained in the Army and had accompanied Colonel Busch to La Paz as his Adjutant. That could be me, he thought, if not for the military.

"*Que pasa, compadre?*" Ramon asked, turning from his dalliance with the orange seller.

"*Nada.* Just got hit by a damned Indian," Carlos answered, massaging his shoulder.

"*Carajo,*" Ramon laughed, his eyes twinkling. "Look who's talking - my friend from Ocampo. Now that you wear a tie and leather shoes, you are worse than the rest of us. Let's keep moving before we get crushed."

Carlos knew Ramon was right. During his two years in La Paz he had changed. He wasn't quite sure when he had changed, or even when he had made the decision to change. It had been gradual, not one specific event, but over a period of time. He hadn't even noticed it at first, it just seemed to happen. The city had shaped him like a flowing stream forms its banks, slowly carrying away the loose dirt and rocks, until one day the bank has changed, what was straight is curved, what was rough is now smooth, or the foundation of a bridge is undercut.

He had become more like Ramon, throwing away his sandals and discarding his poncho. His knitted hat was a thing of the past, replaced by a felt fedora. When he was not in uniform, he dressed in a double breasted suit, white shirt with tie, and leather shoes. If it were cold in the evenings, he used an overcoat. Although he had only chewed coca on special occasions in the past, now he quit altogether because it branded one as an Indian. He no longer drank *chicha*, having cultivated a taste for beer and wine. He had his hair cut at a regular barber shop, short around the ears as dictated by current fashion.

When people spoke to him in Aymara or Quechua, he replied in Spanish. He wanted them to think he was a mestizo. He knew he was denying his Indian ancestry, rejecting his parents, but it was the only way to gain respect in La Paz. He had learned the lesson quickly, watching the Indians step into the street to let the mestizos pass, seeing them denied entrance into the restaurants and better stores. If a man wore a poncho and sandals, with a bulge in his cheek, everyone assumed he was a beggar, come to the city in search of charity.

It didn't matter if one were a full-blooded Indian, as long as one acted like a mestizo. If Carlos dressed like a mestizo, he was treated like one, and if he dressed like an Indian, he would be treated like one. Now that Carlos had experienced life in La Paz, he never intended to return to Ocampo. Since he had no interest in being treated like a second class citizen, he discarded all traces of his former identity.

It wasn't only the city that had forced Carlos to change. He was becoming more important in the Marshal Santa Cruz Lodge and in the government. When the war ended, rather than disappear, the Lodge continued to meet and plot the overthrow of the civilian government. Less than a year after the armistice, in May, 1936, a group of officers led by Lieutenant Colonel German Busch forced the Acting President Tejada Sorzano to resign, and a Military Junta assumed power. The Junta named Colonel David Toro President and Lieutenant Colonel Busch assumed the role of Minister of Defense. The clandestine military Lodge, born in the Chaco, now ran the country, although its members denied its existence, and its meetings were still held in secrecy.

Even though Carlos had served competently as Busch's adjutant for two years, he was surprised when the Colonel promoted him to Captain and gave him the title of Chief of Internal Security. In his new position, Carlos controlled the National Police and the much feared Secret Service. Carlos named Ramon his second in command, so they were always together, both at work and afterwards.

Once the Military Junta assumed power, it wasted little time in implementing the ideas that the young officers debated in the Chaco. The Junta created a new Ministry of Labor and Social Security in 1936, naming a socialist and avowed leftist as its boss. That same year the first national workers' union was founded with encouragement from the Junta.

Under the prodding of Carlos and with the support of Busch, the Junta convened a National Farmers' Conference, and abolished the system of forced labor by Indians through a decree-law. For Carlos, this single decree justified his abandonment of his village, for it meant the poor Indian farmers would now be rewarded for their sacrifice in the Chaco, and would have a chance for a better life.

Also by decree-law, the Junta created a new Ministry of Mines and Petroleum. The three large mining companies, along with the Central Bank, were forced to contribute to the funding of a new Mining Bank, whose purpose was to aid small miners in competition against the large concerns. Bolivia was no longer to be run for the privileged landowners and mining potentates.

In March, 1937, less than a year after assuming power, the Military Junta seized the Bolivian holdings of the Standard Oil Company, settling accounts with the firm for its betrayal of them during the war. The outcry in the United States was instantaneous, since this was the first time ever a U.S. oil company in Latin America had been expropriated. The U.S. government threatened to break off diplomatic relations, but the Junta stood firm. Crowds swarmed through the streets of La Paz to cheer the Junta for their action against the Yankee imperialists.

These were exciting years and Carlos loved being involved in the changes, although at times his job caused him sleepless nights. Running the National Police was easy enough - the underpaid and poorly equipped force was in charge of enforcing the law in the cities, mainly in La Paz. Most of the crimes were straightforward: robberies, murders, rapes, and muggings. Corruption in the force was widespread but tolerated.

The one hundred twenty person Secret Service was another matter. The elite unit was charged with preventing internal subversion within the country; in other words, with keeping the Military Junta in power. Carlos acted only on the directions of Colonel Busch and assumed this was the reason for his appointment. The Colonel needed a loyal officer who would take orders without questions.

If the Colonel sought information on an upcoming labor leader, on an aging politician with aspirations, or on an outspoken university professor, the Secret Service dutifully compiled a dossier. Carlos had inherited extensive files from his civilian predecessor and he continuously expanded these archives. In reading and updating these files, Carlos learned about the dark side of humanity, for he found few persons whose lives were unblemished in one way or another.

There were as many mistresses as there were politicians, hidden away in a "second house". Illegitimate children were everywhere, sometimes acknowledged by their fathers, sometimes not. The poor abused coca and aguardiente; the rich abused cocaine and whisky. Respectable bankers secretly owned whorehouses. Businesses cheated on their taxes as a matter of custom. Industrialists underpaid and mistreated their employees. As everywhere in the world, there were men who liked only men, including a leading priest in the city, and women who preferred the company of other women. As he mastered and extended the files, Carlos realized that the city bred corruption, that the close proximity of hundreds of thousands of people, and the anonymity that the city provided, released the vileness within, and the contamination spread, touching every home and every inhabitant.

The Military Junta was not known for its democratic principles. When Busch wanted someone held for questioning, Carlos brought him in. If the person was to be roughed up, which was only on rare occasions, Carlos gave the order. The Secret Service had its own prison conveniently located in the center of the city, where it was possible to hold a person incognito for as long as the Colonel desired. At first Carlos had been reluctant to have people beaten or secretly imprisoned, but Colonel Bush always came up with a reasonable answer to his infrequent objections. Finally, Carlos told himself that the end justified the means. The Junta was determined to change Bolivia for the better and would not tolerate any interference. If he could help in making the change, so be it.

Also, Carlos' new circumstances overrode his misgivings. He had a luxuriously furnished four bedroom house, compliments of the Junta. His Captain's salary was augmented by payments from people who wanted favors, who paid to have his men look the other way. Graft was a long standing tradition, and Carlos knew that he could not change it. Therefore, he took his share.

Ramon interrupted his thoughts. "I've walked enough. How about some lunch?"

"Let's eat here. I need to get back to headquarters this afternoon."

"On Sunday? You're crazy, *compadre*. Enjoy life while you can."

"I do enjoy it. But police work is full time. You know that."

They purchased two plates of stewed tripe with roasted potatoes, and ate with their fingers, standing alongside the boiling pot and dripping gravy onto the ground. When they finished, they dried their hands with handkerchiefs, and washed the meal down with warm beer from green bottles.

Ramon wiped his lips with the back of his hand.

"That beer was good. Let's go get another at Consuela's, and look over the girls. Maybe she has some new ones."

Carlos handed his empty bottle back to the vendor.

"Don't you ever get tired of the whorehouses? I'll bet you know every single one in La Paz."

"Why should I get tired? A warm pussy is the best thing in life. Especially on a Sunday afternoon." Ramon winked. "I don't remember you protesting when I started showing you around."

Carlos shrugged. "It was okay in the beginning, but I'm getting tired of it. They're all the same. All they want is your money."

"So?"

"So I want something more, a woman who is not for hire."

"There's a new girl at the Negro Negro. She's young, no more than seventeen. Good clear skin, cute tits, and a great backside. We can go there."

Carlos laughed. "You don't give up easily, do you?" He slapped his friend on the back. "You go along. I might come later, but don't wait for me."

He turned and walked away, leaving Ramon and the market behind.

When Carlos arrived at Police Headquarters, he found the incoming reports and correspondence laid out neatly in a large leather-covered folder. At the very top he discovered a note from Colonel Busch with a separate letter attached. The note read:

Carlitos,

If I remember correctly, you were at Pozo Favorita with Lieutenant Kunnert. Could you respond to his wife? Thanks.

German Busch

Intrigued, Carlos detached the note and examined the letter. The return address read Bavaria, Germany, and it was dated April 13, 1937. The letter was addressed to the Minister of Defense, hand written in a clear, feminine penmanship on cream-colored, linen stationery in a text-book Spanish which was grammatically correct but not that of a native.

Dear Sir:

I am writing to ask your help. In September of 1933 my husband, Lieutenant Manfred Kunnert, went missing in action while commanding Bolivian troops of B Company, Eighteenth Infantry Battalion. The war ended in June, 1935, and all prisoners were repatriated over the next six months. Unfortunately, my husband never came home and his whereabouts remain a mystery. For four years I have tried to obtain further information through the offices of the German Embassy in La Paz without success.

Manfred's disappearance has created a terrible situation for me. If my husband is dead, I would like to recover his remains and return them to his native Germany for a proper burial. If that is not possible, it is necessary that I have some legal proof of his death in order to settle his estate and restructure my own life.

Could you please investigate the circumstances of his disappearance and issue a final official report? I am desperate for a solution to this tragedy, which becomes worse as time passes.

As a military officer, I am sure you will look favorably upon this request from an officer's wife.

Yours truly,
Baroness Ingrid Kunnert

Carlos read the letter twice. The writing, the blue ink, the cream colored paper, were all so feminine. He sniffed the paper and thought he could detect a subtle but pleasant perfume, like wild lavender on a sunny day. He unlocked the bottom left hand drawer of his desk and searched among the papers there. He found a brown envelope and extracted a worn photograph, wrinkled and stained with sweat, which he had carried with him throughout the war. Despite its condition, he could still discern the long blond hair and the lithe figure of the woman in the bathing suit, lying on a raft, and remembered the many times he had admired the beauty of this woman.

He thought for a while, and then composed a reply. Not satisfied, he rewrote it two times, struggling for the right words. Finally he transcribed it onto his official stationery:

June 16, 1937

Dear Baroness Kunnert:

The Minister of Defense sent me your letter. I served under your husband in B Company and was with him on the day he went missing. I have additional information and think I can help you solve your problem if we work together.

However, it will be necessary for you to visit Bolivia in person in order to deal with all arrangements here. I put my services at your command.

With all respect,

> Captain Carlos Obregon
> Chief of Internal Security.

He reread his letter several times, trying to imagine its effect on the recipient. Finally satisfied, he smiled to himself, addressed and sealed the envelope, turned and leaned back in his chair, contemplating the light outside his window. It was a perfect day.

Chapter 2

The note, dated December 12, 1937, was marked URGENT, and requested that Carlos come to Colonel Bush's office as quickly as possible. When he arrived, the Colonel's door was shut and the Adjutant asked him to wait. After seven minutes the door opened and the Colonel appeared with a tall man whom Carlos did not recognize. He was obviously a foreigner, for he stood over six feet tall, had fair skin, gray eyes, and light brown hair. Judging from the gray wool, three button suit and paisley tie, Carlos guessed he was an American.

"Ah, *Carlitos*," Busch said, "I didn't know you were waiting. Let me present Mr. Bruce Berkman. Mr. Berkman is the Political Attaché at the U.S. Embassy in La Paz."

Bruce Berkman extended his hand and Carlos took it. It was a strong handshake; Bruce appeared to be in his thirties and in good physical condition. He must be an athlete, thought Carlos, for the man's body was firm and well-built and he moved gracefully. His smile was friendly and seemed genuine, even though his government was not on the best of terms with the Junta.

"Pleased to meet you, Captain Obregon. Colonel Busch has spoken about you often," Bruce offered.

"My pleasure, Mr. Berkman."

"Colonel Busch tells me you fought with him in the Chaco, and that you are one of the few heroes of the war."

Carlos smiled. "It is an honor that he thinks so, but the truth is much less. I served, like thousands of other soldiers."

"How refreshing," Bruce said. "A modest hero. Well, I must run along. Thank you for your time, Colonel. Again, my pleasure, Captain." Bruce shook hands with both men and left.

Colonel Busch ushered Carlos into his office, closing the door behind them, and asked him to sit down. The Colonel leaned back in his leather chair and propped one foot on an open drawer of his desk.

"Mr. Berkman is my main contact with the U.S., *Carlitos*. The American Ambassador doesn't want to get his hands dirty, so he attends the official functions, plays golf at the country club, and entertains U.S. visitors. Berkman talks with me when we have problems."

"I see, Sir." Carlos had not been aware that Busch had a direct contact within the U.S. Embassy. He presumed all foreign affairs were being handled by the President of the Military Junta, Colonel Toro, or by the Foreign Minister, Colonel Garza. "I thought our relations with the U.S. were very difficult now, because of Standard Oil."

"They were for a while, but reasonable men can always find a mutual ground for understanding. The U.S. is important to us, *Carlitos*. If a war breaks out in Europe, we may be cut off from our European ore clients, and the U.S. market will become critical. Also, the Yankees are one of the biggest investors in our industry. U.S. companies own the major cement plant, the biggest paint plant, and the largest textile mill. We need to keep them happy."

"Yes, Sir." Carlos nodded his understanding.

"But that's not why I asked you here today, *Carlitos*. The time has come to make a change, and I want your help."

"What type of change, Sir?" asked Carlos.

"A change of President. It's time for Colonel Toro to step down," Busch responded, returning his foot to the floor and assuming a more serious demeanor.

Carlos was stunned. He knew that David Toro was one of Busch's best friends. The older officer had helped Busch rise rapidly in his military career. Toro had been Best Man at Busch's wedding, and their wives were close. It had even been rumored that Busch himself had been responsible for making Toro President of the Junta, since Toro had been in the Chaco supervising prisoner repatriation when the Junta assumed power.

Recovering, Carlos responded, "Of course you have my support, Sir, but I'm not sure I understand. Why should Colonel Toro give up the Presidency? He's still young; only thirty-eight isn't he?"

"We're all young, *Carlitos*. I'm only thirty-three myself. The future belongs to people our age. But the current situation can't continue. David is pocketing too much money. He has put all his personal friends in key government positions so they can enrich themselves, and they're stealing the country blind."

Carlos assumed this was true since no Bolivian President had ever left office a poor man, but Colonel Busch was not idle either. Certainly his style of life did not come from his military pay.

"Isn't Colonel Toro very popular now for the decree-laws that he has issued, helping the Indians and the miners, and taking over Standard Oil?" Carlos asked.

"Those are laws issued by the Military Junta, *Carlitos*, not by David. In fact, David is the most conservative of all of us. Getting him to act is like trying to move an overloaded llama." Busch paused. "Besides, there has been a stronger backlash than we expected from the mine owners and from the U.S. Some very powerful people and countries are putting pressure on the Junta, *Carlitos*. They want David removed."

"I understand, Sir," Carlos replied, making the connection now between this conversation and the visit of Bruce Berkman to Colonel Busch. "But doesn't Colonel Toro have the support of the Military Junta, Sir?"

"He did, *Carlitos*, he did. I convinced the others to make him President. Now I have convinced them that he should go. I will be the new President."

Colonel Busch said the last sentence with such obvious satisfaction that it unnerved Carlos. For the first time, he recognized the unbridled ambition and deceit in the Colonel's character. For Carlos, Busch had been the most altruistic and bravest of the officers, a source of solidity and strength in an otherwise unscrupulous group. Now a darker side of Busch's personality had surfaced, and it upset Carlos. But why hadn't Busch simply assumed the Presidency when the Junta took power the year before? Maybe too young or not quite sure he could pull it off, Carlos speculated. Perhaps he had maneuvered Colonel Toro into this position, letting Toro take the heat for the reforms, so that Busch could now move in and enjoy the rewards. In either case, Carlos had no love for the vain and aristocratic Colonel Toro.

"How can I help, Sir?"

"Tomorrow morning a group of officers will call on David to demand that he resign. I want you in that group. You represent the National Police and the Secret Service, two important sources of power."

"Who else will be there?"

"All the Lodge members based in La Paz. I have contacted the members serving in other cities and have their total support. All troops throughout the country will be confined to their barracks tomorrow except one battalion, reporting directly to me, which will surround the Palace. I am ordering you to keep your men off the streets during the morning. No Police. No Secret Service agents. To avoid any resistance. Do you understand?"

"Yes, Sir," Carlos said slowly, his doubt showing.

Colonel Busch studied his face, as if reading his mind. "I want to show my gratitude for your cooperation, *Carlitos*. You've been a big help to me. As of tomorrow, assuming all goes well, I am promoting you to Major. We might even be able to find a place for you on the Junta. Is that satisfactory?"

Carlos didn't know what to say. Obviously he was being bought off for his betrayal of Toro, whom he had never liked since his incompetence at Picuiba. He would have helped Busch even without the incentive.

"Of course, Sir. Thank you. What happens to Colonel Toro, Sir?"

"Nothing. He resigns and will be given the opportunity to go into exile. Maybe he'll choose Lima, or Buenos Aires, even Mexico City or Madrid, who knows? Don't take all this too seriously. Nobody will get hurt if we handle it right. Do you know how many Presidents Bolivia has had during the first one hundred years as a republic?"

"No, Sir."

"Twenty-eight. One every three and a half years, even though the constitutional term is for six years. Presidents just don't last very long in this country. Yet we have never had a civil war or any mass uprisings since Independence. The changes are made before the population even knows about them. Meet me here tomorrow at eight o'clock. We will go as a group to see David. It will be over by lunch."

"And afterwards, will there be elections, Sir? The Junta promised elections when they took power."

Colonel Busch threw his head back and laughed. "Bolivia doesn't need elections, *Carlitos*. Bolivia needs a strong leader. You have to understand how the people think. They want a charismatic figure to show them the magic way to an easy life. Someone like Simon Bolivar. A romantic figure, who represents all that they aren't. A man who has power, wealth, and women." Busch was smiling now, exuding confidence. "Someone like me. But they don't want to elect him. They don't want that responsibility. Then when he fails, they can criticize him, but not themselves for having chosen him as their leader. They want a man who takes power on his own."

When Carlos arrived at Colonel Busch's office the next day, he found a group of nine officers. In addition to the Minister of Defense, the Commanding Officer of the La Paz garrison was present, as well as the Commanding Officer of the Military College. All were in full dress uniform. Two or three of the officers nodded at him, but the remainder ignored his presence. Carlos didn't consider any of them friends. While Carlos remained at one side, the other officers talked quietly among themselves, tense and nervous. Only Colonel Busch was in good spirits.

The officers were admitted immediately when they arrived at the Presidential Palace. Colonel Toro was standing behind an enormous oak desk, twice as large as Carlos had ever seen before. Portraits of Bolivar and Santa Cruz hung in elaborate gilded frames behind the desk, surrounding a recent portrait of Toro himself. Despite the presence of a Bolivian flag and a conference table, the office seemed enormous, an effect enhanced by a high ceiling. As he walked across the room, Carlos noted that the Colonel's beautifully pressed uniform jacket was covered with medals and decorations.

"Good morning, gentlemen," Colonel Toro said, smiling. "What brings you here today?"

"A rather grave and unpleasant matter," Colonel Busch answered. The other officers positioned themselves on both sides of the Colonel, facing the President.

Colonel Toro continued smiling. "Nothing can be that serious," he said. "The people seem to be with us now, the economy is picking up, and the opposition is under control. What's the problem?"

"You, David," Busch said coldly. "You're the problem."

The smile vanished from Toro's face. Carlos studied the two men. They reminded him of two proud cocks confronting each other, measuring each other's size, before the cockfight began.

"I don't understand," Colonel Toro said.

"You're stealing too much, David," Busch said bluntly. "You and your friends are bleeding the country dry. Everywhere we look, either you, your wife, your families, or your cronies are raking in money, through bribes, or special privileges, or kickbacks. It's gone too far. The whole country is talking about it. You've taken too much advantage of your position."

Colonel Toro crossed his arms across his chest. "I don't know what you're talking about."

"Yes, you do. You know exactly what I'm talking about. You've stolen more money in the last eleven months than most presidents do in a lifetime. You've become too greedy."

"This is ridiculous. I am President of Bolivia. I won't accept accusations like this."

"You are President because the Lodge wanted you to be," Busch bore in. "Now the Lodge has lost confidence in you. So we want your resignation." Busch took a step forward. "Now."

"Preposterous! You can't treat me like this."

The officers moved closer to Busch, forming a solid wall facing Toro.

"We can, and we are," Busch replied. "You can either resign now and go into exile, at a place you choose, or be arrested."

Toro's face turned red from anger.

"I don't have to take this. I am the President."

"Don't be a fool, David. If you resist, you can be locked up for a long time. If you accept, you can live a comfortable life in exile.

Take your money with you. It will be less painful." Colonel Busch was as calm as a doctor counseling a terminally ill patient.

Colonel Toro glared at Colonel Busch with a hatred that Carlos had rarely seen.

"You, of all people, to do this…"

Carlos searched Busch's face for some sign of sympathy, of past friendship, but saw nothing but cold confidence.

"Exile is the smart choice, David. Nobody suffers that way."

"I want some time to think it over."

"One hour, maximum. After that, we need your decision. Exile or prison? Your choice. We'll wait outside."

Colonel Busch motioned to the other officers to follow him, and left the room. Carlos was the last to leave, and turned to look back at the President as he closed the door. Colonel Toro was still standing behind his desk, his jaw firmly set, his face red, glaring at the open door.

Once outside Toro's office, Carlos took Colonel Busch aside.

"Isn't this dangerous, Sir? He could be rallying support from other officers."

"I presume that is precisely what he is trying to do, *Carlitos*." The Colonel didn't seem to be worried.

"Then shouldn't we cut the telephone lines, Sir? At least we can prevent him from calling outside."

"On the contrary. I want him to reach the officers he calls. They are already committed to us. It's better that he knows this."

When Colonel Toro came out of his office he was no longer defiant, but looked instead as if he had aged several years in the past hour. His customary erect military bearing and courtly manners had vanished; even his uniform hung more loosely on his slumped shoulders. Carlos felt no sympathy for him, for he remembered the Colonel's role in the disaster at Picuiba, his own escape, and his near death from dehydration. Finally, he thought, the son-of-a-bitch is being repaid for his incompetence.

"I will prepare my things, Colonel Busch. My family and I will depart for Lima tomorrow."

Chapter 3

Ingrid Kunnert relaxed in solitude on the edge of the raft, her long, tanned legs dangling in the green water. July was uncommonly hot in Germany this year and the chill of the lake water provided a welcome relief from the sun overhead. She stretched, arching her shoulders, and her firm breasts pushed against the elastic of her one-piece bathing suit. The warmth of the sun imparted a lazy sensuousness. She closed her eyes and locked her legs together to increase the sensation. She had not slept with a man for ages, but the desire still remained. Deep inside. Waiting.

A shout came across the water. She opened her eyes, pushed her wet hair from her face, and saw her father waving to her from the shore. She waved back and he motioned her to come. Ingrid stood on the raft, dove cleanly into the water, and swam effortless fifty yards to the grassy shore, knifing through the water with long, smooth strokes.

She emerged from the water, dripping wet, and picked up her towel from the ground. Her bathing suit clung to every curve.

"Hi, Papa. What is it?"

Her father waved a white envelope over his head.

"A letter from Bolivia. Maybe it's the answer you've been waiting for."

Her eyes lit up. "Open it, Papa. I'm all wet. Tell me what it says." She bent forward and rubbed her blond hair vigorously with the towel.

Her father opened the envelope and read out loud the letter from Captain Carlos Obregon.

"Papa, that's wonderful!" Ingrid cried, straightening up. "It's the first good news in four years. Finally we've found someone interested in helping us."

"Preposterous," his stern voice answered. "This Captain Obregon must be an idiot. There is no way you could travel to Bolivia. My work will not permit me to accompany you, and your mother is not strong enough. We can handle this through our embassy."

"The embassy hasn't found out anything for four years. We've tried and tried and nothing happens. The letter says that I myself should come."

"You've never traveled alone before."

"I could take Wilhelm, Papa," she said excitedly. "It would be an education for him."

"An eight year old boy? Take him across the Atlantic to an Andean country that one can hardly find on the map? What about the sanitation, and his schooling?"

"It would be good for him. He would learn more on a trip like this than in a full school year. We would only be gone a few months." Ingrid finished drying herself.

"Absolutely not. There is no way I will permit this." Her father turned his back on her and stalked toward the house.

Her father's objections made Ingrid even more determined to go. She had been sheltered long enough, her parents always doting over her and telling her what to do, organizing her life to fit their own image of the perfect daughter, selecting her clothes, her schools, even her companions. After her marriage, Manfred had assumed the role of her parents, making all the decisions. Now she wanted to break out of the mold, to do something on her own. This was the opportunity she had been waiting for.

She wrapped the towel around her head like a turban, slipped on her sandals, and followed her father. Walking slowly, she pictured herself as a strong-willed heroine who would travel to a mysterious and exotic foreign land, surmount all obstacles and return triumphantly with a sick and weak husband in her arms. A tough, self-sufficient woman. But leaving Wilhelm behind in Germany was out of the question. He was her son, and she wanted him by her side.

After two weeks of lengthy arguments, Ingrid finally got her way. Her father reluctantly helped her make the travel bookings and arranged for money to be waiting for her at banks in Lima and La Paz. The maids washed and ironed her travel clothes, and Ingrid herself supervised the packing of a steamer trunk and two suitcases, pestered all the time by Wilhelm, couldn't wait to begin the adventure. Three weeks later she left Bavaria with high hopes and a new sense of independence - but the trip started badly.

Ingrid and Wilhelm embarked at Hamburg on a Johnson Line steamer and immediately encountered rough weather in the North Atlantic. Even the experienced travelers became seasick, and Ingrid, on her first ocean voyage, suffered worse than most. The combination cargo and passenger ship made calls at Curacao, Cartagena, Panama, Buenaventura, and Guayaquil, ports with strange names and even more strange inhabitants, before arriving at Lima six weeks later. During most of that time she was confined to her cabin, unable to eat, her stomach rolling uneasily with the never ending waves. The attentions of an attractive ship's doctor made the trip somewhat more bearable, but Ingrid was too sick to encourage him.

After a short rest in coastal Lima, Ingrid and Wilhelm took a train which climbed so steeply into the Andes that switchbacks were needed, traveling from sea level to twelve thousand feet in one day. The train, with engines on both the front and rear, crawled forward for half a mile, then reversed and backed up the next grade, continuing the process as it scaled mountains which were otherwise insurmountable. A delighted Wilhelm ran up and down the first class wagon, all arms and legs, pointing out the sheer drops which threatened their lives, while Ingrid huddled terrified against the opposite side of the car. She was no longer the brave heroine she had imagined herself before leaving. When they crossed the "Devil's Mouth", an enormous gorge with a three thousand foot sheer drop, the train suspended over an empty void by an aged wooden bridge, Ingrid closed her eyes and prayed, while Wilhelm stuck his blond head out the window and shouted excitedly, "Look, Mama, look!"

Then *soroche*, the mountain sickness, hit her. First she felt nauseous, then she developed a terrible headache combined with shortness of breath. She sent Wilhelm to look for a doctor, but he returned with an Indian porter dressed in a white jacket. The porter carried an inflated white canvas bag under his left arm; in his right hand he held a nozzle attached to the bag by means of a flexible rubber tube. When Ingrid explained her symptoms, he positioned the nozzle under her nose, squeezed the bag with his arm, and released a jet of pure oxygen into her nostrils.

It worked. The headache and nausea disappeared instantly. Her breathing stabilized and she smiled gratefully. Unfortunately the sickness returned almost as soon as the porter left the wagon. She made it as far as Huancayo, Peru, gulping additional oxygen every hour on the train.

They rested overnight at the Tourist Hotel in Huancayo, departing the next day for Puno and Lake Titicaca. Traveling along the flat, high Altiplano, Ingrid saw her first herds of llamas, untidy creatures with cleft lips and bright colored ribbons sewn in their ears, that stopped their chewing to examine her questioningly, as if asking why, why did you come? At the lake the two adventurers changed from the train to a small paddle wheeler which would take them across the highest navigable body of water in the world, leaving Peru behind to enter Bolivia.

When they boarded the steamer, Ingrid learned from a plaque on the wall that the metal ship had been designed and built in Europe, disassembled, and shipped in pieces to the lake, where it had been welded together again. This seemed as illogical and frustrating as everything else she had encountered in these backward countries. While they settled into their berth, the motor started, the paddles on both sides of the ship hit the water with solid slaps, and their small cabin vibrated with the shock.

They went on deck for the late afternoon departure. As the ship moved across the smooth water, Ingrid saw hundreds of reed boats returning to their island homes, framed in the last rays of the disappearing sun. Men dressed in wool ponchos stood at the rear of the graceful, curved boats, propelling them forward with long, smooth strokes of bamboo poles sunk into the soft mud bottom. Nets full of glistening perch and brim filled the front and mid-sections of the small craft, which glided across the water like skaters across ice, but more slowly, recognizing that the passage of time held no meaning on this lake. The boats were not much bigger than the men, and rode so low in the water that the more distant fishermen appeared to be standing on the surface, ghostly figures defying nature.

When the sun sank behind the mountains, hundreds of small, wavering lights appeared on the islands, the glow of wood fires as the inhabitants prepared their meager supper. As the horizon darkened, the sky turned a royal blue, and the stars above blended together with the lights on the islands, and cast their reflections on the still water, leaving her suspended in one glorious constellation. She had never seen stars so brilliant or so close or underfoot.

A late, full moon crept furtively over the Andes, hesitant to intrude on the beauty; its pale rays sneaked through the mountain passes like thieves, streaking the dark waters with lines of grainy chalk, and then flooding the entire surface with a thin white cover of breathtaking majesty, invoking gods of another time.

This was another world, a moment of mystic beauty. The train trip into the mountains had been her introduction to the Andes, but the boat passage across the lake was her wedding to this strange land, a severing of all ties to her previous existence. As she dozed off that night, the rhythmic sound of the paddle wheels lulling her to sleep, she realized that she had truly left home.

When Ingrid awoke the next morning, Wilhelm was already up and eager to see the sights. Joining him on deck, she found the lake covered with a thick fog, a dense cloud through which the boat moved blindly, oblivious to the dangers of unseen rocks or hidden islands. By the time they finished breakfast, the fog had dispersed, and she made out the small Bolivian port of Guaqui in the distance.

Approaching the dock, the slowing steamer was surrounded by reed boats, like ants around a dying beetle. Seated women in bright wool sweaters and brown derby hats poled the boats, food and souvenirs spread out before them in their floating shops. Wilhelm pleaded for a brightly colored wooden toy, nothing more than a carved stick linked by cord to a bigger round piece perforated with a hole. Ingrid bought the toy for him, and watched with amusement as he tried unsuccessfully to toss the round piece so that the hole would land on top of the stick.

After disembarking, Ingrid and Wilhelm boarded another train for a half day trip to La Paz, and arrived at the end of September, 1937.

At La Paz she collapsed into a hotel bed and slept for twelve hours. When she awoke at seven the next morning, she felt better, and began to recover from the mountain sickness. The hotel prepared a green tea made from coca leaves, which settled her stomach and eased her headache.

The second day in La Paz she sent a note to Captain Obregon to announce her arrival. Eager to explore the city, she and Wilhelm left the hotel in mid-morning and immediately discovered that the Bolivian capital was built on the floor and walls of a broad canyon, and the main street followed a steep incline. She quickly determined that her leather shoes with medium heels were not going to work on the slick cobblestone streets and sidewalks, and decided to buy something flat with rubber soles.

She descended down the main street in search of a shoe store, holding on to Wilhelm for balance. She found the storefronts uninteresting, lacking any sense of style. Unimaginative window displays featured bolts of cloth, cans of paint, small electric power generators, refrigerators, radios, and other items of basic necessity. There were one or two street vendors in every block, sitting on the sidewalk, their backs against the store walls, merchandise spread out in front of them, but she could not understand how they could possibly make a living. Each vendor sold only one or two items, such as toothbrushes, fountain pens, lemons, or small boxes of handkerchiefs. How many toothbrushes, she wondered, would you need to sell to feed a family?

Two-thirds of the people she passed were dressed in worn and poorly-fitting western style clothing, mostly in dark colors, the type German farmers might wear to church on Sunday. The other third were Indians, who added a touch of brightness to the otherwise drab scene. She found the Indian women to be the most colorful, each wearing three or more skirts, one on top of the other, billowing out from their waists like Christmas trees. Wilhelm gleefully pointed out their comical hats to his mother.

Just as Ingrid was beginning to enjoy herself, they arrived at a street corner and she looked to her right. Not more than three yards from her a man dressed in a black suit was urinating against the wall on a cross street. As her jaw dropped, he turned and smiled at her, showing a gold tooth in the front of his mouth, and shook the last drops from his penis. Ingrid grabbed Wilhelm by the arm and rushed him across the side street, dodging the oncoming cars. To her surprise, she found two more men relieving themselves in public at the next corner.

"Don't they have bathrooms, Mama?" Wilhelm asked.

"I'm not sure, but we've seen enough. Let's go back."

Ingrid crossed the main street with her son in tow and turned back in the direction of the hotel. She was walking uphill now, and the high altitude and steep climb quickly left her without breath.

Wilhelm tugged on her arm and said, "Look, Mama." He pointed to an Indian woman squatting at curbside, her multiple skirts spread around her, half in the street and half on the sidewalk. As they watched, she pulled her skirts together and rose, stepping carefully to one side. A small wisp of smoke rose from the hot excrement she left behind.

Ingrid put her hand over Wilhelm's eyes and hurried him past the spot. She ran most of the way back to the hotel, dragging a reluctant Wilhelm, her heart pounding in her chest. She did not like La Paz.

On her third day there, she felt a burning knot in her stomach and barely made it to the bathroom. For the next four days she was confined to bed with violent diarrhea and vomiting. The hotel doctor said it was something she ate. Fortunately, Wilhelm remained unaffected by either the mountain sickness or stomach problems, but was bored with the hotel.

Normally a healthy person, Ingrid's sickness demoralized her. At home she swam in Lake Constance, played tennis, and rode in the local horse shows. When her husband departed for Bolivia, Ingrid and Wilhelm had moved into her family's home, a big house on large grounds, located next to the lake. Although her family had no title like her husband's, they were wealthy enough to command respect. Her father had made his money in the brewery business and had a good nose for investments. An only child, Ingrid had always been given the best. She had attended a fashionable private school for girls at Munich, made the right acquaintances and acquired the proper social graces. Her passion for horses had brought her into contact with Lieutenant Manfred Kunnert, and she had married young, following the custom of her times.

Her marriage to Manfred had been successful, if not exciting. They rode and played tennis. Manfred considered these activities as a discipline; Ingrid approached them as a diversion. Consequently, they seldom competed as partners.

Their sexual life had been much the same way. He approached lovemaking as a series of steps, one to follow after another, to be perfected with time, always in the proper setting. In this he was unimaginative but persistent. At twenty-one Ingrid gave birth to a healthy baby boy.

When Manfred departed for Bolivia, Ingrid was only twenty-four, but she had her three year old son for company. Together with her parents, she devoted all her love to her beautiful blond toddler.

Then the news came from Bolivia: her husband was missing in action. They had been together only six years. Now he was gone. At first she maintained a youthful optimism that he would return. Then, as the days, months, and years passed, her hope faded. She became resigned to her husband's death. However, since officially Manfred was only missing in action, her situation was complicated.

First, there was the matter of his estate. Although not large, Manfred was the rightful heir to part of the Kunnert wealth. She wanted this inheritance for Wilhelm. Second, she was unable to resume an active social life; her parents forbade her to date any of the many eligible bachelors who found her attractive. At twenty-nine, she had not had sex for five years, and her body reminded her continuously that this was not natural.

Now that she was in La Paz, her confidence disappeared. The sickness left her weak, doubting if she could ever get accustomed to the altitude. Everything was so strange: the people, their dress, their habits, and the food. She had learned Spanish as well as French at her finishing school, but many people didn't seem to understand her. They spoke another language altogether.

Worst of all, her message to Captain Obregon had gone unanswered for three days. Then he had replied that he was too busy to receive her during office hours, but would like to invite her for dinner at his home. She observed from his note that he was now a Major, evidently a recent promotion.

Ingrid didn't like the idea, but she had come too far to think of returning without seeing him. She debated with herself for a full day, then reluctantly accepted the Major's invitation. Now she awaited the car he had offered to send.

Uncertain of what to wear, she had tried on several outfits before selecting an emerald green, silk cocktail dress, with just enough décolletage to suggest the fullness of her breasts. She wore black leather shoes with medium heels, and let her blond hair fall in smooth waves down to her shoulders. She was aware that her attractiveness could possibly be used to her advantage, and she wanted Major Obregon to like her.

Chapter 4

The black Ford bounced through the cobbled streets, turning frequently and leaving her disoriented. Ingrid had never ventured more than a few blocks from her hotel, and she could see very little in the dark night, except for the back of the chauffeur's head. The invitation indicated 9:00 p.m., a typical hour to dine in La Paz she had been told. The automobile rolled past darkened buildings with flat windowless facades. Nobody walked the streets, except for an occasional beggar. After twenty minutes, the car stopped in front of a big double wooden carriage door, and the driver sounded the horn. Moments later, an Indian in a white jacket, black pants, and black shoes, swung back the door. The car drove into a large enclosed courtyard illuminated by lights from the house.

The house was big, much larger than it appeared from the stark outside. After exiting the car, Ingrid saw two stories, with several doors opening onto the patio on the first level. A wooden balcony circled the second floor on three sides. In the center of the courtyard stood a round tiled fountain. Six jets of water sprang into the cold night air and fell softly back into the circular basin. The house exuded a pleasant open feeling, inviting her to enter.

Ingrid followed the Indian houseman through a downstairs waiting room filled with elaborately carved wooden chairs. They climbed a carpeted stairway to the second floor, passing through another smaller waiting room that contained even more ornate wooden chairs with padded cushions, plus several colonial paintings with gilded baroque frames. When the Indian opened the last door,

Ingrid stepped into a large living room. A log fire burned brightly in an oversized, decorated, stone chimney. The furniture was a mixture of Louis XIV copies and Spanish colonial styles. A beautiful woven carpet covered the tiled floor.

"Baroness Kunnert. Let me introduce myself. Major Carlos Obregon."

Ingrid examined the uniformed officer who extended his hand. He was younger than she had expected and not a bad looking man. Slightly shorter than she, he had a broad chest and muscular body. His skin was a smooth bronze except for a small mole on his chin. His jet black hair and dark penetrating eyes glistened like those of a raven.

The thing she noticed most was his odor, a musty, masculine smell, not unpleasant, but like a soldier who had lived in a barracks all his life, or a horse after a workout. Carlos' unusual scent made her uncertain, as though she were dealing with a powerful, unpredictable animal. She almost expected to see a hoof protruding from his pants leg instead of the polished brown boot she saw there. She didn't like the primal feeling he aroused in her.

"I am charmed to meet you, Major Obregon." She held out her right hand, palm down, expecting him to kiss it, but he captured it instead, enveloped her hand with his own two hands, shook it robustly, and held it for a moment.

"My *mayordomo* will take your coat," Carlos said, finally releasing her hand.

"Yes, thank you." She let the man slip her wool coat from her shoulders. He nodded to Carlos and left the room.

Carlos examined her with no attempt to hide his admiration; in Germany his look would have been impolite, and Ingrid was sorry she had not chosen a more conservative dress. She felt uncomfortable with this man.

"Is your wife joining us?" she asked.

Carlos shook his head. "No. I am unmarried."

"I see," Ingrid replied, thrown off by this new revelation.

"You had a long trip, Baroness?"

"Yes, Major. My son and I traveled for over two months to reach La Paz."

149

"Please, take a seat. We will have a sherry before dinner. And call me Carlos. Major is too formal."

"Thank you," Ingrid hesitated, not wanting to offend, "Carlos." She sat down on one of the ornate wooden seats and crossed her shapely legs. Carlos stared at them and she blushed. She needed to establish the right tone for this meeting.

"It has been an exhausting journey. More so than I had expected. But I am very interested in ending this terrible uncertainty regarding my husband." She looked questioningly at Carlos. "Or should I say my late husband?"

Carlos poured two glasses of sherry and handed one to Ingrid.

"We don't know, Baroness, whether he is alive or dead. There are rumors that the Paraguayans still hold a number of our officers, and are using them to build bridges and roads in the Chaco. Your husband may be among them. On the other hand, he may be dead. You are resigned to this possibility?"

Ingrid took a sip of the sherry.

"It has been five years since Manfred left Bavaria, four years since he was declared missing in action. I have accepted that he is most likely dead, but have hoped that by some miracle he might still be alive. That was why I was so encouraged when I received your letter. Should I have hope?"

"I was with him the night he went missing. In fact, I served under him at the time. He disappeared without leaving any trace, so he could have been captured, or killed. Perhaps buried in an unmarked grave."

"Why didn't the Bolivian Army request this information after the armistice? I asked our embassy to follow up, but they couldn't get any cooperation."

Carlos looked up from her legs. "The German officers on loan to my country were not popular with our own officers. Many think it was because of them that we lost the war. I'm sorry, but frankly, our government didn't care what had happened to them."

Ingrid set the glass of sherry on the table and lowered her head. "I appreciate your openness. But isn't there any way of knowing? It's important to me. You said you could help."

"It depends on the Paraguayan officials. Our relations are better now than three years ago. In fact, they have warmed considerably in the last few months. If I use the right channels, perhaps offer some money, they might be willing to help us. It will take some time, and some searching, but I am hopeful that useful information could be obtained. This is the help I could offer. Would you like that?"

"That would be kind of you," she hesitated again, "Carlos. If Manfred is alive, I want him back. If he is dead, I would like to take his remains back to Germany for a decent burial among his own people."

"That seems reasonable."

"Where should we begin? How long will it take?"

"That depends on the cooperation I receive. Maybe six months, maybe more."

Ingrid frowned. "That's much longer than I expected. Longer than I had planned to stay. Wilhelm shouldn't miss too much school. I wouldn't want him to fall behind."

"This is Bolivia. To us, six months is not so long."

"I don't know where I would stay. I'm just not prepared..."

"Enough for now, Baroness. This discussion can wait until after dinner." Carlos finished his drink, stood, extended his arm, and ushered her into the dining room.

The meal was served on a massive wooden table, large enough for twelve, with silver candlesticks and white linen napkins. Carlos sat at the head of the table with Ingrid at his right. The same Indian who had opened the courtyard door served them, having donned a pair of white gloves. Ingrid smiled to herself at the incongruity of an Indian dressed in this fashion, but his serving was flawless. They began with a creamy soup, warm and tasty. She didn't recognize the ingredients, but suspected the soup might be based on potatoes. The main course consisted of a grilled steak with rice on the side.

Carlos ate greedily, ravishing his food in portions too big for his fork, like a man who had suffered from a lifetime of hunger. Ingrid was fascinated by his hands, big rough hands that overwhelmed the silverware he clenched in both fists like weapons. Hunched over his plate, with his elbows extended, he reminded her of a tiger protecting its kill. When he did look up, he seemed ready to devour her next.

Ingrid nibbled at her steak, but finished all the rice. Her stomach felt better now. The first course had been accompanied by a Moselle wine, and the second by a Merlot, both from Germany. When she expressed her surprise, Carlos answered, "We don't make wine in Bolivia, Baroness. I thought you would enjoy wine from your own country."

Although she was accustomed to wine with dinner, the altitude and her recent sickness made its effect more potent.

"If I call you Carlos, Major, then it is only right that you should call me Ingrid," she said, slightly giddy.

During the rest of the meal, Carlos bombarded her with questions regarding her life, her activities, her likes and dislikes. Although he had never been to Europe, he didn't seem to be interested in Germany, only in her. She tried to change the subject several times, but he kept returning to her life. Realizing that she was becoming light-headed, Ingrid stopped drinking and only pretended to take a sip of wine occasionally. Carlos ignored this and drank heartily, although with no visible effects. His eyes bored into her and she felt a growing warmth between her legs.

They had flan for dessert, sweet and soothing to her stomach. The butler removed the plates after each serving, taking them through a swinging wooden door into a large, white tiled kitchen. Ingrid caught a fleeting view of two Indian girls inside the kitchen, laughing as they washed and dried the dishes. The comfort inside the house contrasted with the poverty Ingrid had seen outside in the streets.

"Shall we have coffee in the adjoining room, Ingrid?" Carlos stood and extended his arm.

"Yes, thank you, but I shouldn't stay too late." Ingrid rose and Carlos led her into a smaller sitting room. She could feel the heat of his arm through his jacket, and his odor, his dangerous, musky odor, seemed stronger than ever.

Coffee and liqueurs had been laid out on a small leather table in front of a couch that faced the fireplace. Two comfortable armchairs flanked the sofa. A furry alpaca rug with Indian motifs covered the floor in between. Logs glowed in a small fireplace, providing a pleasant warmth to the room. Carlos sat on the couch, but Ingrid chose one of the chairs, afraid to sit too close to him.

"You have a lovely home, Carlos," she observed.

"One of the privileges of being part of the government. Something to drink with your coffee?" Carlos asked.

"No, thank you. I think I have had enough. More than enough. The altitude seems to multiply the effect of the wine."

"You should try some of our local Pisco. Strong but good." Carlos held up a bottle of clear liquid. When she shook her head, he poured himself a large shot and drank it quickly. Beads of sweat appeared on his forehead, an effect of the sugar cane brandy or the warm fire. Ingrid didn't feel comfortable with the amount Carlos was drinking, and decided to return to the purpose of her visit.

"You said we would talk about my husband's situation after dinner. May we discuss this now?"

"Of course." Carlos took a second drink and looked down at her legs.

She crossed them and tried to ignore his eyes, but there was a tension in the air that she could not ignore. Crossing her legs didn't help, for it only increased the warm sensation she was already feeling.

"Couldn't you start the search for Manfred without my being here? Is it really necessary that I remain in Bolivia?" She uncrossed her legs. A thin film of moisture covered her upper lip. "Was it really necessary that I came?"

"Absolutely," Carlos replied, his eyes still glued on her. "I have wanted to meet you since I first saw your picture. Lt. Kunnert showed it to me. The one on the raft. I knew then that we needed to meet."

Ingrid blushed. "He shouldn't have done that."

"But he did. From that moment I knew that I wanted you. Wanted you more than anything else. During the war, when I thought all was lost, when the desert heat was unbearable, when I was ready to give up, I thought of you on that raft. Your image kept me alive."

"I didn't know you had seen my picture."

"It was my salvation. You can't imagine how much I wanted you here.

Ingrid felt her nipples grow rigid. Her breasts seemed to be on fire. Five years without a man was too long. Five years. And he was devouring her with his eyes.

"I'd like to go back to the hotel, Major."

"Of course." Carlos stood and walked to her chair. He extended his hand to help her rise.

Ingrid took his hand hesitantly, then let him assist her from the chair. When she arose, she brushed against his chest. An electric shock coursed through her body, and she trembled.

She looked at him, a question in her eyes.

Carlos answered her by seizing her in his arms. He kissed her full on the mouth, passionately, his desire burning on his lips.

Ingrid shuddered, pushed him back, then her resistance crumpled. She let go of her inhibitions and returned his kiss with the same burning desire. Five years was too long.

Her knees buckled and they collapsed together on the alpaca rug.

Naked except for his unbuttoned shirt, Carlos sat on the floor with his back against the couch. He took another swig of the Pisco, letting it slowly drain down the back of his throat. The burning sensation was not half as strong as the passion he had felt just minutes before.

He studied Ingrid lying on the rug in front of him. She had rolled onto her right side, half asleep, her rumpled silk dress bunched at her waist, with her back to him.

Carlos leaned forward and crawled to her. He unbuttoned the back of the dress, slipped it from her shoulders and down over her hips, ripping a seam in the process. She sighed and twisted slightly as he undressed her. Then he returned to his former position and studied her again. This was better. She had a splendid lithe body, thinner than he had imagined, but he knew she had been sick. Her creamy white buttocks were smooth and flowing like those of a sleek animal, curved and appetizing. He compared her in his mind to the short fat Bolivian whores with their painted faces, bulging hips, and voluptuous breasts. Ingrid was a vicuna among llamas, the best of the breed. But vicunas were impossible to domesticate, and he planned to tame this one, to make her his own.

He knew that he wanted her - wanted her more than anything else. From the day he had seen her photograph. He had lied to persuade her to come to La Paz. But now she was here, he had taken her, more easily that he could have imagined, and he was not going to

154

let her get away. She was his now - his possession, his property. His vicuna. He studied her for a while, admiring the creamy white skin and smooth dark recesses, and then crawled to her again. He snuggled against her white buttocks and gently took her from behind. Still half asleep, Ingrid moaned with pleasure.

Satisfied, Carlos lay limp on the soft rug next to her, his body pressed against hers, feeling her warmth. This was the best thing that had ever happened to him. He let out a deep breath and fell asleep beside her.

Later that night, when the cleaning maids opened the door of the sitting room, they saw a naked Ingrid curled in the arms of the Major on the alpaca rug, and the bottle of Pisco on the floor next to the couch. Shocked at the scene, they nevertheless took a good look, and one said to the other, "*Es una puta!*"

In that way the Baroness Ingrid Kunnert became known in Bolivia as the German Whore.

Carlos was in his study when Ingrid entered shortly before noon. She had bathed, gathered her hair back in a loose knot, and wore his checkered bathrobe, without underclothes or shoes. It was hard for her to maintain her dignity dressed in this fashion.

Carlos looked up in admiration.

"Good morning," he said, smiling. "You were sleeping so soundly I didn't want to wake you."

Ingrid stopped at the door and crossed her arms in front of her. "I can't find my clothes," she said.

"Your clothes are being repaired and cleaned. I'm afraid the dress was torn. They will be returned to you in the early afternoon, as good as new."

She pulled the robe tighter around her.

"Last night was a mistake," she said. "I don't know what happened to me. Maybe the wine, or maybe because I've been ill. But what we did wasn't right. It shouldn't have happened."

"It was good," Carlos replied. "Nothing to be ashamed of."

"I'm a married woman. And a mother."

Carlos swiveled his chair to face her.

"We don't know if your husband is alive. Maybe you're a widow. Would that make a difference?"

"Not really. I've just met you. It isn't correct."

"Why not? If people want each other, why isn't it correct?"

She looked at the floor.

"I need to go back to Germany. Nothing in this trip has turned out the way I wanted it to. I feel so lost…so out of place."

"If you want to resolve the situation of your husband, you need to stay here."

"Why?"

"Because it may require money, or for you to sign documents."

Ingrid studied him carefully.

"Or because you want me here."

"That also. You could live here with me. Only as friends, if that is what you want. It will save the cost of a hotel."

"Impossible."

Carlos rose and moved to the window overlooking the courtyard.

"Please, have a look."

Ingrid went to the window and looked down. Her eight year old son was in the courtyard, his blond hair setting him apart from the dark hair of the two Indian boys with him. They were playing with a wooden top and had drawn a crude circle with chalk on the paved courtyard.

"What is my son doing here?" Ingrid demanded. "I left him in the hotel with a sitter."

"I thought he should have someone to play with, so my men brought him here this morning. You told me that he was bored at the hotel, and the cook's children are close to his age. He seems to be having a good time. There is a very good European school here in La Paz. If you choose to stay, you both could live with me and he could go to this school."

"I can't stay, Carlos. Not in this house and not in this country. It's…it's not right."

"It's right if it feels right. Last night it felt right for me. Did it feel right for you?"

Ingrid's lower lip quivered.

156

"Don't you understand? I'm married. I shouldn't be doing this. I feel cheap."

Carlos hesitated a moment before answering.

"You're doing this for your husband. It's the only way to get him back. Stay here and I'll do my best to find him."

Ingrid collapsed on a couch, burying her face in her hands, weeping. Her body shook uncontrollably as she sobbed.

Carlos watched from his place at the window. She was still incredibly beautiful, even in despair. With her head bowed, the dressing gown hung forward, and he could glimpse the round whiteness of her breasts. He crossed the room slowly and sat on the couch beside her, placed an arm over her shoulder, and pulled her to him. She didn't resist. Her spasms subsided as he held her close, cuddling her like a wounded bird.

He reached inside the robe and caressed her breasts, first one, then the other. He removed his hand to untie the bow that fastened the robe. Gently he lay Ingrid down on the couch, kissing her tears, and whispering, "It's all right. It's all right now. I'll take care of you." He pushed apart the robe, and made love to her slowly and tenderly. Much to his surprise, the Baroness had an orgasm.

Chapter 5

In the days that followed, Ingrid's life settled into a calm domestic routine she would never have believed possible in a foreign country. Carlos had her luggage brought from the hotel and settled her bill, installing her in his home in her own separate bedroom. He enrolled her son at the European School, and arranged to have his driver take Wilhelm to and from the institution. Carlos left early, before she was awake, so she had the mornings to herself. When her son returned in the afternoon, she helped him with his homework and sat with him while he had an early supper. After Wilhelm was tucked away for the evening, Ingrid and Carlos dined alone.

At first she was awkward with Carlos, whom she hardly knew, and careful not to do anything that might ignite the passion she had experienced the first night. But as time passed, she realized that he was not going to sleep with her again until she herself was ready. She had free run of the house, but he warned her not to go out on the streets alone. For her own safety, he cautioned.

With little to do, she spent hours debating with herself what action to take. Should she depart Bolivia now, before their relationship became more involved? This would mean giving up on Manfred, leaving her in the same unbearable situation as before. If she stayed, should she wait for Carlos to make the first move, or should she take the initiative? His patience exasperated her.

After ten days she went to him voluntarily, unable to forbid herself the pleasure that had been awakened after lying dormant so long. When she opened the door to his bedroom, he was reading in bed. Without registering surprise, he calmly laid his book on the night stand, then folded back the covers to make room for her.

She approached slowly and stopped at the edge of the bed.

"I didn't know if I should come," she whispered.

"You have waited too long already," he replied, taking her hand and pulling her to him.

He made love to her three times that night, exciting her more than she had thought possible. At the end of the second week, she made up her mind about her situation, and moved her things into his bedroom.

Carlos was not a talkative man by nature, so Ingrid found it difficult to get to know him despite their intimacy. He never spoke of his work, which Ingrid attributed to its delicate nature, and volunteered very little on his background. She learned that he came from a village in the Andes, that his mother and sister were still there, and that he had fought in the Chaco. She knew little else, for he avoided answering her questions. He didn't seem to mind the long silences, but it made her uncomfortable since she was accustomed to sharing her day with her father and mother.

One night after three weeks, when the silences had become unbearable for Ingrid, Carlos invited Ramon to dine with them, and his presence changed everything. When Ramon entered the room, Ingrid could sense the spark inside the tall, slender, curly haired officer, who could have easily passed for a southern European.

"Baroness Kunnert. Delighted to meet you. Carlos told me that you were beautiful, but I didn't realize until now that he had made an understatement."

Ingrid smiled and extended her hand. "And he told me that you were a charmer and to beware."

"Bad advice, Ingrid. May I call you Ingrid?" Ramon took her hand and touched his lips to the back of it. "Anyway, Carlos shouldn't have kept you hidden so long. How long have you been in La Paz?"

Ingrid withdrew her hand. "About a month now."

"So long?" Ramon feigned surprise. "Then Carlos truly has been keeping you hidden. What brings you to La Paz?"

Ingrid's smile faded from her lips. "I'm searching for information regarding my husband, Lieutenant Manfred Kunnert. He was listed as missing in action in September of 1933 in the Chaco, and has not been heard from since that time. Carlos has offered to find out what happened to him."

Ramon's face went blank. He turned to glance at Carlos, who registered no emotion, then again to Ingrid. "If there is anyone who could help you solve the mystery, it would be Carlos."

Ingrid smiled again. "I agree. Carlos has been very kind to offer his assistance and his hospitality. I had almost given up all hope."

"One should never give up hope, Ingrid." Ramon looked at Carlos. "For example, I'm hoping that this invitation for dinner will result in a full and satisfied stomach. Now that you're here, I'm sure that the culinary quality of Carlos' table has greatly improved.

Carlos turned toward the dining room. "Ramon is always hungry…and thirsty. We had better give him something to keep up his strength so he can continue talking."

"Exactly! I won't deny it. Lead the way, Ingrid."

During dinner, Ramon kept up a constant monologue, enlivening the table with his stories about growing up in La Paz. He related the more amusing police reports of the past week: a drunk who stole a taxi cab; a fight between a mistress and a wife; a cockfight which ended with both roosters dead and the spectators in a melee. Ingrid found herself liking Ramon more and more as the evening progressed.

"You make La Paz sound so interesting, Ramon. My first impression of the city was not very good."

"Then we should change that. I would be happy to show you the city. Carlos, do I have your permission?"

Carlos looked up from his food. He seemed to be considering his answer. Then he said, "Of course. But take care of her. La Paz can be dangerous."

The next week Ramon showed Ingrid how to shop in La Paz. Leaving the center behind, he took her to the small back streets where the native women did their buying. She discovered that each side street specialized in one category of product. Rows of stores on one block sold only vegetables and fruits: oranges and lemons, peppers and beans, potatoes and tubers. In the next block bolts of loose cloth were stacked carelessly outside of textile shops. Ten stores in a narrow side street sold only coca leaves.

At the local meat market, Ingrid nearly choked as Ramon walked her past dissected carcasses displayed on flat wooden tables soaked with blood or hanging from overhead hooks in the fetid air, covered with flies. Buckets of entrails sat at the sides of the tables, awaiting their conversion to tripe soup, and skinless heads of llamas stared back at her with white unseeing eyes, which were considered a delicacy when boiled.

Wandering in and out of the shops, Ramon taught Ingrid how to bargain, never to accept the first price, and to compare prices at the next store before making her purchase. She learned to stand up to the aggressive women vendors, who, recognizing her as a foreigner, tried to place their merchandise in her shopping bag before she could say no. And she mastered a few choice refusals in the local dialect, to show her firmness.

The following week Ramon took her to the huge cemetery in the Indian Quarter, spread out over an entire hillside. He led her through the long, low mortuary chapel where humble funeral services were held, just inside the entrance. As they watched, a young Indian man dressed in black entered the chapel carrying a tiny, unpainted wooden coffin on his shoulders, followed by three silent women with black shawls hiding their faces. The coffin which they laid before the altar was no longer than her forearm.

Later, Ramon and Ingrid walked for an hour among the tall, gray, common mausoleums with their thousands of niches. Only the rich of La Paz could afford to be buried in the ground; the poor were stacked in layer after layer in a dead city of concrete tombs. Flowers decorated the front ledges of the newer niches, their colors highlighted by the new white cement used to seal the tombs. Sometimes a photograph was pasted onto the flat panel.

Ingrid noticed that some of the older niches had been broken open and the protective bricks removed, leaving their crumbling edges framing empty black holes. Ramon explained there were men who stole skulls and sold these for use in religious festivals, where they were said to have supernatural powers.

As they left, he pointed out the crippled men sitting by the front gate whom one could hire to pray for the departed.

When they got outside the gate, Ingrid sighed with relief. "That was interesting, Ramon, but a little morbid. Why did you take me there?"

"Because I wanted you to understand the Indians better. Death is a big part of their life, almost as important as living. Because of their misery here on earth, they don't fear dying like you and I. One in eight will die in childbirth, at least that many more before they're twenty. They feel that they have little control over death, and don't trust doctors. When death comes, it is almost a relief, a time of peace." He was silent for a moment.

"I've seen Indians soldiers die in the Chaco without a word. Men with a shattered arm, or a leg blown off, or a hole in their chest the size of a fist. I would have been screaming in pain. They just lay there, no emotion in their faces, waiting calmly to pass away." He paused to look back at the massive cemetery. "It's eerie."

On the next outing they went to the Valley of the Moon. Excited by the name, Ingrid talked almost as much as Ramon during the one hour drive south of La Paz. Ramon finally turned the borrowed car onto a pitted dirt road, and after ten more minutes parked on a slight elevation. When she got out, Ingrid felt she was on another planet. The earth before her had been etched by a massive acid bath, or clawed by a mystical beast from outer space. Irregular forty-foot columns rose straight from the sunken ground and then ended abruptly in smooth flat tops, all at the same height, as though they had been neatly trimmed by a pair of gigantic scissors. The closely-spaced, unnatural formations continued for as far as she could see, each different from the other in shape, but all a uniform gray.

"Ramon, it's unbelievable! What happened here?"

"Nobody knows for sure. Some scientists think this was caused by erosion, that wind and water carved the spaces between the columns. But there's no water here now. And how could the wind excavate so far into the earth, yet leave the columns so tall and flat? It's a mystery."

"What a wonderful mystery! I've never seen anything like it before. Thank you for sharing it with me." She took his arm in hers. "And thank you for being such a wonderful guide and friend."

Ramon grinned with pleasure and squeezed her arm against his body.

He had brought a picnic which they spread out on a blanket. As they ate, Ingrid kept looking back to the carved ground, fascinated by the endless formations. She knew that if she went down into the bottom, into the center of the columns, it would be impossible to find her way out of the maze without a guide, and wondered if her situation in Bolivia were the same. Was there a way out for her, and if so, was Ramon her guide?

When they finished eating, Ingrid pulled her knees up to her chest and rested her chin on her crossed arms.

"Ramon, what can you tell me about Carlos?"

"What do you mean?"

"I know so little about him. He doesn't share his feelings with me. In fact, he won't even talk about his past. You are his best friend. That's why I ask."

Ramon lay back on the blanket, supporting himself on his elbows, before speaking, "I doubt if you will ever know what he really thinks and feels. I don't, and I've known him for over four years now."

"Why is he so closed?"

"I can only guess. Remember, he is an Indian, and Indians aren't talkative. Although he now lives in La Paz, he grew up in a small village, in a mud brick house, working the land. No matter how much he tries to change, there are some traits which he will probably never lose."

"What are Indians like?" asked Ingrid.

"Our writers and historians have been arguing over that for four hundred years. The old view was that they are lazy and stupid, cruel and vindictive. They seldom smile, rarely laugh, and are suspicious by nature. They chew coca, drink too much, and are animals in bed. And they hate mestizos."

"Not a very pretty picture," Ingrid observed.

"Our more modern writers have tried to change the image, making them more romantic figures, capable of suffering great pain with stoicism, loyal to their families and their villages. Hard workers. Oppressed but not beaten."

"Which is true?"

"I don't know, Ingrid. Carlos doesn't seem to fall in the first group. Maybe the truth is somewhere in between. Maybe he's like the rest of us, part good, part bad." He paused. "But both schools agree that Indian men and women don't show their affection. You never see an Indian couple holding hands, walking arm in arm, or kissing in public. They just don't demonstrate much tenderness between them. So don't feel bad if Carlos acts this way."

Ramon laughed. "There's a typical saying among the Indian women: the more he hits me, the more he loves me."

Ingrid didn't smile. "I don't want him to hit me. I just wish I understood him better." Her eyes wandered back to the maze.

"He changes a little each day, Ingrid. He isn't the same person I first met in the Chaco. The war left its marks on him. On all of us. Now that he is in La Paz, he has completely changed the way he lives and dresses. Maybe his beliefs and values are also changing. Our work is not for the squeamish."

"Then why do you continue? Why not leave the Army?"

Ramon's face turned serious. He did not answer for a while, and then replied in a slow, measured voice. "Thousands of men died in the Chaco. Men who knew nothing of war and didn't want to be there. If we ignore their sacrifice, if we don't try to change the country, then these men will have died for nothing." Ramon paused. "Right now only the Army has the power to change Bolivia."

Encouraged by Ingrid's interest in exploring La Paz, Carlos insisted that Ramon dine with them once a week, an obligation which Ramon readily accepted.

While Ramon showed her the city by day, Carlos used the nights to initiate Ingrid in the sexual techniques he had learned in the whorehouses, leading her more and more into unknown areas. At first she was reluctant, feeling degraded and cheap, but she gradually began to accept and even enjoy the variety, so different from her love life with Manfred.

Carlos was a voracious lover, with an insatiable erotic appetite, always exploring, going farther and farther, but he was never again as out of control as he had been on the first night. Now he was more gentle, but always in command. Sometimes he spent hours just looking at her without speaking, which made Ingrid blush. She would look up from her reading, or glance in a mirror when she was brushing her hair, and his eyes would be upon her, a silent presence in the room.

After they had visited most of La Paz and surroundings, the excursions with Ramon ended and the days became longer and longer for Ingrid. When Carlos and Wilhelm left the house each morning, a sullen emptiness settled on her. The maids took care of the housework, the butler organized the meals, and the cook did the shopping, so there was little for her to do. She avoided the small German colony in La Paz in view of her living arrangements. At first she used her time perfecting her Spanish, studying alone and reading anything she could lay her hands on, but after a while this also bored her.

Her idle life in Bolivia was completely different from her former active life in Germany. She would unconsciously duck her left shoulder and execute an imaginary forehand as she walked through the empty rooms, but she knew there were no tennis courts in La Paz due to the high altitude. Lying in the bathtub she daydreamed of swimming in Lake Constance, taking long smooth strokes through the cold green water, arriving at the raft exhausted but fresh at the same time, but there were no lakes near La Paz, and the water supply was not dependable enough for pools.

Resting during the obligatory early afternoon siesta, with her eyes closed but very much awake, she would imagine hearing the voices of her German girlfriends, laughing as they played cards or exchanged gossip. But she had no friends in La Paz, no friends that she had grown up with, gone to school with, no friends at all except Ramon. Carlos didn't even belong to a social club.

As each day passed more slowly, she began to resent her confinement. The butler, who was always ready to do her bidding, smothered her with his servility and offended her with his bad breath. The cook, an Indian woman, couldn't or wouldn't speak Spanish. The two young maids were too intimidated to talk with her, and didn't do much but giggle between themselves anyway. Ingrid felt she had to get out, to do something.

One afternoon she carefully selected a white silk blouse with small flowers, a gray wool skirt, cut narrow as was the fashion in

Munich, plus a blue jacket purchased especially for the trip to Bolivia, and, defying Carlos' instructions, went for a walk. The sky was clear, the air was fresh, and she stepped out with a brisk pace, headed for anywhere.

Ingrid had not gone more than three blocks before a man in a worn dark suit fell in behind her, matching his pace with hers. At the next corner another man looked her up and down, eying her trim ankles, her shapely calves, and her blond hair. He leered and said something she didn't understand. She quickened her step, pretending not to have heard.

But the same thing happened again, two blocks further on, with another man. She turned and saw the first man still following her, but closer now. He smiled at her, a knowing smile. She hastily crossed the street and ran back to the house, stumbling on the cobblestones in her high heels. When she arrived breathless, the man was still behind her, and motioned to her to come to him as she fled through the door.

One week later she decided to try again. This time she dressed in a conservative tailored brown suit with delicate stripes, patent leather flat heels with sensible rubber soles, and a long tan raincoat. She took a taxi to the center of La Paz, near the hotel where Wilhelm and she had stayed, and got out on the main shopping street.

She walked slowly downhill past drab, uninteresting store windows, taking care not to step on the trinkets spread out on the sidewalk by street vendors. The day was warm so she slipped off the raincoat and carried it over her arm. She stopped in front of a shoe store, which displayed two rows of unpaired shoes neatly lined up in the window on unpainted shelves, one higher than the other. Women's shoes, brown with low heels and a minimum of decoration occupied the bottom row. Men's shoes, black with plain toes except for a pair of brown workman's boots in the right corner, filled the top row.

She felt a tug on her elbow. Turning, she looked down on a round oily face with close-set eyes. "How much?" the voice said. "How much do you charge?"

Ingrid tore herself loose and ran into the shoe store, her body shaking. When she looked back, the man was still outside, his obese figure blocking part of the window, waiting.

"Call me a taxi," she blurted out to the startled clerk. "Please," she pleaded, emptying her purse and leaving bills scattered across the counter top. "Please call me a taxi."

When Carlos arrived home that night, he found her in the bedroom, stretched out on the bed, crying. "What's the matter?" he asked as he sat down beside her.

She told him what had happened. "I don't understand," she sobbed. "I wasn't doing anything wrong. It was four in the afternoon. In full daylight. I was trying to look at store windows."

"Ingrid," he explained, "I told you never to go out alone. Day or night. If you insist, take a maid with you. A well dressed woman is always with someone. Otherwise she is a *puta*."

"But why? It wasn't like this at home. I could spend all day shopping on the streets of Munich without ever being approached. That's a bigger city than La Paz."

"This is not Munich," insisted Carlos in a stern voice. "This is La Paz. And decent women don't go out alone. Don't ever do it again."

She buried her head in the pillow. "I hate this city! And I hate this house! I want to go home!"

Carlos gently put his hand on her back. His voice lost its hardness. "*Bien, bien.* We'll find something."

The following week Carlos presented her with a beautiful brown three year old mare. After that she spent her mornings at the stables. The riding provided a release from her inner tensions and a connection with her former life. When her frustration reached the breaking point, she would drive the horse until they were both drenched with sweat, too exhausted to think. Sometimes Ramon would appear at the stables and watch her ride in the show ring.

At first she questioned Carlos weekly about his progress in locating Manfred or his remains. She wanted to finish her business in La Paz and return home. He always answered the same - he was working on it, but it was difficult to make the right connections with the Paraguayan officials who could help. He explained that things always moved slowly in Bolivia, and when two Latin countries were involved, even more unhurried. After a while she asked less frequently. She realized that Carlos did not like her to bring up the subject.

Carlos had other things on his mind. Now a Major and a member of the Military Junta, he was one of only six officers who ran the country. As a precaution against another coup, Busch kept the Ministry of Defense, but with the responsibilities of President, he had less time to oversee Carlos, so Carlos was free to run the National Police and the Secret Service as he saw fit. Consequently, he became better known in La Paz. His picture appeared in the newspapers, and strangers greeted him on the streets. He enjoyed the recognition and paid more attention to how he dressed.

Colonel Busch ruled the country pragmatically, but totally unpredictable. He appeared to be bowing to the conservatives when he suspended work on a new Socialist Constitution. Yet he made no move to reverse the expropriation of Standard Oil, and his speeches glorified the new ideas born in the Chaco.

During this time Carlos received an unexpected visitor. Juan Lechin, now leader of the Bolivian Miner's Union, asked for an appointment. Carlos agreed immediately, remembering the letter the union organizer had sent when his father was killed. Since the war's end, the miners' union had expanded nationwide, gained recognition from the owners, and was a considerable power in the country. Juan was its undisputed leader. The meeting took place in Carlos' office.

Carlos greeted him warmly. "Mr. Lechin. It's a pleasure to meet you. Please take a seat." Carlos pointed to the chair in front of his desk, waited for Juan to be seated, and then sat down.

"Coffee?"

Juan shifted his weight in the chair. "Not today, Major. I know you're a busy man and I appreciate your receiving me."

Carlos studied the older man whose hair showed premature streaks of gray.

"I remember the letter you wrote when my father died."

"When he was murdered, Major." Wrinkles appeared on Juan's forehead. "I have no doubt, no doubt at all, that the mine owners had him killed because he was helping us organize the workers at Catavi. He was a brave man. I hope you know that."

Carlos leaned back comfortably, distancing himself from the union leader.

"Actually, I only saw my father once a year, when he came home for vacation. To me, he was a kind, gentle man who loved his family."

"He also loved his fellow mine workers. He gave his life for them. Thanks to your father and others like him, we now have a strong national union that can stand up to the owners. You should be proud of him, Major."

Before Carlos could respond, Juan continued, "You should be proud of yourself too, Major. For being named a member of the Junta."

"Why?" asked Carlos. "Because I am the only Indian in the Junta?"

Juan looked offended. "Of course not. Because you have risen from a modest background, become a war hero, and have reached your present position due to your own merits. Plus you have a reputation for being honest and straightforward in your dealings."

Carlos recognized the flattery for what it was.

"Thank you, Mr. Lechin. I shall remember your words. Now, what can I do for you?"

Juan's left foot began to tap the floor.

"Major, my mine workers are worried and we need some reassurance. When the Military Junta took power in May, 1936, they promised a new social order, one that would protect the miners and the Indians. We felt that the military was on our side, that we shared the same goals."

Carlos smiled. "I remember, and I think the Junta has done what it could do. We created the first Ministry of Labor and Social Security just for that reason."

"That was an excellent step," Juan agreed.

"And the Junta consulted you on the choice of the new Minister."

"True. The Minister is a friend and a Socialist."

"Then what exactly is your concern?" Carlos asked.

"Since Colonel Busch replaced Colonel Toro in July, 1937, we see a swing back toward the mining interests. Nothing has been done since that time. The mine owners are becoming bolder, returning to their old habits. They refuse to listen to our demands. We want the government to support our claims."

"Aren't your strikes effective? Every day I read in the papers that some mine is closed down because of labor problems."

"The mine owners are fighting back. They've hired thugs to beat up our members. They've threatened even worse things. Those people are evil, Major. You, of all people, should know that in view of what they did to your father."

"I didn't realize the situation was so bad."

"The mine owners have exploited the country and their workers for years. Now it is our turn. Two thirds of our union members served in the Chaco. You know the hardships they endured. Many were killed." Juan leaned forward in his seat and his foot stopped its nervous tapping.

"Yet the workers still labor in inhuman conditions, for a despicable wage, without adequate vacations or medical assistance, dependent on the company store for credit to survive, while the government does nothing. We will not be denied our rights any longer, and we want to know where the Junta stands."

"I understand, Mr. Lechin." Carlos paused. "Let me talk to Colonel Busch. Maybe I can persuade him to see you. Then you can discuss your concerns directly with him. Would this be satisfactory?"

"That would be excellent, Major. I have tried for months without success to get an appointment with the Colonel. He has always been too busy or previously engaged. I turned to you knowing that the son of Luis Obregon would not deny me. Your help would be greatly appreciated."

The men shook hands and Juan left. Carlos picked up the telephone and dialed a number he knew by heart. The following week Juan Lechin had his first meeting with Colonel Busch.

Chapter 6

Forty-nine, fifty, fifty-one. Bruce Berkman counted to himself as he did sit-ups on the bedroom floor of his rented apartment in the center of La Paz. Fifty-two, fifty-three, fifty-four. Sweat poured down his face and chest but he kept going. Fifty-five, fifty-six, fifty-seven. He normally stopped at fifty but he was frustrated today. When he was frustrated, he needed to take it out on his body. Fifty-eight, fifty-nine, sixty.

Goddamn bastard! That tricky son-of-a-bitch Busch. Sixty-one, sixty-two, sixty-three. What the hell was happening? The Colonel had promised that he would reverse the expropriation of Standard Oil. Sixty-four, sixty-five, sixty-six. Bruce grimaced as his stomach muscles shouted at him to stop. Six months since Busch overthrew Toro. The money had been deposited in Busch's numbered bank account in Panama. Yet nothing's happened. Sixty-seven, sixty-eight, sixty-nine. He fought the pain. Yesterday the s.o.b. made his State-of-the-Union speech, and blabbered for two hours about national aggrandizement and social justice. Another fucking Mussolini!

Bruce stopped at seventy and collapsed on the floor. Rolling on his side, he wiped his brow with a towel. Busch is a damned crook, that's what he is. They had a deal, and Busch hasn't done his part. The money is paid and nothing has happened. And now Busch won't even return my calls. In Texas, where I grew up, a man's word was his honor. Well, Busch evidently doesn't have any honor. Fucking Bolivian mestizo!

Now Bruce himself was in trouble. He had assured the Ambassador that he could make it happen. The Ambassador had relayed the message to Washington and to Standard Oil, who put up the cash. He was dealing with powerful interests. Although Bruce's parents had only been modest cotton farmers north of Dallas, he knew the power of oil money in Texas and the U.S. Standard Oil was the biggest and most ruthless of them all.

Bruce spat into his towel. The Colonel was not playing by the rules. In the small town where Bruce had been raised, you played hard, gave it your all, but you played fair. He had been a high school football player, a member of the basketball squad, and a tennis player in off-season. He played to win, but he always played by the rules.

When he went to Princeton, he had not been good enough to play collegiate sports, but he had learned another lesson: to serve your country. His Princeton years opened up a whole new world to Bruce. There he was surrounded by classmates who were better educated and more urbane, prep school types whose parents were wealthy and important. Bruce wanted desperately to be like them. The first two years he studied furiously just to make passing grades and stay in. Then he blossomed and finished in the top quarter of his class. At the university he had developed a love for Latin America and the diplomatic corps. The corps offered a chance to serve his country and to enjoy life abroad at the same time.

Bruce was now thirty-seven and in his fifteenth year with the U.S. Foreign Service. In his first years he had done consular work in Guatemala and Chile and some desk work in Washington, developing a reputation as an achiever, a person who got things done. Some of his co-workers considered him self-centered and overly ambitious, but he wrote this off to professional jealousy. Political Attaché for Bolivia was his highest position so far, and could possibly lead to Chief-of-Mission at his next posting, or even to Ambassador in a small country. He had to succeed here.

Now that son-of-a-bitch Busch had stabbed him in the back. Bruce himself had conceived the idea of bribing Busch to overthrow Toro and recover the expropriated properties of Standard Oil. Shit, the company had over seventeen million dollars of U.S. money invested in the Chaco. They had drilled twenty-eight wells, built two small refineries, and all sorts of infrastructure before the socialist Military

Junta just took it all away. That was not fair! Bruce had decided to help Standard Oil get back their property, and make some points for himself at the same time.

Face it, he thought, Busch has outfoxed me. He has one million dollars of Standard Oil's money in his Panama account, and he knows we can't make it public. Now he refuses to even give me an appointment. Bastard!

Bruce stepped into the shower and ran cold water over his body. The shock helped clear his mind. He had to find another angle. Someone else who could right this injustice. This time, though, no money changes hands until Standard Oil has its property back. Who could help? Who?

By the time he reached the Embassy, Bruce had formulated a plan. He asked his secretary to set an appointment with Major Carlos Obregon.

Carlos sat patiently at the broad conference table, waiting for Colonel Busch to make his appearance so the July, 1938, monthly meeting of the Junta could begin. The other four members were huddled as a group at the window, ignoring him. Like himself, they had all served in the Chaco and were members of the still secret Marshal Santa Cruz Lodge. Unlike Carlos, who distrusted anything from the outside, they were convinced that national socialism, as practiced in Italy and Germany, was the best method of government for Bolivia, the only one that could pull the country out of its decadent poverty. The recent successes of Mussolini and Hitler had reinforced their belief.

Since Carlos didn't share their idols, and perhaps because he was an Aymara, they seldom included him in their private discussions. Captain Gutierrez glanced over at him and then said something to the other three officers. They all laughed.

Carlos wondered why he hadn't yet taken revenge on Gutierrez, and then answered his own question. Because he hadn't found the best way, because when it happened, he wanted Gutierrez to suffer. He could have ordered one of his Secret Service agents to assassinate Gutierrez, but that would have been too quick, too painless. He wanted something slow, something painful and humiliating.

Carlos wondered why the others were in such a good mood. Certainly not because of any great accomplishments. After two years of military rule, realism should have dampened their enthusiasm. Each time the Junta tried to take a step forward with a new decree, they encountered fierce resistance from the mining interests, the wealthy landowners, and the conservative politicians, and consequently very little had been accomplished.

Their greatest success had come during their first year in power, when they expropriated the holdings of Standard Oil, created Bolivia's own national oil company, and gave it a monopoly on future exploration. This had gained them popular support for a few months, but so far no new oil had been discovered, and even the old wells weren't producing as much as before.

The door opened and Colonel Busch strode into the room with a folder of papers under his arm and a frown on his face. Carlos stood up until the Colonel took his seat at the head of the table, then sat down again. The other officers stopped talking and arranged themselves around the table with Major Melendez, the Minister of Finance, at the opposite end, flanked by Captain Gutierrez.

"Gentlemen." Colonel Busch opened the folder and pulled out the top sheet. He held the document up for the other officers to see. Carlos recognized the yellow page and bold black print that one of his men had brought him earlier in the week.

"Pass this around," Busch ordered.

"What is it?" Major Melendez asked.

"A manifesto picked up at the university calling on the public to join a general demonstration against the Junta," Busch answered. "Among other things, it accuses us of despotism and corruption."

Major Melendez shrugged. "Why worry? It's just a bunch of students. They're always against the government."

"Because one year ago these same students applauded us, and because the students normally have a good sense of what the people are thinking." Busch raised both hands in frustration. "Don't you see, this is a sign that the populace doesn't support us. Otherwise the students wouldn't dare to call for a general demonstration."

"Arrest the student leaders," Major Melendez counseled.

"If that doesn't stop them, we can always close the university," Captain Gutierrez added.

Busch shook his head. "Just what they would want us to do. Then they would have legitimate grievances. If we're going to change this country, we need the support of all the people. Right now, we don't have it."

"As far as I'm concerned, the students aren't our biggest problem," Major Melendez said. "Right now our tax collections have dropped much lower than our expenses. Within six months, I doubt if we will have enough money to pay the government employees, or even our own military. Then we will have a problem."

"What's causing the drop in income?" Busch asked.

"The three big mining companies are holding back their tax payments. That's almost half the government budget. They're mad because we established the new Mining Bank, and made them contribute to the capitalization. They say it's the same as financing their competitors."

Busch nodded. "That was the idea, to break their monopoly. But what about our decree forcing them to sell all their foreign currency receipts to the new bank at an artificial rate of exchange? That should bring in plenty of money."

Melendez shrugged. "It should be, but it's not. The companies are hiding receipts and using black market transactions to get around the law."

"So they are trying to bring down the Junta by bankrupting the government?" Busch asked.

"Essentially, that's what they're doing," Melendez replied.

Colonel Garza, the Minister of Foreign Affairs, spoke up. "Colonel, if the Junta has lost the support of the people and is running out of money, why don't we consider holding elections and restoring a civilian government? I'm getting pressure from some of the ambassadors."

"No. Definitely not," Busch answered angrily. "This country isn't ready for democracy. Ninety per cent of our population doesn't even participate in the economy. They live on barter instead. Seventy percent can't read or write. Uneducated. Unthinking. How can they be expected to elect a good government? We would be turning the country back into the hands of the same people that ran it previously. All our work, all our ideas, would be lost." Busch pounded the table to make his point. "Over sixty thousand men would have died in the Chaco for nothing."

Major Melendez added, "We can't let go of the government now. The people are still wondering why the military lost the war. We don't want any civilian investigations into that. None of us might survive."

"It wasn't our fault," Captain Gutierrez protested. "General Kundt was responsible for the defeat at Campo Via."

"Yes, but our own native officers lost the first major battle at Boqueron, and the last at Piquiba," Garza replied. "The public is not happy with us."

"They never were," Major Melendez countered. "Be realistic. Nobody asked us to kick out the elected President."

"Enough," Busch intervened. "We have enough enemies outside of this room. We don't need bickering among ourselves. We need another big step forward, something that will be popular with the masses, something to get their attention, like the expropriation of Standard Oil." He paused. "And I think I know what it is."

The officers stopped arguing to listen to Colonel Busch's latest idea.

"I have asked the Minister of Labor and Social Security to draft a new labor code - a law to bring our country out of the dark ages and put us on a level with Italy and Germany. An all-embracing labor law that will place the power in the hands of the workers, whose support we need. It should be ready in six months."

"Is that wise?" Major Melendez asked. "Our main problem now is lack of money. If we antagonize the mine owners and industrialists even more, the Treasury will be empty."

"I agree with the Major," Captain Gutierrez said pompously. "We keep trying to buy the workers with new laws, but they just laugh at us and demand more. Juan Lechin is never satisfied."

Carlos frowned when Gutierrez spoke. He suspected both Melendez and Gutierrez were receiving money on the side from the big mining companies, and decided to intervene.

"Maybe that's because we make all these new laws, but nothing changes. We never enforce them," Carlos said.

"It's because we're dealing with a bunch of ignorant Indians who think more about chewing coca and getting drunk than working for the good of their country," Gutierrez answered. He looked straight at Carlos. "You should understand that."

Carlos eyes narrowed. He had postponed his revenge on Gutierrez too long.

"Let's wait until we see the draft of the new labor code, then we'll make a decision," Busch said.

There were murmurs of agreement around the table, and Busch adjourned the meeting. All the officers left with the exception of Busch and Carlos, who remained seated at the conference table.

Busch spoke first. "A word of advice, Carlos."

"Yes, Sir."

"Before challenging another officer, make sure you have the strength behind you to win. Otherwise you look foolish."

Carlos nodded his head.

"What do you think about the new labor law, *Carlitos*? Will it work?" Busch asked.

"Perhaps, Sir. The people are restless now. It will gain you support from the miners and from factory workers, but what about the farmers, who are a much bigger group? The Indians who work the land still haven't seen any change in the way they live. They work from sunrise to sunset just to stay alive. They're still waiting for the land we promised them. Nothing has changed for them, yet many more farmers died in the war than miners. The mine workers are organized and getting most of their demands, but the Indian farmers don't see any difference from before the war. Those farmers who served in the Chaco are bitter, Sir."

Busch raised his eyebrows. "What about the National Conference of Farm Workers? We organized that."

"Nothing but a lot of speeches. Nothing came of it. When the conference was over, the Indians went home, and nothing happened."

"We passed a law abolishing *pongueaje*," Busch said gruffly. "What more do you want?"

"But nothing has changed," Carlos answered back. "The big landowners have ignored the decree. The farmers still have to work three days a week without pay on the owners' lands, in order for the patrons to let them have a small plot of land to farm for themselves. If any of the farmers protest, the landlords take away the land they need to survive. We could send troops into the countryside and have them enforce the new law. If the landowners refuse to cooperate, we could take their land and give it to the Indians. We could make the law work."

Busch stood up at the table and went to the window. Then he turned to face Carlos.

"Don't be naive, Carlos. The Indian farmers can't help us. They aren't organized. They don't have rifles. They're spread out in isolated communities all over the country. The workers are concentrated at the mines and here in La Paz. They have power. Even the landowners are more help to us than the farmers. At least they have money."

Carlos' eyes narrowed and his jaw became rigid. "I am a farmer," he declared. "These are my people. We promised to help them. You promised to help them."

"When did I make these promises?" Busch asked.

"At our Lodge meetings in the Chaco. You said the Indian farmer would be given his own land, be provided with money and equipment, and be made part of the economy. Don't you remember?"

"Don't raise your voice at me, Major." Busch glared at Carlos. "You're no longer a farmer. You're an army officer, and a member of the Junta. We have more important things to accomplish."

Busch softened his tone. "Look, Carlos, it's hard to change this country. Damned hard. We have too many enemies and not enough popular support. We have to be practical…and patient."

Carlos clenched his fists underneath the table. "You promised to help my people."

The Colonel left the window and approached Carlos, who tried to hide his anger. "Don't look so mad. I have some other news for you. Good news!"

Carlos' fingernails were digging into his own palms.

"What is it, Sir?"

"How would you like to spend three months in the U.S.?"

"Me, Sir?" His fists relaxed a little.

"Yes, you. As you know, it appears that Hitler may be preparing for war in Europe. If so, that cuts off our connection with the German military for the duration. The U.S. has offered to train our officers in the future. They suggested we send one man up to Fort Benning, Georgia, to go through a three month class with their new officers. I remembered that you never went to our own Military College here. It would be good for you and you could check out their training at the same time. Interested?"

"Yes, Sir," Carlos replied with mixed emotions, knowing that Busch expected him to go, but reluctant to leave Ingrid.

"Good. All the arrangements can be made through Bruce Berkman at the U.S. Embassy. You met him at my office. Remember him?"

"Yes, Sir." Carlos not only remembered him, but Bruce had visited his office several times during the last three months, obviously trying to cultivate some sort of friendship. He decided to say nothing of these meetings to Busch.

Carlos told Ingrid of his proposed trip that same evening after dinner, in the sanctity of their bedroom. Ingrid was sitting at her dressing table, removing her lipstick with a Kleenex. She turned to face him.

"You will be gone for three months? That's a long time."

"It will go quickly. You'll see." Carlos unbuttoned his uniform shirt and hung it in the wardrobe. "I'll be back as soon as possible."

Ingrid turned to the mirror again so he would not see the tears forming in her eyes. She crushed the tissue in her hand. "If you are going for such a long time, I should return to Germany. Wilhelm and I have been here almost a year, and there's still no news of Manfred. Wilhelm will fall behind in his studies."

Carlos sat on the bed and removed his shoes. "I told you that I've had some encouraging news. I've made contact with a Colonel Ortiz of the Paraguayan Army. He's looking into your husband's disappearance. Maybe we'll have some information by the time I return." He took off each sock and folded them carefully in his shoes. "Besides, Wilhelm seems to like the European School here. He's made a lot of friends."

Ingrid moved her head so that she could see Carlos in the mirror.

"The Headmaster told me that Wilhelm is one of his best students," Carlos said, lifting his shoes from the floor.

She watched him take his shoes to the wardrobe and bend to place them neatly along one side. Then he stood and removed his trousers. He took a hanger from the wardrobe, folded the trousers neatly over it, and hung them in their place. He was dressed only in his undershorts and she could see his flat stomach and the strong muscles in his arms and legs.

"My parents will be worried if Wilhelm and I stay any longer in Bolivia. I think they are already suspicious about why we have stayed this long."

She watched Carlos close the wardrobe and approach her from behind. He knelt, slipped a hand under each breast, lifted them slightly, and began to massage them through her silk nightgown.

"And why have you stayed so long?" he asked, looking at her in the mirror.

Ingrid closed her eyes. She felt his fingers tease her nipples, and then gently squeeze each one. Her nipples stood erect, embarrassing her with their response.

"Is there something here you like?" he teased, as one hand moved down her stomach.

"Don't, Carlos. I'm serious." Ingrid removed his hand.

"So am I," Carlos said, and placed his hand on her back. He ran his fingers lightly down her spine, stroking her, stopping ever so often to move up a few inches, but always going lower. He reached the crease of her buttocks, and gently ran one finger up and down the indentation in the silk nightgown.

Ingrid shivered and felt herself becoming moist. He knew her so well, what she liked, how to please her. She felt him lift the nightgown and fold it over her shoulders, exposing her back and buttocks.

Then she felt something else on her back, teasing her, making little circles. Something hard yet soft at the same time. He was playing with himself while playing with her. He placed his hands under her armpits and lifted her from her chair.

Before she could protest, he bent her forward over the chair. She gasped as he entered her, then looked up to see his face in the mirror. He was smiling as he grasped her hips, pulled her against him, and thrust deeper and deeper.

Chapter 7

"Geronimo," he shouted as he leaped through the open door of the airplane. The air stream slapped his face and spun him sideways. The plane's gray tail rudder passed his helmet too close to be comfortable. He saw the ground two thousand feet below him and his body stiffened. A shock yanked him upward as the parachute opened, and his fear turned into exhilaration. All noise vanished as the plane disappeared and he floated slowly down toward the target area, surrounded by white parachutes below and above him. Now he knew how a condor must feel, soaring above the world, untouchable in the sky, omnipotent.

This was Carlos' eighth week at Fort Benning and his first jump. Damn it was good! The American officers were disciplined and professional. Jump school was new; his was only the sixth class. The military called it the wave of the future - mass deployment of a well trained fighting force behind enemy lines. If the Bolivians had used parachute troops in the Chaco, who knows what might have happened. Certainly not the slaughter at Nanawa when the German General sent thousands of soldiers directly into enemy machine gun fire.

His fellow officers in the training program came from all parts of the U.S.: blond farmers from Arkansas, dark haired city boys from New York, a Mexican-American from San Antonio, all young and enthusiastic, and supremely confident in themselves and their country.

Mostly, though, Carlos found them naive. They felt that if you trained hard, you could defeat anybody and change the world. The good guys always won.

Carlos knew better - he had been on the losing side in the Chaco. He believed that life flowed in circles and destiny played tricks, sometimes killing the most able, sometimes rewarding the wicked. The same officers who betrayed their troops in the Chaco were running Bolivia now. Hadn't he been promoted after killing his own Commanding Officer? Man has little control over his life, or the timing of his death. Therefore, better to take advantage of opportunities when they appear. They believed in slide rules; he believed in earthquakes and storms. Nevertheless, he kept his opinions to himself, made more acquaintances than friends due to his reserve, and learned some basic English.

As the ground came closer and closer, Carlos forced himself to relax and bend his knees. Upon impact he ducked one shoulder and rolled forward, pulling the chute cords around him as he fell. The chute dragged him a short distance, then collapsed. Carlos stood, wrapped in the cords, and ran forward to stand on the closed chute. He looked up at the sky and watched the airplane disappear into the clouds. He had survived. Defied nature and survived.

Two weeks before his training ended, Carlos received a phone call from Bruce Berkman, inviting Carlos to join him in Washington, D.C., after graduation. Bruce indicated that he was in the U.S. capital on government business and wanted Carlos to meet some of his associates.

Bruce met him at the Washington train station and took him to the Whitehall, a small hotel distant from the city center, but nicely furnished with a big double bed, a welcome change from the Spartan officers' quarters he had shared for three months at Fort Benning. The first afternoon Bruce took Carlos to see the tourist sights: the White House; the Capitol Building; the Washington and Lincoln monuments. The dynamism in this young nation impressed Carlos. That evening they dined in a French restaurant, and Bruce questioned him about his experience at Fort Benning. The time passed quickly, with no mention of Bolivia. They agreed to meet at nine the next morning.

Carlos was undressing in his hotel room when he heard a discreet knock on the door. He buttoned his pants, walked to the door, and opened it. In the corridor he saw a pretty redhead in her early twenties, dressed provocatively in a tight black satin skirt and clinging red blouse. Both her fingernails and her toenails were painted in the same bright red.

"May I come in?" she asked. Her voice was soft and sensuous.

"There must be a mistake," Carlos said, not taking his eyes off her.

"I think not, Major. Mr. Berkman told me that you had been with nothing but men for the last three months. He thought you might appreciate some female companionship. Compliments of the U.S. government." She didn't wait for an answer, pushing the door open and entering as if she knew the room well.

Carlos watched her pass him, taking in the rolling movement of her buttocks under the tight skirt. She turned and smiled at him. Slowly she unbuttoned her blouse, starting with the top button. "I understand that you Latin men are really macho. Why don't you show me?"

The next morning she rose, bathed, and dressed before eight. When she reached the door, she turned to Carlos. "It was good, Major. I hope you enjoyed yourself. Mr. Berkman wants you to be happy. If you wish, I can come back tonight. Otherwise, there are plenty of other girls in Washington who would consider themselves fortunate to spend the night with you. What will it be?"

Carlos was still in bed, propped up on one elbow, nude and thoroughly satisfied. He studied her body and remembered the night with pleasure. Smiling he answered, "Variety is good. Tell Mr. Berkman I like variety."

She closed the door quietly and left, also smiling.

The next two days fell into a standard pattern. Bruce would pick up Carlos after breakfast and they would go to the State Department. There he would meet with different officers who wanted to know more about Bolivia and its military Junta. The Foreign Service men pumped him for information; they were interested in everything he could tell them, and filled several notebooks with their hasty scribbling. When one officer finished with him, another would begin, mostly covering the same ground. They even discussed Bolivia during lunch. The long meetings were difficult for Carlos, who was unaccustomed to talking so much. He was tired, and they often had to use a translator. He wasn't getting much sleep at night.

On the third day Bruce asked Carlos to put on his best uniform for a special meeting and picked him up earlier than usual. Bruce seemed nervous, checking his watch several times and fidgeting with his tie. When they arrived at the State Department building, Bruce accompanied Carlos to a reception room on the third floor, where an attractive middle-aged woman announced them. Then Bruce led Carlos into a spacious corner office decorated with dark wood paneling, thick beige carpeting, and light blue curtains. A leather sofa with two matching arm chairs and a center table occupied the right side of the room. Above the sofa was a framed and autographed photograph of President Franklin Roosevelt from the chest up, jauntily sporting his trademark cigarette holder. A silver coffee service sat on top of a low credenza placed against the second wall.

Sun from the window fell across a massive mahogany desk in the center of the room and illuminated a draped U.S. flag positioned on the left. Two polished wooden chairs faced the desk and the leather swivel chair behind it. A tall slim man with patrician features and gray at his temples rose from the swivel chair as they approached. Dressed in a three-button, dark gray suit with light gray pinstripes, a white oxford cloth shirt, and a blue and green striped tie, he was the most distinguished man Carlos had ever seen.

Bruce made the introduction. "Major, I would like you to meet Dana Gardner, Assistant Secretary of State for Latin American Affairs. Mr. Secretary, this is Major Carlos Obregon."

The Assistant Secretary extended his hand. "Welcome, Major. I hope your visit to the U.S. has been pleasant so far."

Carlos shook his hand, and replied, "Yes. Excellent. Thank you."

"Bruce has told me quite a bit about you and the current situation in Bolivia. Have a seat on the couch and we can talk more comfortably," Gardner said, maneuvering Carlos toward the sofa.

Bruce and Carlos took seats at opposite ends of the couch. Gardner sat in the right armchair, slightly higher than the other men, his head framed by the outside light.

Smooth, thought Bruce, admiring the subtlety of the seating arrangement. Gardner is so smooth. A background of old New England money, years of attending the right schools, joining the right clubs, and mixing with the right people. Bruce knew Gardner didn't have to work; his family had left him enough to do whatever he wanted for the rest of his life. But Gardner had joined the Foreign Service after Harvard law school and had risen rapidly due to his money and influential friends. Ambassador to Guatemala at the age of thirty-five, Ambassador to Colombia at forty-two, several years on important committees in Washington, and Assistant Secretary of State at fifty-one. Bruce envied his money and his career, and always felt intimidated in the presence of this man. Now coffee had been served and Bruce waited for Gardner to speak - this was his show.

"Major, I wanted to meet you personally and discuss some of my government's concerns," began Gardner.

Carlos nodded but did not answer.

"As you know, we are unhappy with the Junta's expropriation of Standard Oil. We respect the right of private property in the U.S. and we expect other countries to honor this principle, particularly when formal contracts have been signed between the local government and the oil companies."

Carlos moved his head slightly and took a sip of coffee. Bruce could not tell if he had agreed or not.

Gardner hesitated a minute for effect, then continued, "We also understand the difficulty of reversing an expropriation after eighteen months, particularly when the local population has strongly supported the measure."

"We agree on that," Carlos answered.

"Let me continue, please, Major," Gardner said with a smooth but forceful tone. "I want to urge your government to reconsider the expropriation at the appropriate time. Maybe six months from now, maybe a year. If the properties are not returned, then the U.S. Government expects Bolivia to indemnify Standard Oil for every cent of their investment."

"Colonel Busch has no intention of undoing the expropriation. I doubt that he will ever pay any compensation," Carlos replied. "He is stubborn once he makes up his mind."

Gardner set his coffee cup on the table and replied, "Colonel Busch will not always be in power, Major. Governments change."

Carlos didn't respond, so Gardner continued, "My government is also concerned about the obvious sympathies the Junta has for Germany and Italy. The U.S. does not agree with the political philosophies of the Nazis and the Fascists. We fear that they are leading Europe into a new war with their strident nationalism. If a war starts, Bolivia will have to choose sides. We expect Bolivia to be on the side of the U.S."

"Why must we pick sides?" asked Carlos.

"Because the military powers will need Bolivian tin, Major. If the U.S. gets involved in the conflict, we will want an uninterrupted flow of Bolivian ore. And we don't want any of that ore going to our enemies."

"So you will fight against Hitler?"

"I don't know," Gardner answered. "That decision would be up to the President. But even if we didn't send troops, the U.S. would become the arsenal for the countries fighting Hitler, and that arsenal would require tin."

"I see," Carlos replied, "and I understand your situation. But you are speaking to one member of the Junta, Mr. Gardner. Why not talk to all of the members, or better yet, to Colonel Busch?"

"Frankly, Major, we have been disappointed in our dealings with Colonel Busch. We prefer someone who knows the U.S., who has met our people and seen something of our country. Someone like yourself." Gardner smiled at him, a conspiratorial smile.

"Colonel Busch makes the final decisions in the Junta," Carlos said, folding his arms across his chest.

"He does now, Major. But as I said before, we both know that governments can change. In fact, they change quite often in Bolivia. Think about it. Remember that the U.S. is a strong ally." Gardner indicated by his tone that the conversation was over. The three men stood and exchanged handshakes. Bruce escorted Carlos out of the office and down to the first floor, where he left him with another Foreign Service officer.

When Bruce returned to the third floor office, Gardner was seated behind his desk, looking out the window, thinking. He turned when Bruce entered, and asked, "Do we have the right man?"

"Yes," Bruce answered, taking a seat at the desk. "We can work with Major Obregon."

"Why?" Gardner leaned back in his chair. "He seemed unresponsive to me."

"Because he is ambitious. He comes from a poor family, but has now tasted money. Father was a miner, now dead. Mother and sister still live in a remote village. He likes power, money, and women."

"So does Busch, from what I've heard."

"Yes, but Busch is unreliable. He has already cheated us on the Standard Oil deal. Besides, Busch is the son of a German immigrant married to a Bolivian woman. He is more likely to be sympathetic to the Germans than Obregon."

"Why not approach one of the other members of the Junta?"

"I've tried. But they all believe in national socialism. They worship Hitler and Mussolini, and they don't like the U.S. Yankee imperialists, they call us."

"What a mess," Gardner said, swiveling his chair toward the window again. "I guess we go with Obregon. Continue to work on him and keep me advised."

"If he takes power, he will be another dictator," Bruce warned.

Gardner swiveled back to face him. "We can work with dictators, Bruce. We just don't want any fascists or commies in our backyard." He thought for a minute, and then added, "What about Obregon's mistress? Isn't she German?"

Good God, thought Bruce, Gardner really does his homework. "Yes Sir, she is. But from what I've seen in the last few days, Obregon doesn't seem to be very loyal to her."

Chapter 8

Clad only in her robe, Ingrid studied the open suitcase on her bed. For the third time during Carlos' absence, she had taken her suitcase from the closet with the intention of packing. If she and Wilhelm were to get out of Bolivia, now was the time to depart, while Carlos was in the U.S. Once he returned, she knew that she would not be strong enough to leave. Once he touched her, her resolve would disappear.

She picked up one of the many white envelopes inside the suitcase and rubbed the letter slowly across her upper lip, feeling the smoothness of the linen paper. During the year that she had been here, her parents had written several times urging her to return to Germany. Each time she answered that she was making progress in discovering what had happened to Manfred, but she had lied - she knew Carlos would never push the search for her husband as long as she remained his mistress.

Ingrid pulled the envelope away from her lip and studied her own name and address written in her mother's neat handwriting. She had told her parents that she was staying with a Bolivian family. She shuddered when she thought what they would do if they knew she was living with an unmarried Bolivian Army Major. She dropped the envelope back in the suitcase and sighed. How had she gotten herself into this mess?

She glanced at her watch and saw that it was almost eight p.m., the time when Carlos normally returned home, and she was still not dressed. She closed her eyes and tried to recreate his image in her mind. Without thinking, she opened the robe, crossed her arms across her chest and caressed her bare breasts. Her left nipple responded immediately, but her right nipple remained sunken in her soft flesh. She licked her finger and touched the nipple, rubbing the aureola gently, coaxing the nipple to come up. The nipple rose erect from its hiding place, and she smiled. She massaged her breasts tenderly and felt a warm sensation in her lower belly.

Carlos was an animal, and was turning her into one as well. He loved to arouse her, to tease her, bringing her to the heights of lust. Then he made her do whatever he wanted before he would satisfy her. But when he did, he would never stop. He kept her on a high tension wire, forcing orgasm after orgasm. When he finally finished, she was wet with perspiration and totally exhausted. Carlos delighted in making her behave like a hungry animal, like a cat in heat, bringing her down to his level. She shivered with the thought.

Ingrid opened her eyes and turned to study her new sexuality in the mirror. She had never looked more beautiful; her tall frame had developed more gentle curves; and her blond hair glistened as though it were alive. Her breasts were larger and her buttocks more rounded. Lovemaking agreed with her.

She hated herself for having become Carlos' sexual pawn, but she loved the sex. She felt degraded and cheap, but she also felt satisfied and full. Before Bolivia, she would never have imagined herself capable of this behavior. Now she knew herself better. Maybe there was a side of her which relished the pure lust, the depravity, and the domination. Maybe she was falling in love with Carlos. She turned again to the empty suitcase and gently closed the lid. She was not ready to leave.

Ramon waited impatiently for Ingrid in the drawing room. The Thursday dinners with her marked the high point of his week. He looked forward to them, his anxiety and anticipation increasing each day, until his chest was ready to burst. When the evening was over, the process began again, a continuous cycle of anticipation and pleasure, anticipation and pleasure. With Carlos away, Ramon enjoyed the dinners even more, for he was getting to know Ingrid better each time, and he was falling more in love with her each day.

When Ramon first set eyes on her at Carlos' house, he had been struck by her beauty, and she had become even more attractive the past year. During their outings he had discovered she was kind, intelligent, and extremely sensitive. When the two of them were together, conversation came easily. What had begun as a friendship had developed into much more for Ramon.

He studied the furniture and other items that belonged to Carlos and felt a twinge of guilt. Ingrid had never explained why she was living with Carlos, but the contrast between them was so marked that Ramon found it impossible to accept, and that gave him hope. He didn't know what hold Carlos had over her, but Ramon could sense her uncertainty and her vulnerability.

Ingrid walked into the room and he rose from his chair.

"Hello, Ramon." She extended her hand. "Excuse me for being late. I wasn't sure you were coming this week."

Ramon brushed his lips across the back of her hand and released it. "Why wouldn't I come? Dinner with you is the most exciting part of my week."

Ingrid motioned to the chair. "I doubt that, considering your job. Anyway, I'm always happy to see you. Have a chair and I'll tell the *mayordomo* that we are ready to eat."

Ramon sat down again and watched her walk away from him. He rehearsed in his mind what new stories about La Paz he would tell her tonight. He tried to disguise his feelings by recounting amusing anecdotes, telling jokes, engaging in playful banter, but he assumed that she must be aware of his affection for her.

Ingrid returned from the dining room. "Dinner will be ready in a few minutes."

Ramon rose and retrieved a paper sack from the coffee table. "A present for Wilhelm."

Ingrid took the package from him. "Ramon, you don't have to do this. You're spoiling him with all these gifts. What is it this time?"

"A bamboo flute. I found it in the market."

"That's very kind of you. You're a good friend to keep me company while Carlos is away, and to think of Wilhelm. Thank you."

Ingrid leaned forward and kissed him on the cheek. Ramon could smell the clean, delicate, intoxicating perfume of her body. He started to embrace her but the Indian butler entered the room to announce that dinner was served.

At the table, Ramon began with the story he thought would interest her the most.

"Have you heard about the accident suffered by our Mayor?" he asked.

"No," Ingrid replied, lifting her napkin from the table and spreading it on her lap. "You mean the Mayor of La Paz."

"Yes."

"What happened to the poor man?"

The butler set their plates before them and Ramon waited until he left before replying.

"It seems that he has been having an affair with the wife of a prominent local surgeon." Ramon watched Ingrid lift one eyebrow. He knew he had her attention.

"Anyway, this week, I think it was Tuesday afternoon, the two of them, the Mayor and the doctor's wife, that is, were having a romantic moment together in the doctor's bed while the doctor himself was supposed to be at the hospital."

"I see," Ingrid said, lifting her fork, and then holding it half-way. "But I thought the Mayor was also married."

"He is." Ramon loved every movement Ingrid made.

Ingrid kept her food suspended in the air. "I've seen her picture in the newspapers. She's very attractive."

"One of the most desirable women in La Paz." Ramon smiled. "Present company excluded."

Ingrid took a bite from the fork, chewed it slowly, and then replaced the fork on the table. "Then why would the Mayor want to have another woman?"

Ramon placed his own fork on his plate. "It's a Latin thing. *Machismo.* Most Latin men need to prove to themselves that they are good lovers. Not only with their wives, but with other women. As many as possible."

"Interesting," Ingrid replied, and resumed her eating. After a minute she asked, "And what happened to the Mayor?"

"The poor man heard the doctor arrive home. Rather than be caught in the doctor's bed, he hastily threw on his pants and, clothes in his arms, jumped from the bedroom window."

"Oh, my." Ingrid giggled and Ramon's heart skipped a beat.

"Unfortunately, the bedroom was on the second floor. The Mayor not only sprained his ankle, but he also broke his arm."

Ingrid laughed out loud, and then her face became serious. "It serves him right. He shouldn't have been taking advantage of the doctor's wife."

Ramon loved the way she thought.

"That's not the end," he continued. "When the Mayor was rushed to the hospital to be treated, guess who set his broken arm?"

Ingrid laughed again. "The doctor himself."

"Yes!" Ramon laughed with her. "The doctor himself. He was called from his home to attend the unfortunate man."

Ingrid wiped her eyes. "Oh, Ramon. Sometimes I think you make up these stories, just to please me."

"No," Ramon protested. "It's true. I swear it." He thought to himself, *but I would make up the stories if I thought it would make you happy.*

Every time she laughed, he felt joy in his own heart. When they fell silent, he looked at her across the table and could feel his love growing. Every thing she did, the way she cut her meat and raised it to her mouth, the way she tossed her head to remove her hair from her eyes, the way she lifted an eyebrow in doubt, every movement was perfection in his eyes.

By the end of the evening, Ramon could no longer hold back the tension that had been building in him all night. As they rose after coffee, instead of departing, he took Ingrid in his arms and kissed her long and hard on the mouth. His move was so unexpected that at first Ingrid did not resist. He could feel her legs tremble, and he pressed his chest harder against her, while burying his face in her blond hair.

"Don't Ramon. Please don't," she said, pushing him away.

Still clinging to her with his arms around her waist, he blurted out, "I love you, Ingrid. I can't help it, but I do."

"No. You shouldn't." She turned her face, denying him her lips.

"Why, Ingrid? Don't you have any feelings for me?" He tried to squeeze her close again, and felt his own hardness betraying him.

"It's not that, Ramon," she said, untangling herself from his arms. She was breathing heavily. "You're very handsome, and I am attracted to you. But you are Carlos' best friend."

Ramon gritted his teeth. "I am also a man. A man who loves you. I have never felt this way about anyone. I'm not lying, Ingrid. You're on my mind day and night. I can't control my feeling any longer." He raised his arms and shook his head in despair. "You don't belong to Carlos. You are not married." He regretted the words as soon as he spoke them.

"No," she replied, "but I live with him in his home. He is taking care of me and my child. No matter what they say, Ramon, I am not a whore. And I am not the doctor's wife. I have my pride." She looked down.

"I know that, Ingrid." He softened his tone. "It's just that I love you so much that I can't keep it inside me any longer." He took her hand in his. "It's stronger than anything I have ever felt before."

Ingrid withdrew her hand. "Are you sure it's love, Ramon? Or are you just taking advantage of Carlos' absence?" she asked with her face turned away from him.

"Don't insult yourself, Ingrid. I love you. More than anyone in this world."

She answered slowly, still not looking at him. "The timing is wrong. Perhaps if I had met you before Carlos, or if Carlos were dead. But not now, Ramon. I like you as a friend, but that's all it can be for now. Please try to understand."

"I respect your decision, Ingrid, but I can't stop loving you."

"Then please go now. Don't come again until Carlos has returned." She went to the door and opened it for him. Ramon hesitated, looking for the right words, but couldn't find them. He left in silence.

Chapter 9

Carlos recognized the jumble of modest, one story adobe houses which marked the outskirts of La Paz from his window seat on the train. They weren't much different from the crude, thatch-roofed hut where he had grown up in Ocampo. Half-clothed Indian children played in the unpaved streets, and a stooped Indian woman carried a bucket of water on her shoulder. As the train moved on, the adobe houses gave way to cylinder block, then brick and stone. The rutted dirt roadways became smoother, and were replaced by paved streets.

The journey from Washington had taken a long ten days, first by train to New York, then by steamship to Lima, on by train to Lake Titicaca, paddle wheeler across the lake, and then train once more. He wondered how much longer it might be before airplanes could be used to reach La Paz, but he knew it would be one of the last Latin American capitals to be serviced due to its location in the Andes. Maybe it's better, he thought, we're not ready for what I saw in the U.S. Isolation does have some advantages.

The ageing steam engine slowed as it approached the corrugated tin canopies of the La Paz terminal. Vendors ran alongside the slowing train, balancing trays of local cigarettes, painted clay pottery, steaming potatoes, and ribboned hats, and shouting their offers at the passengers. Carlos ignored them and searched for Ramon in the crowd without success.

When the train finally stopped, Carlos retrieved his suitcase from the overhead luggage rack, and made his way to the front of the wagon, pushing past noisy families still organizing their belongings.

Stepping down from the train, the first thing he saw was the outstretched, dirty hand of a nine-year old Indian girl.

"*Limosna?*" she begged.

Carlos searched in his pocket for a coin, and dropped it into her palm.

"Welcome home, *compadre*."

He looked up and saw Ramon standing in front of him. Carlos rested his suitcase on the paved platform and embraced his friend. For some reason Ramon seemed to draw back from his arms.

"Let me carry that," Ramon said, and picked up the suitcase. "You must be tired. The car is this way."

"I slept on the boat last night," Carlos said, and fell in alongside Ramon as he moved toward the exit. "How is Ingrid?"

Ramon seemed to stumble, then continued. "Fine, I guess. I haven't seen her for a while."

"Weren't you going to keep an eye on her for me?" Carlos asked.

Evidently Ramon did not hear his question, for he walked faster. "The car is over here."

When the suitcase had been stowed, and they were installed in the rear seat of the car, Carlos settled back to enjoy the ride. The city had not changed much during his four month absence, but the contrast between the dynamic U.S. capital, with its bustling traffic, well dressed pedestrians, fine hotels and restaurants, and the Bolivian capital left him pensive. Only when the military chauffeur swerved to avoid a pothole, did he remember that Ramon was at his side.

"How is the situation here?"

"Terrible." Ramon shifted to face him. "The Junta is more unpopular than ever before. Inflation has destroyed the economy and most people aren't earning enough to feed themselves. Every political party has called for Presidential elections. As you probably know, Colonel Busch dissolved Congress last month and assumed all governmental powers by Supreme Decree."

Carlos noticed that the number of Indian beggars at every street corner had increased. "I read about it in Washington."

"Well, it's probably worse than anything you read." Ramon glanced at the chauffeur and lowered his voice. "Colonel Busch is drinking heavily and is completely unpredictable. One day he is full of enthusiasm and plans for a new Bolivia. The next day he is despondent and complaining about his enemies. He's determined to stay in power at all costs, but I don't know if he can. Too many people want him out."

Carlos leaned forward and tapped the chauffeur on his shoulder. "Corporal, take me to my office, please."

The driver made a left turn and headed toward the center.

"Don't you want to go home and see Ingrid?" Ramon asked, perplexed.

"I can call her from headquarters. From what you've said, I want to learn more about what's going on. The sooner the better."

Ramon jerked his head sideways and stared sullenly out of the car window.

Five months later, on a sunny morning in May, 1939, Carlos was sitting in his office, reviewing intelligence reports, when Ramon burst into his office and laid a thick sheaf of papers on his desk.

"You'd better take a look at this," Ramon said.

Carlos glanced at the papers. "What is it?"

"Colonel Busch's new labor code. The one you told me about before you went to the U.S. This is evidently the finished document."

Carlos picked up the papers. "Where did you get it?"

"The Colonel had it delivered early this morning to the major newspapers. One of our men picked up this copy at *El Diario*. They plan to print a summary in a special edition today."

Carlos examined the front page, which listed the number and date of the new decree, titled "The Busch Code". He flipped to the back page and saw that the Colonel himself had signed it.

"Dammit!" Carlos exclaimed. "He issued this on his own, without consulting the Junta. The man is getting impossible to deal with."

"What do you think will happen?" Ramon asked. "Will the other members let him get away with it?"

"I don't know. But he's made a mistake. We knew he was working on a new labor law, but he swore we would discuss the draft in the Junta before taking any action. Better let me read it and then we'll talk."

Ramon left the room and Carlos opened the thick document. As he read, he shook his head in disbelief.

The new decree law was the most comprehensive piece of labor legislation he had ever seen. Its provisions regulated contracts of employment, apprenticeship, wages, hours of work and rest, paid vacations, labor of women and minors, promotion and retirement, safety, medical aid, workers' housing and food supply, workmen's compensation, organization of workers and employers, conciliation and arbitration, strikes and lockouts, everything a union leader could possibly desire. Carlos spent four hours just reading the document. The comprehensive law might have been appropriate for a modern, industrialized nation, such as the U.S., Germany, or France, but in Bolivia's undeveloped economy Busch's Code was a farce.

The following day, thousands of workers poured into the streets of La Paz in support of the new law. Spontaneous celebrations erupted among the union members in the mining camps. Juan Lechin called on Busch to congratulate him. The mine owners and industrialists fumed in their offices; with strikes legalized and everything else regulated, they had lost control over their own work force.

Bruce Berkman came to see Carlos that same afternoon. He didn't waste time with formalities.

"What the hell is that madman doing now?" Bruce asked before even shutting the door.

Carlos offered him a seat.

"Which madman, Mr. Berkman?"

"You know who I mean, Major. Colonel Busch. This new labor code is madness, complete madness."

Carlos smiled. "If I recall correctly, your own President Roosevelt is progressive in labor matters."

"That's different, Major. Franklin Roosevelt is no Socialist. This stuff comes directly from Europe. More specifically, from Italy and Germany. No other country in Latin America has a labor law so obviously pro-labor. Busch will ruin the mining industry this way. The U.S. needs tin, Major. War is getting closer each day now."

"I see your point," Carlos answered. He had heard the same thing in Washington six months earlier. "What would you propose I do?"

"Stop him. Reason with him and tell him what he is doing will cause a disaster. The owners will close the mines before accepting this new law." Bruce's impatience was obvious.

"Colonel Busch is very rigid. Once he makes up his mind, he won't listen to reason."

"Then get rid of him. Get him out of power."

Carlos shrugged and shook his head. "He is very popular now because of the new Labor Code, the most popular he has ever been. The unions wouldn't like to see him go."

"You could find a way, Major. You are smart, smart enough to find a solution. Eliminate him if necessary."

"Why would I want to do that?" Carlos asked.

"Because you could be the next President. You could have all the power and money that Busch has now. Think of it - President Carlos Obregon. Absolute power. Everybody in Bolivia would know you. You could run the country the way you want. You could do something for the farmers, and lay off the mining industry." Bruce paused to let his message sink in.

"The U.S. will take care of you, Major. Eliminate Busch, repeal this stupid decree, and name your price. The U.S. helps those who help the U.S. We can make it worth your while."

Carlos cocked his head at this suggestion.

"We don't want to control your country, Major," Bruce insisted. "We just want what is correct. We will help you in any way we can to get rid of Busch, and will give you our full support once you are in power. I can guarantee you immediate U.S. recognition of your government if you succeed."

"I see." Carlos turned his chair away from Bruce and gazed out the window. Could I do it, he wondered. Could an Aymara Indian ever be President of Bolivia? It is a long way from a mud brick hut in Ocampo to the Presidential Palace in La Paz. Yet each time I've taken a risk and broken the rules, fortune has smiled on me. Killing Lieutenant Kunnert. Escaping from Picuiba. Eliminating Don Simon. Lying to Ingrid about her husband. So far fate had been on my side, but how far can I go? How far can I go?

Carlos couldn't see the Presidential Palace from his window, but the distance between his headquarters and the President's residence was only seven blocks. *If I've come this far, what would keep me from going the rest of the way? To the top? The very top!*

He thought for a while longer, then turned back to face Bruce. "When I was in the U.S., I saw a new development there. A silencer, I think they call it. It fits over the barrel of a gun, and muffles the explosion so that no noise can be heard."

Bruce leaned forward with anticipation. "Yes, I know these silencers."

Carlos took his Luger pistol from its holster and passed the gun across the desk to Bruce. "Then get me a silencer for this weapon, the quietist ever built."

Bruce smiled, took the gun, and leaned back in his chair. "Consider it done, Major."

The next meeting of the Junta started badly. As usual, Colonel Busch arrived late and Carlos could smell stale alcohol on his breath. Busch ignored the cold reception of the remaining members and opened the meeting.

Colonel Melendez began the attack. "Since the publication of your so-called Busch Code, I have received protests from all three of the major mining companies, Colonel. They all oppose it. You might at least have had the courtesy to consult us before acting."

Busch grimaced and rubbed his forehead. "I had my reasons."

Colonel Garza spoke next. "Representatives of the same three companies have been to see me as well. They're incensed and threatening to retaliate."

"I know. I know," Colonel Busch said. "They've probably been to see every damn one of you. But the workers are happy."

"You have gone too far this time, Colonel Busch. I propose that the Busch Code be rescinded. Your new labor code will ruin our country. Before accepting it, the mines and factories will fire workers and stop production altogether if necessary," Colonel Melendez alleged.

"In the long run we will lose more than we gain. Foreign investment has already slowed to a trickle after the expropriation of

Standard Oil. The new labor code will kill it altogether," Major
Gutierrez added in support.

Busch raised his hand for silence and glared at them with
bloodshot eyes. "They're rapists! Rapists and Exploiters! Those
gringo bastards come here, take our natural resources, and leave us
nothing."

"It is their money that buys our ore and builds the factories.
Where would we get the means to develop the country if all the
foreigners quit investing?" Melendez asked.

Busch answered in a hoarse voice. "They need our tin. It's
vital for their own industries. Even more so now that Europe is
rearming."

"And how," Melendez asked, "will we sell them tin ore if the
mine owners shut down their mines? If the mines stop production, the
Treasury will be broke within two weeks. We're living from month
to month right now. We've already had to delay payments to the
military two times."

"The owners wouldn't dare shut down the mines," Busch
answered.

"And if they do?"

"Then, godamnit, we will nationalize the tin mines," Busch
shouted.

A hush fell over the room. The Colonel had suggested the
unthinkable. The largest tin mines in the world, expropriated by a
military government. Even Carlos recognized the enormity of
Busch's suggestion.

"I'm tired of the threats of those rich bastards, Patino,
Hoschild, and Aramayo, with their English estates and Swiss chalets.
They're parasites! Did they help us during the war? No! Yet their
riches come from the mountains of Bolivia. Not their mountains.
The Andes belong to the country."

Busch slammed his hand down on the table and stood up. "To
hell with their threats! Tomorrow I will issue a new decree which
will show them who runs this country for once and all."

There was complete silence in the room and all eyes were
riveted on Busch.

"Starting tomorrow the mining companies will have to deliver
all their foreign exchange earnings to the Central Bank, to be

exchanged into local currency at the rate of exchange I choose. Also, I am raising taxes on these companies, and will insist they bring back to Bolivia all the money they have deposited in foreign banks. If any company directors try to hinder the working of this new decree, there will be an automatic death penalty, and By God I intend to apply it."

Carlos shifted uneasily in his seat. The other members of the Junta stared at Busch.

Colonel Melendez spoke first, "This will kill the mining industry."

"No, Colonel. It won't kill it. From now on the profits will go to the country and not to three men," Busch responded, glaring at Melendez down the table.

The other officers remained silent. They knew not to tangle with Busch when he had a hangover.

"Any other comments?"

No one spoke.

"Very well. This meeting is adjourned."

Carlos waited until the others had left and then approached Busch. "Sir, I'm worried about Colonel Melendez and Major Gutierrez."

"Worried? About what?"

"I'm almost certain that they both receive money from the mining companies. Now I fear they are plotting against you, Sir. I don't trust them. I suggest you relieve them of their commands… immediately."

"That's asking for trouble, *Carlitos*. Both men are members of the Lodge and have troops at their disposal. Melendez is the Commander of the La Paz garrison, and Gutierrez is head of the military college here. They're dangerous adversaries."

"You could do it if it was handled swiftly, Sir."

"You and Major Gutierrez have never got along. How can I be sure that this isn't just a vendetta on your part? Do you have any proof of your allegations?"

"No, Sir."

"Then I don't think it's wise to act. A false move on my part could trigger the very action you are worried about."

"May I have your permission to investigate further, Sir?"

Busch buried his head in his hands and mumbled, "Yes, of course. No harm in that."

Carlos called Ramon into his office the following day, informing him about his suspicions of Colonel Melendez and Major Gutierrez, and gave instructions to put them under surveillance. For the next two months Secret Service men followed them everywhere, making notes on where they went and whom they met.

At the end of the period, there was still no clear evidence of a conspiracy. Carlos summoned Ramon to his office and closed the door.

"This is taking too long," Carlos said. "What have we found out so far?"

"Nothing concrete. We recorded one lunch with Don Alfonso Sotomayor, the lawyer who represents the mining consortium. Both Melendez and Gutierrez attended. Melendez had another lunch with a lawyer who works for Hochschild. Gutierrez wasn't there."

"Did we get any of their conversation?"

"Nothing. They ate at the Club Potosi. Our men couldn't even get in the front door, much less close to their table."

"They could have been plotting to overthrow Busch."

"Possibly, but we couldn't say. Maybe the mine owners are just complaining to them. They're members of the Junta. Nothing illegal in that."

Carlos frowned. "What else do we have on them?"

Ramon reviewed the paper in his hand. "Both Melendez and Gutierrez have met several times with other officers. Colonel Ochoa, who commands the garrison at Cochabamba, was in La Paz two weeks ago and met with Gutierrez three times. It's in the reports."

"That looks suspicious."

"Maybe. Or maybe Ochoa just wanted to talk about sending some of his men to the War College. Or maybe he and Gutierrez are old friends. Who knows?"

"They could be asking for help to overthrow Busch."

"Carlos, officers meet with each other all the time. It's part of their job. The meetings don't prove anything."

"Don't we have any informers who could provide some information?"

"Not at that level. These are high-ranking officers. "They have their own staffs, loyal to them."

Carlos closed his eyes and rested his right cheek on his clenched fist.

Ramon waited patiently. He knew Carlos was thinking. Sometimes the solution came quickly, sometimes not.

Carlos opened his eyes. "Pick up Gutierrez Friday night on his way home. Take him to the Secret Service prison for questioning. Post some men at his house and keep his family from contacting anyone. This has to be handled in secret."

"What's the charge?"

"Plotting to overthrow the government. I want a full confession signed by the Major. Use any methods you want, but I want a signed statement by Saturday afternoon."

Ramon arched his eyebrows. "Carlos, I don't like this. You're taking a big risk."

"I'll take the responsibility. You just follow orders."

"And what if Gutierrez doesn't cooperate?"

"Then I would be disappointed in our men. I will be at the prison at eight on Saturday. I want to take part in this one."

Chapter 10

Major Gutierrez was a mess. The right cheekbone of his once round face protruded upward and his nose sat at an awkward angle. A two-inch, jagged red cut split the eyebrow above his swollen right eye, now reduced to a narrow black slit. He slumped completely naked on a wooden chair with his arms strapped behind him, his legs tied at the ankles. Purple welts covered his flabby body, and his feet lay in a shallow pan of water.

The room in the basement of the Secret Service prison had no windows and only one solid metal door. No pictures, calendars, or mirrors decorated the bare white walls, and no rug covered the cold cement floor. It was a room without personality, devoid of any human warmth. The only other furniture in the room besides the chair was a wooden table, placed in one corner. Two short lengths of rubber hose rested on the table, and the Major's crumpled uniform and shoes had been thrown under it. A large automobile battery connected to an electric cattle prod lay at the Major's feet. Four men surrounded the slumped figure.

"How long has he been out this time?" Carlos asked.

Ramon looked at his watch. "About thirty minutes. He's getting weaker and can't take much before losing consciousness."

"He's tougher than I thought."

"He put up quite a fight when we arrested him, threatening that Colonel Melendez would have us shot."

Carlos looked at the Major's scorched genitals. "Let's try the pepper. That should keep him awake longer."

Ramon frowned, then gave the order and the other two men left the room. As soon as they had gone, Ramon closed the door and pulled Carlos to one corner.

"I don't like this," he said in a low voice, his eyes on the unconscious prisoner. "This is the farthest we've ever gone, Carlos. We've never worked over anybody like this before. Anymore could kill him."

Carlos looked at him impassively. "So?"

"So it's not right. I mean, what if Major Gutierrez doesn't know anything? Maybe he and Melendez are innocent."

"Maybe."

"Then why are we torturing this guy? He's an officer, you know. Like you and me. I sure as hell wouldn't want to be in his place right now."

"I want Melendez and Gutierrez in prison."

"I can understand that. You've never liked Gutierrez. But there must be another way."

Carlos moved closer and two deep creases formed between his eyebrows. "Why do you care about this son-of-a-bitch?"

"It's not him, Carlos. It's you. You're going too far. This is not human. Don't you have any pity for the poor bastard?"

Carlos considered this for a moment. "No more than he showed for me when he came to my village. He made me suffer. Now it's his turn."

"But goddamnit, that doesn't make it right, Carlos. You're playing God now."

Before Carlos could answer, the door opened and the other two men entered. One was shaking a liter bottle filled with clear liquid. Red particles whirled about, suspended in the water.

"Wake him up," Carlos ordered, and left Ramon in the corner.

The two men used a sponge, dipping it in the water pan at the prisoner's feet.

"Major, can you hear me?" asked Carlos.

The Major nodded his head, and then spoke, slurring his words, "I didn't do anything."

"Would you be willing to sign your name to a piece of paper I have, Major? Then all of this can stop and you can go home. I'm ready to forget our problems once you sign."

The prisoner seemed dazed; then he slowly shook his head.

"Too bad," sighed Carlos.

He motioned the two men forward. One pulled the Major's head back and braced it between his arms. The other poured the red pepper and water mixture down the Major's nostrils until he gagged violently. When they stopped, the prisoner coughed and choked at the same time. His face turned a deep red. The intense pain was reflected in his distorted features and involuntary twitching. This lasted for four minutes. Although the Major was visibly weaker, he didn't pass out. Carlos could see his will had collapsed.

"Are you ready to sign now?" Carlos repeated.

The nod was barely perceptible.

"Good. Bring up the table and untie his arms," Carlos ordered. When this was done, Carlos pulled a typed sheet from his jacket pocket.

Ramon looked questioningly at him. Obviously Carlos had prepared the statement in advance.

"This is too much, Carlos. I'm not having any more of it." Ramon walked to the door, yanked it open, and went out, slamming it behind him.

Carlos watched him go. He turned to the table and pulled out a pen.

"Sign here, Major."

After the officer signed, Carlos examined the signature carefully. "Let me have his military identification papers," he ordered. Carlos compared the two signatures, was satisfied, and put both the confession and the identification papers in his jacket pocket.

"What shall we do with him now?" asked one of the men.

"Kill him. Otherwise, someday he will kill us." Carlos left the room.

Carlos greeted the guards at the Palace gate and said hello to the military driver who was waiting for Colonel Busch in the courtyard. They knew him well as one of Colonel Busch's closest collaborators.

When Carlos entered the Colonel's office, he could see the President was in a bad mood. It was after ten on Saturday night and the Colonel enjoyed his weekends free of trouble. He had enough problems during the week; Saturday night was his night for women. Carlos had telephoned him, insisting that it was extremely urgent, and Colonel Busch has reluctantly agreed to meet him at his office in the Presidential Palace.

Carlos closed the door behind him and Busch spoke first.

"Well, *Carlitos*, this had better be good. I've had to delay a very important engagement."

"I'm sorry, Sir, but it is urgent. I've uncovered a plot to overthrow you. Colonel Melendez and Major Gutierrez are behind it."

"That's a serious accusation, Major." The Colonel became more formal. "Do you have proof?"

"Yes, Sir. Major Gutierrez has confessed. I have his full statement here. Dates, meetings, everything." Carlos opened his attaché case and handed over the signed confession and the identification papers.

Busch took the papers from Carlos as if he had been handed a snake. "How did you get this?"

"I had him followed for two months. Remember, you gave me permission to investigate. When I had enough evidence, I had him picked up. He confessed immediately when he saw what we had."

"You arrested him without my permission?"

"For your own good, Sir. Read what he says."

Colonel Busch sat down at his desk and spread the documents before him. He read the confession slowly and carefully, and then examined the identification papers.

"*Madre de Dios*, this says the coup is planned for this Monday." Busch looked shocked.

"Yes, Sir. That's why I came right away." Carlos had moved behind the Colonel, as though he were looking over his shoulder. He withdrew two more papers from his attaché case. "I have prepared formal arrest orders for Colonel Melendez and Major Gutierrez. In view of their rank, the orders need your signature, even though we already have Gutierrez."

Busch scanned the orders. "This is a hard thing for me to do. *Mierda*, these are two of the original members of the Lodge. We served in the Chaco together. Bastards!" He signed and handed the orders back to Carlos, who placed them in his briefcase.

"This is the final document, Sir," said Carlos, handing the Colonel another paper.

Busch began reading, frowned, and continued. His head bent closer to the paper. The letter read:

In view of the lack of confidence in my leadership, as evidenced by the plot of Colonel Melendez and Major Gutierrez to replace me, I feel it is my duty to resign as President of the Military Junta. The actions of these two officers have seriously demoralized me, and I can no longer continue in office.

"Is this a joke?"

Carlos pressed the six inch barrel of the silencer against Busch's head, over his right ear.

"This pistol is not a joke, Colonel. Please sign and you will not get hurt," Carlos clicked the safety on the Luger to make his point. "It is time for you to step aside, Colonel."

"But why you, Carlos? We were friends." The voice was almost plaintive. "I'm the one who made you an officer. I brought you to La Paz, and made you a member of the Junta. Doesn't that mean anything to you?"

"You were my teacher, Sir. Remember Colonel Toro. He was your friend."

"What makes you think you can depose me like this? What other officers are with you?"

"This gun is my support," Carlos answered.

Busch turned his head slightly. "I don't think you would kill me, Carlos."

"Don't tempt me. I am offering you exile."

The room was so silent that Carlos could hear the grandfather clock against the wall. His eyes turned cold, without feeling. He knew Busch was plotting his next move.

Busch took a deep breath and sighed. "I would like to go to Buenos Aires, Carlos. I've always enjoyed that city." He signed the paper and pushed it aside. "But I need some time to pack. Maybe you could leave me alone for a while?"

"Of course, Sir. Have a good trip," Carlos said, and pulled the trigger. There was almost no noise, but the Colonel's head jerked to the left and fell forward on the desk.

Carlos didn't touch the last paper Busch had signed. He unscrewed the silencer from the gun barrel, placing it in his attaché case. Carlos wiped the gun clean, then put it in the right hand of the Colonel, curling the dead man's still warm fingers around the weapon. He placed Busch's right arm on the desk where the pistol was clearly visible. Finally he inspected the room carefully, making sure that he had left nothing behind. Satisfied, he left the office, closing the door on his way out.

He stopped to speak with the Colonel's driver in the courtyard. "The Colonel said to go on home. He has a lot to do, and will be working late. Poor man, he has so many troubles recently."

The driver saluted and left. Carlos said good-bye to the guards at the gate and walked to his own car. He returned to the Secret Service offices where Ramon was waiting for him. Withdrawing the signed arrest orders from his briefcase, he said, "Here are the arrest orders. Take some men and pick up Colonel Melendez at his home. Make sure our men are armed. There may be some resistance. Also put two hundred of our best National Police troops on alert in case of trouble."

A guard found Colonel's Busch's body on Sunday morning. Carlos was the first member of the Junta to be notified, and he went immediately to the Palace, placing the guards there under his command. He reinforced the Palace with two hundred troops from the National Police. Then he called the other two members of the Junta to enlist their support. Busch was dead, he told them, an apparent suicide. Melendez and Gutierrez were in prison on orders of Busch himself. They had betrayed him. Carlos said he was taking over the Presidency. To smooth the way, he offered the previous commands of Melendez and Gutierrez to the officers. Duty at La Paz was the dream of most career officers; it was the only true city in Bolivia. After they agreed, Carlos issued a communiqué announcing Busch's death and his own assumption of the Presidency, sending it to the two La Paz newspapers along with some Secret Service men to ensure that it would be published in the Monday morning editions.

He instructed the Secret Service men to review the entire newspapers, front to back, and censor any possible criticism.

By late Sunday evening Carlos was exhausted. He had been up all Saturday night, and had worked all Sunday. He made one last call, to Ingrid. "Prepare your things. We're moving into the Presidential Palace."

BOOK III

EL PRESIDENTE

1939—1942

Chapter 1

The Presidential Palace, a brown, U-shaped, three story, stone building constructed in the 1800's, occupied one full side of the Plaza Murillo. An ornate, black metal fence, over ten feet tall and crowned with gilded spikes, enclosed the open side of the U, which faced the large square in the city center. An iron grill gate, wide enough for two cars side by side, provided access into the paved courtyard. Metal letters formed the words *Libertad y Patria* at the apex of the gate, a reminder that Bolivia was once a Spanish colony.

From the spacious, bricked courtyard, three curved marble steps led up to a massive wooden door that remained open during the day. Ceremonial Guards, dressed in red tunics, white pants with red stripes, high black leather boots, and white gloves, kept watch at the gate and at the door. They wore embossed metal helmets of colonial design painted in gold, with black plumes gracing the crowns, and carried long swords in glistening silver sheaths.

Their attire, like the building, was designed to impress and inspire. In some ways the Palace was beautiful, particularly the ornate metal gate and the carved wood main door. But the somber, brown mass of stone overwhelmed the touches of gold and the red tunics of the guards, leaving one with the impression of a fortress rather than a palace. Gold paint could not disguise the sharpness of the metal spikes which topped the fence, a fence designed to discourage unwanted intruders. Although the main door remained open during the day, only well dressed lawyers, dignitaries, and uniformed officers were seen passing between the armed guards.

The left wing of the Palace served as offices and living quarters for the President, his family, and servants. There were over twenty rooms in this area, all with high ceilings, which invoked grandeur but contributed to a permanent chill inside. Wooden beams on the ceilings added a sense of solidity and timelessness. Priceless oil paintings from Colonial days, in ornate gilt frames, decorated the interior walls. Mounted conquistadors and martyred saints, assured of their places in history and impervious to the cold, looked down smugly on the current residents. Heavy wooden furniture covered in rich velvet upholstery filled the main rooms. Solid oak doors, which remained closed, led both to the courtyard and directly to the street on the wing's opposite side.

The center of the building was used for receiving dignitaries, for state diners, and meeting rooms. The reception rooms were draped in royal blue and purple velvet, and contained high-backed, wooden chairs bearing the carved seal of Bolivia. The kitchen occupied the back of the first floor. An enormous ballroom with a high, painted ceiling and a decorative parquet floor filled the second and third floors.

The right wing of the building served as offices for the Presidential staff and barracks for the Presidential Guard. After Carlos assumed power, he increased the number of Guards and strengthened their training. He appointed Captain of the Guard a soldier of unquestionable loyalty who had served with him in the Chaco. The fifty new Guards were given the latest automatic weapons and brown combat uniforms. Somber, threatening presences, they maintained positions behind the Ceremonial Guards at the main gate and at the two side entrances to the Palace, where pedestrians crossed the street to avoid passing in front of their loaded guns.

Carlos sat behind a massive, dark oak desk in the President's Office in the left wing. Ten days had passed since he assumed power. The blood stains had been cleaned from the desk and carpet, and a new green sheet of blotter paper had been inserted in the leather holder on top of the desk.

Despite his tight censorship over the newspapers, Carlos knew rumors were circulating by word of mouth in La Paz regarding the suspicious circumstances of Colonel Busch's death. Also, there were many people in the capital who considered it demeaning to the country to have a full-blooded Indian as their new President, an insult to Bolivia's educated Spaniards and mestizos. Carlos was certain this group included the gray-haired man in the dark wool suit now sitting in his office.

Don Alfonso Sotomayor was the best, or at least the most highly paid, lawyer in Bolivia, and represented the three big tin mining companies.

"Thank you for the coffee, Major," said Don Alfonso, delicately resting his empty cup on the credenza next to his chair.

"My pleasure, Don Alfonso," replied Carlos, pushing his own cup away from him on the desk. "You are probably wondering why I asked for this meeting?"

"Not at all, Major. I had expected that we would need to meet." Don Alfonso's tone had the air of a Spanish hidalgo addressing a peasant, and he kept emphasizing Carlos' rank rather than his new position as head of the country.

"I want the support of the mining companies for my Presidency," stated Carlos.

Don Alfonso smiled a thin, closed-lipped smile. "You are smart to seek an accommodation, Major. My clients have not been happy with our former President. Bolivia's economy depends on the mining companies, and so does her government."

"What do I need to do to get their backing?"

"For a start, repeal the Busch Code. The mining companies will never accept all those restrictions."

"I can't repeal the Code publicly," replied Carlos, shifting in his high-backed chair. "It is too popular. But I could stop it from being implemented. I can let it die a slow death in the government administrative offices. Would that be satisfactory?"

Don Alfonso pushed up his steel rimmed glasses with his index finger. "That would be acceptable, provided that the right to strike was annulled outright."

"I could declare strikes to be illegal unless they have prior approval of the government."

"In that case, it would be necessary for the mining companies to have one of their men in the government, to protect their interests."

"In what position, Don Alfonso?"

215

"Minister of Finance."

Carlos nodded.

"My clients would insist that government control over foreign exchange be loosened. They need the flexibility to keep some money abroad to pay their foreign obligations. The exchange rate would have to reflect our currency's true value."

"What would they give in return?" asked Carlos, shifting his weight to the other side of the chair.

"Payment of all taxes and export duties in full and on time, so the government can meet its obligations. Withdrawal of financing from political parties." Don Alfonso smiled his thin smile again. "And no encouragement to those officers who think they are more qualified than you to be occupying the President's seat."

"I would like something more," said Carlos.

Don Alfonso had expected this. He knew they were all alike once in power. He waited for Carlos to state his price.

"One percent of the value of all tin ore exported."

Don Alfonso betrayed no emotion. "That is too much, Major. Perhaps at the maximum a quarter of one percent. That would make you a wealthy man within a year."

"Three-quarters of one percent would be more reasonable, Don Alfonso. I am offering the companies an opportunity to operate without restrictions. I merely ask that they share a small part, a very small part, of their profits."

"Why should they share anything?" Don Alfonso countered.

"Because I could ruin them if I wanted. I could apply the Busch Code. I could freeze their foreign exchange."

"You would hurt your own government. The economy would collapse. I doubt if you would remain in power very long."

"I am willing to take that risk," Carlos answered.

The two men looked at each other across the desk, their faces blank.

Finally, Don Alfonso spoke. "One-half of one percent is acceptable. Our final offer. Where would you like it deposited?"

"The money will go to the new Agrarian Bank I am establishing by Presidential decree."

For the first time in the meeting Don Alfonso's eyes widened and a tiny crease appeared on his forehead, lifting his spectacles ever so slightly.

"The bank will loan money to the Indian farmers, so that they can buy seed, farm tools, and machinery, and purchase their own land." Carlos leaned back in his chair. "The Indians who fought in the Chaco will be given preference, to replay them for their sacrifice. I will give you the details before the end of the week."

Carlos stood and extended his hand. "Are we in agreement?"

Don Alfonso rose and took the extended hand. "We are in agreement, Mr. President."

After his meeting with Don Alfonso, Carlos moved quickly to consolidate his power. To prevent another military coup, he retained the title of Minister of Defense, as well as President. In this way he could transfer unfriendly officers out of command responsibilities and keep them away from La Paz. Within the first two months, he appointed the two remaining members of the Junta as ambassadors to Spain and to Argentina, effectively abolishing the group.

Carlos assumed all the dictatorial powers Busch had established for himself. He promoted Ramon to Head of Internal Security and instructed him to crack down hard on dissidents. Ramon increased the number of paid informers and the size of the Secret Service. There were no unauthorized gatherings, no political rallies, and no criticism in the newspapers. Any newspaper that did not support the government found itself unable to buy newsprint from the government import monopoly. If the editors were too critical or inflexible, they ended up in the Secret Service prison.

In September, 1939, only one month after Carlos assumed power, German troops overran Poland and set off World War II. The demand for tin ore boomed and prices doubled overnight. Bolivian tin was mixed with copper to form bronze and other alloys that went into tanks, airplanes, trucks, and cannons. Tin was needed for shells, tin cans, tinfoil, and soft solders, and there was never enough. True to his word, Carlos forbade strikes unless authorized by the government, saying it was necessary to prevent any fall in production. Authorization never came. Labor agitators were closely watched and thrown in jail when necessary. Carlos' government was not popular, but the mines worked at full output, factories operated normally, and the U.S. got the tin ore it badly needed.

Bruce Berkman waited patiently in the reception room outside the President's office. He ignored the other supplicants who had arrived before him, aware that Carlos would not keep him waiting long. He glanced through the folder in his lap, organizing the papers in order of importance. When the adjutant nodded in his direction, Bruce stood and walked through the office door as if he were in his own home.

Carlos rose from behind his desk and extended his hand.

"Good morning, Bruce."

Bruce shook Carlos' hand firmly.

"Good morning, Major." He took a seat in front of the desk before being asked.

"Isn't it time you promoted yourself to a higher rank. As President of Bolivia, you should be at least a Colonel. General would be better."

Carlos showed no emotion and sat down. His lack of expression, of feeling, always annoyed Bruce. It was so hard for Bruce to tell what Carlos was thinking.

"Every thing in its own time. The difference in military pay isn't all that big."

"It would give you more status, and make for a bigger pension."

Again Carlos registered no emotion. Bruce had never seen the man laugh.

"I doubt that I will ever reach retirement. The position of President of Bolivia is not very stable. How is the Ambassador?"

Bruce frowned. Since Carlos had taken power, Bruce himself had conducted all U.S. business with the President. He loved the role and didn't want to share it with anybody.

"He's fine, Carlos. Working on his memoirs and busy entertaining U.S. visitors."

Bruce sat up higher in his chair. It won't be long, he thought, if relations with Bolivia continue this well, before I will be an ambassador.

Carlos picked up a pen from his desk. "What do you have for me today?"

Bruce opened the folder and took out the first paper. "W.R. Grace & Co. would like to expand their cement plant in La Paz with a new kiln, which will double their capacity. Since it's a foreign investment, it needs your authorization."

He handed the paper to Carlos, who glanced at it briefly. "Grace has a monopoly on cement in Bolivia."

Bruce leaned forward. "Yes, but they're a good company. They treat their workers fairly and keep reinvesting in Bolivia. This is good for everyone."

Carlos shrugged, signed the paper, and handed it back to Bruce.

Bruce removed another paper from the folder and passed it to Carlos.

"General Electric Co. wants to name a new managing director for Bolivia, to replace their man who is leaving. Since the new executive is a U.S. citizen, he needs your approval for his working papers."

Carlos laid the sheet on his desk. "Why can't General Electric appoint a Bolivian national to this position? Someone who already knows the country."

Bruce raised his hands. "It's the way U.S. companies operate, Carlos. They want to have one of their own men as head of their operations in every foreign country. It's a question of trust."

Carlos signed the paper and returned it to Bruce.

"It's dumb. What's next?"

Bruce handed the third paper to Carlos, this time more hesitantly.

"Standard Oil needs your permission to export capital from the country."

"How much?"

Bruce tried to sound casual. "Half a million dollars. It's the down payment and the first royalties for technical assistance to the national petroleum company. Remember? You signed the agreement six months ago."

Carlos lay down his pen. "I don't remember it being this much, this quick."

"It's strictly according to the terms of the agreement, Carlos. The agreement you signed. It's the only way Bolivia will ever get its oil production to rise again. The national company definitely needs assistance from abroad. Production at existing wells has fallen, and no new wells have been discovered for four years. No other international oil company will touch Bolivia until Standard Oil recoups some of the money it lost from the expropriation."

Carlos hesitated for a moment, then signed the document and passed it back to Bruce.

"Is that all?"

"Yes." Bruce sighed with relief.

"When will the U.S. agricultural team arrive?" Carlos asked.

"Within two months," Bruce replied, now on safe ground. "The Ambassador passed on your request, and the State Department said it was delighted to assist. They're assembling a team of our best farm experts. They can stay in Bolivia on a rotating basis for as long as you wish, at no charge to your government."

"Good. We've already set up two farmers' cooperatives at Milpu and Oyate, on land bought from big landowners by the government. I want these cooperatives to succeed. We have plenty of money in the Agrarian Bank, but we need modern farming methods."

"Don't worry," Bruce assured him. "The U.S. has the most productive farmers in the world. We'll be able to help."

Bruce relaxed in his chair. This was the part of the meetings with Carlos he liked best, a time to review how things were overall. *Here I am, a small town Texas boy, giving advice to the President of a foreign country.*

"How were tin ore shipments last month?" Bruce asked.

"Up five percent over June. The best month ever, and production continues to rise."

"Wonderful!" Bruce clapped his hands.

"Not as good as it could be," Carlos said. "Still no progress in negotiating a new treaty with Chile regarding port taxes and loading fees at Antofagasta. The current treaty expires in 1941. Without the Chilean port, we have no way to ship our tin ore anywhere."

Bruce leaned forward again.

"What does General Bustamante want?"

"I'm not sure. He's been in power for twelve years now and rules his country with an iron hand. Why doesn't your government put some pressure on him to reach a reasonable settlement? You need the ore."

Bruce rubbed his forehead. "I've spoken to the Ambassador about it, but we have to tread lightly. Chile supplies most of the copper ore used by our industry. It's vital for our military buildup. We don't want to jeopardize that."

"Well, without a treaty, tin ore shipments will stop in 1941."

"Why don't you invite the General to La Paz for one-on-one discussions? This would be much more effective than negotiating through your representatives. You're both army officers. You should be able to reach an agreement."

Carlos rested his chin on his fist and closed his eyes. After a minute, he spoke.

"Maybe you're right. I will invite him. What harm could come of it?"

Chapter 2

Ingrid sat at her dressing table in her slip and applied a touch of flesh colored face powder to her cheeks, then dusted most of it off. She applied a soft pink lipstick to her full lips. At thirty-two, she used very little make-up, preferring the freshness of her own natural beauty.

"I like your hair that way, Mama."

Ingrid turned to Wilhelm, who sat cross-legged on the floor watching her preparations. He was eleven now, a thin gangling boy who attended school all day during the week, and half a day on Saturdays.

"The hairdresser came today. He thought it would look good in an upward sweep, exposing the neck. What do you think?"

"I think it looks great. You look like a queen. What's the occasion?"

Ingrid rose and walked to the bed, where the maid had laid out her dress. "Carlos has invited the President of Chile to dinner at the Palace." She slipped on a dark green velvet evening dress, low cut with bare shoulders. "Give me a hand and zip me up."

Wilhelm got up from the floor. "Sure." He closed the zipper at the back of Ingrid's dress.

"Thanks," she said, and returned to the dressing table.

Wilhelm flopped on the bed. "This is the life."

Ingrid picked up an emerald pendant from Colombia, a gift from Carlos, and suspended it from her neck with a fine gold chain.

She adjusted the pendant so that it would draw attention to the cleavage between her breasts.

"Do you like living here at the Palace?"

"Sure. It's great. Don't you?"

She fastened two emerald earrings, perfectly coordinated with the pendant, to her earlobes. The sparkling green of the emeralds highlighted the deep green of her eyes.

"I don't know. The old house was more of a home." She turned to face him. "It was certainly more pleasant to look out on the fountain in the patio instead of beggars and vendors in the street."

Wilhelm sat up on the bed. "Yeah, but here we all have our own rooms. And look at all the servants."

Ingrid sighed. "I preferred it the old way. I don't know half of the staff here. And those armed guards make me nervous. It's too big."

Dimples formed on Wilhelm's cheeks, a sure sign that he was going to tease her. "We could always go back to Germany," he said.

"Some days I wish we could." Ingrid turned again to the dressing table and picked up a perfume bottle. "With the war on, it's too dangerous to cross the Atlantic. They say there are submarines everywhere. And the North Sea is heavily mined. I haven't even received any letters from your grandparents recently." She dabbed perfume behind each ear and between her breasts. "Would you like to go back?"

Wilhelm hopped off the bed and came closer to admire his mother. "No. I'm happy here. All my friends think it's great that I live in the Presidential Palace. And Carlos told me I can go to the Military College when I'm old enough."

Ingrid winced when she heard his words. He was becoming more independent, and as a good mother, she knew that she must let him go, but it hurt her to see him growing. One day he would be gone forever.

"I'm not sure I'd like another officer in the family."

"Why not? Carlos is an officer."

Ingrid turned and took his hands in hers. "You really like Carlos, don't you?"

Wilhelm grinned from ear to ear. "Sure. Don't you?"

Ingrid smiled and stood up. "Get out of here before I spank you, young man. You're getting too fresh for your own good."

Wilhelm raised his hands in mock fear. "Okay. Okay. I'm going." He backed out of the room, laughing.

Ingrid sat down again and studied herself in the mirror. Her smile faded, replaced by a wistful sadness. Her relationship with Carlos was nothing to joke about. She wondered whether or not he loved her. He was a quiet man and never disclosed his emotions. Now that he was President, she saw less of him than before. But even though his visits to her bedroom were not as frequent, his sexual appetite was as strong as ever once there.

She thought she loved him. It had been so long now - over three years since she came to Bolivia, three years of searching futilely for Manfred, three years of living with Carlos. Yet Carlos had never spoken to her of love…nor of marriage.

By installing her in the Palace, he had acknowledged their relationship to all the world, but the so-called society of La Paz had no interest in either Carlos or her; Carlos, because he was an Indian, uneducated, rough, a soldier who had risen through the ranks; she, because she was his mistress - not his wife. A foreigner living in open sin with the President, installed in the Presidential Palace, a blatant defiance of their mores. She couldn't blame them. In Bavaria, she and her family would have acted the same way confronted with a similar situation. She and Carlos were socially unacceptable, and it hurt her.

She decided the dress was a little too daring. To add a touch of modesty, she went to her armoire and retrieved a black lace Spanish shawl, which she draped over her pearl white shoulders. The effect was simple, but stunning. Satisfied, she left the room, holding her head high, like a queen.

Much to Ingrid's surprise, only Carlos and the Chilean President were waiting for her in the reception room. She had assumed there would be more guests, perhaps the Ambassador of Chile and his wife, or the Bolivian Minister of Foreign Affairs and his wife. But after the introductions were made, and time passed over cocktails, she realized it was to be only the three of them.

Her disappointment disappeared as the evening progressed. General Bustamante was a charming man. At fifty-nine his hair was almost entirely gray, but he had a lean body on a tall frame and distinct European features.

"I understand you are from Bavaria, Baroness."

"Yes, General. I was born and grew up in a town on the Bodensee."

"I have been there and found it very lovely. But I am more fond of Munich. The opera season there is magnificent. And the women are both beautiful and fashionable. Their clothes are among the most attractive in the world."

"You flatter us, General. When most visitors think of Munich, they think only of the beer halls. It seems that you know Germany well."

"Very well, Baroness. My mother was from Northern Italy, and my parents sent me to a preparatory school in Switzerland when I was sixteen. Since then I have returned to Europe on every occasion I could find. I spent three years in Berlin as Military Attaché at the Chilean Embassy. What an exciting experience! I traveled to England and attended Ascot and the Henley races. I visited Paris, dined at Fouchet's, and saw the cabaret shows. But Germany was my favorite country. Don't you miss it?"

Ingrid glanced at Carlos before replying. "Of course I do, General. But Bolivia also has its attractions."

They spent the rest of the evening discussing Germany. They talked about the opera, the best symphony orchestras, the latest fashions, the newest plays. The General had returned to Berlin on an official visit only two years before and, because the economy was going well, had found the people in high spirits. He brought Ingrid up-to-date on all the things she had missed.

The General was also an equestrian. He had participated in many of the same horse shows that Ingrid had, although at an earlier time. Carlos listened but said nothing. The conversation was between two people charmed to have found so much in common, with many similar likes and dislikes, and Carlos had nothing to contribute. The General was at times serious, at times gay, always alert to catch her replies. Ingrid was radiant. She hadn't enjoyed this type of repartee for three years. The dinner passed in a flash.

225

When they returned to the drawing room for brandy and cigars, Ingrid knew the protocol. Carlos would want to be alone with the General to discuss the treaty. She excused herself with regret. The General kissed her hand as she left. She returned to her room humming to herself and thinking of the wonderful evening.

After Ingrid left, a butler offered cigars and brandy to Carlos and the General. The General accepted but Carlos declined. Both men settled into deep leather armchairs.

"So, General, have you thought about my proposals for the new treaty?" Carlos began.

Before replying, the General rolled the Havana under his nose, savoring the aroma. "Yes, Major, I have. It appears to me that you are only offering a renewal on the same conditions as before."

"Not so, General. As you know, I am offering increased fees for loading the ore. More than what the current treaty allows."

The General snipped one end of his cigar with a cigar cutter, then lit a match and held it to the other end, slowly rotating the cigar. "That is very little, Major."

"That is only the official part. You know my other offer. A percentage for you, General, of all the receipts for ore exported through Antofagasta. I know now that you love Europe, and have lived in Switzerland. I could arrange to have the money deposited there."

"That is more tempting," replied the General, raising the lit tobacco to his lips. He inhaled deeply.

"We are both military men, General, and realists. Our time as heads of our countries is limited. There is always an ambitious politician or another officer who wants our place. You have done well - twelve years as President of Chile is remarkable. But it can't last forever. You need to take care of yourself now for an uncertain future."

"True, Major. Very true. But I am not without my own personal savings." The General relaxed comfortably in his armchair and slowly exhaled the cigar smoke, closing his eyes to enjoy the aroma.

Carlos eyed him questioningly. His offer could add a half-million dollars a year to the General's savings. "We seem to understand each other well, General. What else can I offer that will persuade you to sign the treaty?" Carlos sat back himself and waited.

The General's eyes were still closed. He raised the brandy glass under his nose, inhaled the bouquet, then took a sip. A faint smile appeared at the corners of his mouth. Carlos wasn't sure that the General had heard him, because he waited a long time before replying. When he spoke, it was as if he were talking about another subject, "Baroness Kunnert is a strikingly attractive woman, Major. I congratulate you on your good taste."

Carlos studied him carefully as he sat almost dreaming, sipping his brandy and enjoying his cigar. The man was a sensualist, without a doubt. The smile on his lips took on a double meaning.

"It seems that the Baroness was impressed by you also, General. I suggest that we retire now. Perhaps something can be arranged." Carlos stood up, extended his hand, and accompanied the General to the guest quarters.

When Carlos entered her bedroom, Ingrid was sitting in front of a mirror brushing her hair. The long golden strands fell below her shoulders in soft waves. She had removed her make-up and her skin looked as fresh and soft as a baby's. She was wearing a white silk nightgown tied at the waist.

Carlos put his hands on her shoulders and massaged them gently. She leaned her head against his arm and closed her eyes, wishing this to go on forever.

"Did you enjoy the evening?" Carlos asked.

"It was wonderful," she replied, rubbing her cheek on his arm. "The General is a charming man."

"It appears that he likes you as well." Carlos continued massaging her shoulders. "He wants you to spend the night with him." He said it casually, without changing the tone of his voice.

"What?" Ingrid jerked free and spun in her chair. "What did you say?" Her eyes were furious.

"I said he wants you to spend the night with him. And I want you to do it." His tone was firm now.

"This is crazy. I just met that man. I have no interest in him sexually. Besides, I am your —," she groped for the right word. Mistress? Whore? Lover? "woman," she finally said.

"Yes, you are my woman," he replied, "and I want you to do this for me. The new treaty between Bolivia and Chile is vital for my presidency. If we get it on our conditions, Bolivia will be rich. The world is desperate for our tin ore. There will be money for everybody and everything - new roads, new schools, new factories, and enough to fund the Agrarian Bank for years. I can create a new Bolivia. If Chile gets tough, then all that money will go for railroad freight, for loading charges, and for export fees. Chile will be rich and Bolivia will remain poor. And my presidency will be gone and forgotten. I want you to do it for me and for my country."

Ingrid stared at him as if seeing him for the first time, thinking this can't be true. He can't be asking me to do this. She began to cry. "I am not a whore," she sobbed. "I am not a whore."

"Of course you are not," he spoke gently, placing his hand on her shoulder. "You are a good person. But I need your help. It is important that you help me now."

Ingrid continued to cry. She buried her face in her hands and the tears ran through her fingers. When she spoke, her voice was scarcely audible, muffled by her hands and her emotions. "Do you love me?"

Carlos replied without hesitating, "Yes, I do."

She heard it clearly. The unbroachable subject had been broached. The unsayable word had been said. He loved her. "Then how can you ask me to do this?"

"Because my love is strong enough to accept this situation. And yours must be too. You are my woman and you must do this for me."

She looked up at him. Her eyes were full of sadness and love. "I don't want to do it," she whispered.

"I know you don't. But you will do it for me." He reached into his jacket and withdrew a small metal case. Opening it, he grasped a small amount of white powder between his thumb and index finger, and placed it on the open palm of his left hand, offering it to Ingrid. "Here, inhale this. You'll feel better."

Ingrid looked at the unfamiliar substance. "What is it?"

"Something to pick you up. Here, sniff deeply," he said, extending his hand below her nostrils.

She inhaled cautiously.

"Harder," he said, "Sniff harder."

She closed her eyes and inhaled deeply. Within seconds she saw vivid yellows, oranges, blues, and greens flash behind her closed eyes. They spun and melted into one glorious revolving rainbow. She opened her eyes after a minute and the colors disappeared but her mind felt as clear and alert as she had ever experienced. Her brain raced with the wonderful confidence that it could solve all problems. None were too big to be overcome. She was strong and intelligent and clear-minded.

Carlos removed his handkerchief to dry her eyes, and it appeared before her like a sheet, enormous and white - such a brilliant white. He wiped her eyes and lifted her by her right arm. When he touched her she could feel his strength flowing into her body. The spot where he held her was warm and flushed, while the rest of her body was cool. He smiled and a tingling began in the calves of her legs and worked its way up to her neck. Even the ends of her hair were full of some electric power.

As Carlos led her down the hall she saw everything in a new light. The patterns on the carpets stood out for the first time, and she understood the message the weaver had intended. Each painting took on new and significant meaning, even though she glanced at them only briefly. She could not feel her feet moving. She was floating - floating alongside Carlos, with his warm, dominant touch.

When they arrived at the guest quarters, Carlos knocked softly and stepped away from the door. The General opened in his pajamas, and saw Ingrid standing in front of him in her nightgown. Her eyes were big, bigger than he had remembered, and she was smiling a faint smile.

He took her arm and led her through the door. "Thank you for coming, my dear." He closed and locked the door behind them.

He placed both his hands on her upper arms and drew her to him. He kissed her on the mouth, forcing his tongue between her lips. She tasted the brandy and the cigar as though she herself had just finished them. He stepped back without releasing her, and examined her approvingly, starting with her blond hair and continuing to her bare feet. She could see the desire in his eyes. Bursting through every vein. She felt her body tremble. Her breasts seemed to expand and her nipples became rigid. The tingling in her body increased.

His hands dropped from her shoulders to her waist, and his fingers deftly undid the bow of her nightgown. His hands slipped under the folds of her gown and moved up to her neck, igniting her as they went. Gently, he pushed the folds of the gown from her shoulders, and it floated to the ground around her feet. She was naked before him.

He kissed her right nipple with his tongue, and it jutted out tense and trembling. He repeated this on her other nipple, and an electric shock coursed from the nipple down her smooth flat stomach to between her long legs. He hastily removed his pajamas while she watched in a trance. Then he led her to the bed, and laid her across it, with her legs dangling over the side.

He bent over her and kissed her breasts, fondling them with his hands at the same time. He sucked each nipple like a baby, and Ingrid imagined milk flowing forth. Then he moved down her body, kissing her as he went. He stuck his tongue in her navel, and it felt strangely sensitive. When he reached her abdomen, he parted her legs, putting one over each of his shoulders. And then he kissed her there.

Ingrid could no longer contain herself. She arched her back, shoving herself into his face, and moaned with pleasure. This excited him and he moved his tongue faster, exploring more deeply. She began to buck under his attack, gyrating from one side to the other, always thrusting herself forward, while he went deeper and faster. She exploded with her first orgasm and shook violently. He laughed and continued. Now the pleasure was unbearable and she came again and again, with his laughter taunting her.

Then he stopped and stood up. Her legs were weak from exhaustion, but he held them in his arms, riding on his hips. She felt her flesh parting, opening, and he was inside her. He was enormous, and his penis grew within her, taking on a life of its own, expanding to fill every part of her, like a balloon inside a jar. And yet it began moving, and she couldn't understand how anything that big could move inside of her. She gasped as it moved back and forth, like a battering ram trying to break down a gate. But the gate was already down. She was open completely to it. Yet it kept thrusting and growing and expanding, until finally she felt a great gush of liquid burst inside her like a waterfall, and heard him cry out with pleasure.

At the same moment, her own cascade opened to meet his, her body jerked with ecstasy, and she moaned with joy. She felt his body collapse on her, and exhaustion overcame her.

When she awoke, it was four in the morning. A noise had awakened her - an unfamiliar noise. She was lying on her side in a strange bed, facing the wall. The noise came from behind her. She turned slowly and saw the General lying on his back, snoring loudly. His gray hair, which had made him so distinguished the night before, was uncombed and matted. His face in repose was flaccid and wrinkled. He looked old, old and corrupt and repulsive.

Ingrid felt the stickiness between her legs and nearly vomited. She was ashamed and disgusted with herself. Making as little noise as possible, she crept from the bed and retrieved her nightgown from the floor. She slipped out the door and rushed to her room, where she threw up in the toilet, then ran a hot bath. She washed herself from head to toe, let out the water, refilled the tub, and lay soaking and crying in the warm water. When the water turned cold, she got out, dried herself, and crawled into her own bed. She had never felt more depressed in her life.

The General rose late and came down to breakfast at ten. Carlos was waiting for him.

"An extraordinary woman, Major. My compliments again."

"Do we have a treaty, General?"

"Of course we do. Your terms were acceptable from the start" He smirked just enough to be noticeable. "We can sign the treaty today if you like. One of my men will contact you regarding a numbered account in Switzerland. That arrangement between you and me should begin the same day as the treaty, don't you think?"

"I perfectly agree, General," Carlos answered with a slight smile.

"Another thing, Major."

"Yes."

"I would have signed without the extra incentive of last night, but it was a nice gesture on your part. Please say good-bye to the Baroness for me," he hesitated, "and please visit me in Chile sometime. Perhaps I can return the favor there. We have some beautiful women in our country."

231

At mid-afternoon Ingrid had not left her bedroom, so Carlos went up to see her. He found her still in bed, her eyes red from crying.

"Has he gone?" she asked.

"Yes," Carlos answered, "he left at one o'clock, after signing the new treaty."

"I hate him," she said, turning her face away from him in the in bed. "And I hate you for doing this to me." Fresh tears appeared on her cheeks. "I feel cheap."

He sat down on the bed next to her. "It was necessary, Ingrid. You have helped me greatly. You can't imagine how much." He tried to take her in his arms, but she recoiled from his touch. He sighed and removed the metal case from his jacket.

"Here, take this. You will feel better."

She turned and looked at the white powder before her. After a moment of hesitation, she grabbed his hand. This time she sniffed deeply. A feeling of well-being engulfed her instantaneously. Her pupils dilated. The bed became softer and more inviting. She lay back and stared at the ceiling. A pleasant euphoria settled over her.

Carlos stood up and looked down on her, knowing she was far away, on some other planet. "If you want more, let me know. We have plenty of cocaine here in Bolivia." He left the room, closing the door behind him.

Chapter 3

By September, 1942, President Carlos Obregon had been in power for three years. When the U.S. entered World War II in December, 1941, following the Japanese attack on Pearl Harbor, Bolivian tin ore exports exploded; the U.S. took everything the Andean country could produce. The shortage was such that children in the U.S. saved tinfoil from their chewing gum wrappers, rolled them into tight tennis-sized balls, and proudly brought them to designated pick-up points as part of the war effort. The price for tin ore skyrocketed and the Bolivian economy was awash with dollars. Money flowed into the new Agrarian Bank and out again to the poor farmers. Things should have been perfect, but they weren't.

Despite the booming economy and land reform, agitators still demanded the end to a military dictatorship. Using the war as an excuse, Carlos cracked down on dissidents. The Secret Service jail was overflowing, so he had political prisoners transferred to the infamous Isle of the Moon prison on Lake Titicaca, and threw them in with hardened criminals, but even the island prison was now overcrowded. Unrepentant dissidents somehow fell sick and mysteriously died on the island with regularity. Their deaths freed up space, but created new groups of hard-core enemies among the deceased's family and friends.

Newsprint was in short supply due to the war, so Carlos closed one of the two La Paz newspapers - the one he considered more critical of his government. Despite these measures, there was unrest throughout the country, fed by rampant inflation.

The mine owners were quiet. They were making enormous profits and one of their lawyers was Minister of Finance. The big landowners had few complaints; prices for agricultural products were inflated and land prices were increasing now that Indian farmers could borrow money to buy their own farms.

But the politicians, the university students, and the labor unions were a continual threat. Three times in the last two years they had forced Carlos to declare a State-of-Siege and suspend all constitutional guarantees. Although political parties were outlawed and Congress had been disbanded, secret meetings took place in homes, private clubs, and classrooms. The politicians and students wanted free elections, the renewal of Congress, a civilian President - in short, they wanted a democracy - even though there had never been a true democracy in Bolivia's history.

The labor unions were worse than the politicians. They had tasted power under Toro and Busch, and as a result were hard to control. Theoretically all strikes needed the prior authorization of the government, but lately the unions had staged independent actions. Carlos looked the other way when the bus drivers went out for two weeks, and was only mildly worried when workers shut down a cement factory for almost a month. But the mines had to produce - they kept Bolivia solvent and the Agrarian Bank growing. Therefore, he was annoyed that Juan Lechin, head of the National Miners' Union, was back again, requesting another meeting, the third time in six months.

Nevertheless, he rose from behind his ornate wooden desk as Juan entered his office, forced himself to smile, and extended his hand. Though in his forties, the lawyer had aged considerably over the last ten years. Strands of gray ran through his thinning hair, but his grip was still firm.

"Hello, Mr. Lechin. How are you today?"

"Not good, Mr. President, not good."

This is abrupt, thought Carlos. Custom required that the first few minutes of any meeting be devoted to pleasantries. Carlos tried again. "And the family, Mr. Lechin? How are your wife and daughter?"

"They are fine, Mr. President. It is my larger family, the miners, who are suffering."

"I'm sorry to hear that."

Carlos motioned to one of the two chairs facing the desk. "Please, take a seat."

After Juan sat down, Carlos returned to his own chair, facing Juan across the desk. "Would you like a cup of coffee?"

"No. Thank you. I've had some already this morning."

"Something else? A glass of water?"

"No. Nothing."

Carlos gave up on the pleasantries.

"What seems to be the problem with your larger family, Mr. Lechin?"

"They are starving, Mr. President. In the last year, inflation has increased over two hundred percent. Yet wages for my men have increased only sixty percent."

Carlos knew this to be true. He also knew that negotiations between the mining companies and the national union had recently collapsed. The Minister of Finance kept him informed.

"But you are in negotiations with the companies, aren't you?"

"We have presented our demands for a one hundred percent increase, but they have refused to discuss it," Juan stated.

Carlos feigned surprise. "Well, I don't want to take sides," he lied, "but I am sure that ore prices haven't increased by one hundred and sixty percent."

"No, Mr. President, they have not. But wages are only one part of the total ore costs, and the mine owners are reaping bigger profits now than ever before in their history, while the workers are starving. We want our share, Mr. President." Juan leaned forward and looked him straight in the eye.

Carlos picked up a silver letter opener from his desk, examined it, and then leaned back in his chair. "You are an intelligent man, Mr. Lechin. You know Bolivian ore costs are high already due to our tunneling, rail charges to Antofagasta, and ocean freight. We compete against lower cost producers in Asia."

"There is enough money for all with the war," Juan answered.

Carlos slowly rotated the letter opener in his hands. "Even though inflation is high, miners still have the company stores. Prices there surely haven't risen so much."

"Almost as quickly, Mr. President. The company stores are abusing their monopoly. My union has requested the abolition of all company stores and asked for the freedom to install cooperative stores to be owned by the workers, in each of the mining camps. It's time to put an end to debtor enslavement."

"I see. What other demands have you made?" Carlos queried, keeping his eyes on the letter opener.

"We want payment of our wages in full at the end of each month. The mining companies have been holding back a part of each month's wages to ensure that we do not strike. This is unjust coercion. Not only are the wages too low, but they are not paid on time."

Carlos was aware of the practice and approved of it as an effective way to prevent strikes and preserve production. "You have many demands."

"Demands that are just, Mr. President. The owners refuse to concede anything. They are greedy, full of money and a sense of power. But we are strong, too, and we will not be denied. That's why I am here."

Carlos tapped the blunt end of the letter opener on the desk, avoiding Juan's eyes. "What is it you want from me, Mr. Lechin?"

"I want government approval to strike the Twentieth Century and Llallagua tin mines for an indefinite period. And I want approval to call out all my miners in solidarity on December twenty-first."

Carlos' face remained impassive, but he quickly replaced the letter opener in its original position. Those were the two largest tin mines in Bolivia, both owned by Patino. Loss of their production would be a disaster. "I'm sorry, but I cannot authorize this strike, Mr. Lechin."

"Why, Mr. President?"

"The country needs the revenues from our tin exports. You know that. Go back to the owners and find some compromise."

"We have talked enough. They walked out of our last meeting. Now we are going to show them that they must meet our demands."

"I told you, Mr. Lechin, I will not authorize this strike." Carlos was annoyed with the man.

"What if we strike anyway?"

"That would be illegal," Carlos replied. "I could have you thrown in jail right now just for suggesting it." He could feel the tension rising inside him; the man was exasperating.

Juan studied Carlos for a long time before he spoke again.

"Am I talking to the son of Luis Obregon, the miner who gave his life so that other miners could live better than he did? Are you the same man who fought in the Chaco with courage for his fellow soldiers, the same man who as part of the Junta promised a better life for the workers and Indians? What happened to the ideas born in the Chaco, Major? Have you sold out your father and your race?"

Carlos sprang from his chair and leaned over the desk.

"You are talking to the President of Bolivia, Mr. Lechin. Because you were my father's friend, I will not have you arrested immediately."

"But why not help us, Mr. President? You, of all people, know what it is like to be oppressed," Juan pleaded.

"Because you are a dreamer, Mr. Lechin. You asked my father to share your dreams, and it cost him his life. You want to strike, to call out all your men, but that will only lead to violence. You preach justice, but you bring chaos. Why should I listen to you?"

"Because the mine workers have the right to a better life. I have a cause, Mr. President, a cause to help them live like humans, not like animals. Don't you have one? Don't you believe in anything?" Juan challenged.

"Why should I have a cause?" Carlos shot back. "I have seen every form of evil since I left my village. I have seen soldiers slaughtered for nothing in war, while their officers fled. I have watched them die of thirst, their bodies dry, their tongues swollen. I have seen men butchered by the *Macheteros*, their intestines hung on bushes."

Carlos drew a deep breath and looked down at him. "Here in La Paz I have seen corruption beyond anything I could have imagined. Perversions of every type." Carlos sneered. "And you want me to have a cause."

"In your position, you could change the lives of these men. You could change Bolivia."

"I have done what I can - the Agrarian Bank is a good example - but I have also learned to accept my country as it is. Full of

237

lies, betrayals, corruption. And it won't change because of you or me. Fifty years from now, when you and I are both dead, the miners will still be working in miserable conditions, starving and underpaid, provided there is a demand for tin ore. Accept the situation. Make a deal with the owners. They will take care of you."

Juan stared at him in disbelief. "You are suggesting I take a bribe? You insult me!"

"I am suggesting that you accept reality. Our meeting is over."

Juan rose and walked toward the door. As he grasped the handle, he turned to face Carlos and tried one last time.

"Mr. President, in your father's memory, I ask you once again to authorize this strike."

Carlos glared at him across the room. "No, Mr. Lechin. No!"

Juan spoke softly in a sad voice, "We will strike on December twenty-first, Mr. President," and disappeared through the door.

Carlos looked at the door for a long time, weighing his options. He summoned his adjutant, who appeared immediately. "Get me Mr. Bruce Berkman at the American Embassy."

Chapter 4

At first Ramon would not believe it, refused to believe it, but the signs were unmistakable: the dilated pupils; the changes in mood; sometimes bright and alert, other times depressed and listless, always irritable. He said to himself, it can't be, it is not possible. She is too beautiful, too intelligent, too sensitive, to ruin her life like this. For twelve months he had watched Ingrid deteriorate, watched hollows grow in her cheeks and dark circles form under her eyes. The woman he loved was destroying herself, and because he loved her, she was destroying him as well.

At last he decided to confront her. He waited until an afternoon when he knew Carlos had a meeting outside the Palace, then appeared unannounced, asking to see the Baroness. When Ingrid entered the drawing room, she looked tired and unkempt.

"What brings you here, Ramon?" She extended her hand. "I'm not sure where Carlos is."

"I came to see you, Ingrid." He brushed his lips against the back of her hand.

"Oh," she said uncertainly, "please take a seat."

She sat in a comfortable armchair and Ramon sat across from her on a sofa.

"I've missed you. You rarely come to our weekly suppers anymore, and when you do, you never stay and talk as before. Is anything wrong?" Ramon asked.

Ingrid adjusted her skirt to cover her knees. "I've been feeling tired, that's all."

"You've given up your riding. The stablehands tell me they haven't seen you for months."

Ingrid sighed. "I've lost interest. I've been around horses most of my life. Maybe I've just had too much of them."

Ramon leaned forward, his elbows resting on his knees, and asked in a concerned voice, "Can I help you, Ingrid?"

She hesitated before answering, "No, I'm fine. Just a little tired."

"Have you seen a doctor? You look as if you've lost weight."

Her hand twitched. "A doctor? No...I don't need a doctor."

Ramon observed the dark circles under her dull eyes and her hastily combed hair. Even her dress seemed too big for her. He debated with himself whether the time was right, whether a confrontation might ruin their relationship forever, but her appearance convinced him to continue.

"Where are you getting it, Ingrid?"

She looked surprised. "Getting what?"

"Cocaine. The cocaine you have been taking for almost a year now."

She looked away from him, and smoothed her skirt with nervous fingers. "I don't know what you're talking about."

"Yes, you do, Ingrid. I've been around cocaine all my life. The coca leaves are grown here in the jungle, and are readily available and legal. The factories that process the leaves into the white powder you are using, these factories are either owned by the government which sell the powder as medicine, or are clandestine. Either way, it's easy to get your hands on illegal cocaine."

Ingrid drew back in her chair. "That doesn't concern me."

Ramon clenched his fists. "Yes it does. The production of cocaine is limited because it's a dangerous, addictive drug. I can spot the users, Ingrid, because I see them every day in my work. You're a user."

Both of her hands were now trembling. "That's not true."

"Don't deny it, Ingrid. If you deny you have a problem, you will grow more and more dependent on it. It destroys lives. I've seen young women end up in the streets, selling their bodies, to get cocaine. They will do anything. And in the end, it will kill you."

240

She turned on him, her eyes flashing, "Who gave you permission to pry into my life? I'm a grown woman, capable of making my own decisions. What I do, or don't do, is no business of yours."

Ramon rose and came to her chair. Taking her shaking hands into his, he said gently, "I love you, Ingrid. I love you more than anything else in my life. I can't let you destroy yourself like this. I want to help. Tell me where you are getting it."

She began to cry and shook her head slowly.

Ramon rose and said angrily, "Then I'll find out by myself, and when I do, I'll kill the person who has done this to you."

Chapter 5

As Juan Lechin walked down the dirt road into the Catavi Basin, surrounded by other union leaders, he stopped to study the huge natural crater spread out before him. Nobody had been able to explain to him how this gigantic circular hole in the central Altiplano, almost five hundred yards across and up to fifty yards deep, had been formed. Had a large meteor plunged to earth thousands of years ago? Had the earth's surface collapsed into the molten center? The immense mystery of the basin caused him to pause, but a cold morning wind that curled over the rim hastened him on after a few seconds.

He had chosen the basin as the site to hold the solidarity assembly for the strike of December 21, 1942, because it was a natural theater. The passing of time had flattened the bottom to accommodate thousands, and the high side walls provided protection from the wind, shutting out sound from above and giving resonance to voices below. Looking at it now, though, the steep dirt and rock walls surrounding the basin seemed more threatening than protective, and he wondered if he had made the right choice.

Since dawn, workers from the Twentieth Century and Llallagua tin mines, along with union representatives from all the other mines, had been filing down the one path to the basin's bottom. They brought their families with them, along with food and crude camp stoves, in preparation for a long day of speeches. They brought *pisco* and *chicha* as well, to liven their spirits and ward off the cold.

By nine in the morning over six thousand men, women, and children were assembled around a makeshift wooden speakers' platform in the center of the basin, under an overcast and leaden sky. Bright red banners waved over their heads, in sharp contrast to the brown walls of the basin and the gray sky. Hundreds of fires blinked among the masses, and family groups huddled around them for warmth.

As Juan and his group passed, individual workers yelled their support. When the union leaders mounted the platform and took their seats, a smattering of applause could be heard. At nine a.m., a young union leader from the Twentieth Century mine stood to deliver the first speech.

One hour later, Juan stepped to the front of the platform to give his own speech, the third of the day. Spontaneous applause rose from the crowd, which Juan silenced by raising his left hand high above his head.

"Comrades," he announced in his clear voice, "today is a glorious day. A day of celebration. A day to remember forever." The basin walls echoed and magnified his words. "Today is the day we show the mine owners, and the government, that we, the united mine workers, control our own destiny."

Applause rang out, along with cries of *"Viva Lechin!"* Again, Juan raised his arm to silence the outburst.

"Today, for the first time in history, all the workers of the two largest tin mines in Bolivia, have laid down their tools at the same time. United under one union, we have shown our courage, and our strength. They say patience is a virtue. But we have been patient too long, waiting in misery, hungry and desperate, while the mine owners ignored our requests for just wages and decent working conditions. Ignored while the same owners dined in London and Paris."

The miners broke into applause. As Juan raised his arm once more for silence, he noticed movement at the basin's rim. He continued speaking, trying to ignore the distraction, while khaki-clad troops of the Bolivian Army spread out and formed a row around the entire lip of the basin, blocking the single exit. Methodically they set up trench mortars and machine guns, filling in the gaps with riflemen. The crowd below also saw the troops, and a growing murmur spread throughout the assembly, rising in volume until Juan was forced to stop speaking.

Juan raised his arm once more.

"Look around you. Do you see what I see? Armed soldiers."

Thousands of heads craned and bobbed to get a better look at the troops that encircled them.

"This is the response of a frightened government, a government afraid of its own people. But we are not cowards!" Juan shouted. "Does Major Carlos Obregon think that a show of rifles will force us back to work? Is he that stupid? We are not cowards!" Sweat ran down his face despite the cold weather.

"We have done nothing wrong. We are here peacefully. We have destroyed nothing. Force cannot overcome right!"

"*Viva Lechin!*" someone in the crowd yelled, and others picked up the chant.

"To the mines!" Juan screamed. "Let's go as a group to the mines, and lay our complaints before the management. Let them hear our voices, and see our strength. Then they will know we are not cowards!"

"To the mines," the crowd roared back.

Juan leaped off the platform, and pushed his way though the masses, heading toward the road leading out of the basin. The other union leaders hurried to fall in beside him. A phalanx of bodies formed around Juan as he pushed forward.

Franco looked derisively at the young army lieutenant standing at his side at the entrance to the basin. The lieutenant scratched nervously at his left hand with pale white fingers.

"*Mierda,*" the lieutenant exclaimed. "They're coming up here!"

"What did you expect?" Franco asked. "I told you to start shooting while you had them trapped in the basin."

"Those weren't my orders," the lieutenant answered angrily. "My orders are to guard the mines to make sure no damage is done, not to kill miners. It was your idea to surround the basin."

"Damned good thing we did," Franco countered. "I know these people. That's why the owners asked me to work with you. Once they get loose, you can't stop them. They'll burn the mine offices and sabotage the equipment if you give them a chance. They're animals." He spat on the ground. "The only thing they understand is force. Show some guts."

"There are women and children down there. I can't fire on them."

"Why not?" Franco sneered. "They're all in this together. If they weren't looking for trouble, they shouldn't have come."

By now Juan had initiated the climb, followed by the crowd. As they approached, the union leaders in front linked arms in solidarity, with Juan in the middle.

"Company," the lieutenant shouted, "Form ranks."

Twenty soldiers formed a line across the roadway, blocking any possibility of passage.

"Ready arms," the lieutenant ordered, and twenty rifles were raised to firing position. The sharp click of twenty bolts settling the cartridges into place carried through the air.

The sound was like cold water on the face of Juan, calming the fire inside him. He unlinked his left arm and raised it in the air.

"Stop," Juan cried.

The body of miners came to rest twenty yards from Franco and the lieutenant.

"We have no quarrel with the Army," Juan shouted to the lieutenant. "We want only to present our grievances to the owners."

"They will destroy the buildings if you let them through," Franco whispered to the officer, who had unbuckled his pistol holder.

"Return to the basin," the lieutenant shouted to Juan. "Here you cannot pass."

"Why not?" Juan asked.

"I have my orders. Don't try to force your way through. Return to the basin and continue your meeting if you want. But don't try to pass."

Juan looked up and down the line of union leaders. Some faces were blank, others nodded their heads in agreement. To proceed would be insanity, not courage. He turned to address the other miners.

Before he could open his mouth, an Indian woman boldly pushed through the group. Miners parted to let her pass.

"We are not cowards!" she shouted, repeating Juan's earlier words. "To the mines!"

A second woman, carrying a baby in her arms, ran up beside her. "Yes. To the mines!"

A body of miners followed the women, bursting through the front row of union leaders, advancing toward the soldiers.

"No! No! Stop!" Juan shouted, fighting to hold back the men and women marching past him.

"Stop or we will fire!" the lieutenant screamed, drawing his pistol from its holster.

"Fire, you idiot," Franco said. "Don't let them through."

Sweat poured down the lieutenant's forehead.

"Fire or they'll kill us," Franco said, shaking the lieutenant.

The young lieutenant's arm remained frozen.

"Goddamn you!" Franco cried as he seized the lieutenant's gun from his hand. He aimed at the woman leading the crowd and pulled the trigger. She lurched backwards, an expression of surprise on her face, and dropped to her knees.

"Fire," Franco screamed and the soldiers around him opened fire. The woman with the baby fell with the first row of advancing miners.

The shock of watching his comrades go down was almost as deafening to Juan as the volley of rifle shots. Tears came to his eyes as he bent over a wounded miner and lifted him from the ground. Juan turned and stumbled back down the road, struggling to keep the man on his feet. A second volley of shots rang out and the man he was carrying jerked and coughed up blood. Juan dropped the dying man and ran down the slope, surrounded by retreating miners and their families.

People pushed him from all sides. He stepped on the back of a fallen miner and heard the man groan. He almost fell himself. Screams and crying assaulted his ears. In front of him the multitude of fleeing miners and their families poured onto the flat floor of the crater, spreading out like blood on cement.

The first mortar round landed twenty yards from the speakers' platform, in the midst of the people. Women screamed, a cloud of dust rose, tangled bodies lay in a rough circle on the ground. More rifle shots rang out, at first slowly, then in rapid succession. A second mortar round exploded. One side of the speakers' platform collapsed, crushing those who had sought shelter under it. The rat-tat-tat of machine guns caused Juan's whole body to shiver.

All around him, people dropped to the ground individually and in groups, singled out by riflemen or raked by machine gun fire. Juan ran past a woman without a leg, past a man who lay on top of his wife to protect her, past a mother curled around her child on the ground. He searched desperately for any shelter, any slight depression in the earth, any small rock outcropping, but he found nothing. He looked toward the basin rim, half-blinded by tears, raised both arms in the air, and screamed, "Stop it! Stop it!"

The chaos swallowed his screams as the slaughter continued. Dead and wounded bodies lay all around him. Frantically he stacked one body on top of the other, paying no attention to the sex or age, until he had built a small circle of bodies. He flung himself into the center, and flattened himself against the ground. A moan came from nearby, but he ignored it and covered his ears with his hands.

Even with his eyes closed and his ears blocked, he could visualize the carnage. Mortar rounds fell at irregular intervals. Machine guns chattered, stopped when they became overheated or finished a cartridge belt, and started again. The rifle shots were more spaced, seeking out those who moved. He willed himself to lie motionless, feigning death, but he couldn't control his sobbing.

He had no idea how long he lay there, listening to the dull thuds of bullets hitting the bodies around him, and the loud booms of explosives churning the earth. It might have been an hour, a day, or a week, for his mind no longer functioned. He refused to acknowledge that this atrocity was happening, that some higher power would let it happen.

Finally the shooting stopped. An eerie wailing arose from the floor of the basin, like the howling of dogs. Juan did not dare to move. Then he heard cries of pain and moaning. He slowly drew his hands away from his head, and the lamentations increased in volume. Nearby a child bawled.

Juan lifted his head and peered cautiously over the corpses. Grayish smoke, rising from exploded mortars, floated low off the ground. A mass of prone bodies, some dead, some wounded, some feigning death like himself, covered the basin floor. As he watched, a lone individual slowly rose to his feet, followed by a second, then by others, like ghostly souls rising from a lake of dead.

He pushed himself to his knees and stared at the basin rim. The soldiers were gone.

The world was collapsing around Ramon. For the last five days he had been working almost without sleep. His Department of Internal Security was laboring around the clock to round up the leaders of the miners union, all of whom had gone into hiding since the Catavi massacre. He had achieved some success - seven of the twelve national leaders were in jail, but Juan Lechin, the union President, was still at large. Ramon had led raids at midnight and early morning, breaking into houses, threatening wives and mistresses, bullying children for information, but it was hard work. He had not been home except to change uniforms, sleeping at the office between raids. His nerves were frayed. Carlos was pressuring him to capture Lechin at once. At the same time, reports of clandestine meetings were coming in from all over the country. It was the worst situation he had seen since Carlos became President, and he wasn't sure that he could control it.

Then, on top of all this, he had uncovered the source. Since his conversation with Ingrid, he had been searching for her cocaine supplier. His men questioned employees at the government factory but came away with nothing. Then they raided two clandestine cocaine producers, but netted only a considerable quantity of illicit money. Finally he fell back on one of his informers, a cleaning maid in the Presidential Palace who had worked there for several years. Carlos had developed her as an informant when he was Head of Internal Security, and Ramon continued to use her services. Not against Carlos, but as a means to protect the President, by identifying any possible dangers within his own household.

Now the worst had happened. The maid had reported that Carlos himself was supplying the cocaine to Ingrid. Carlos had made his own mistress a drug addict. At first Ramon refused to believe it, but then it all fell in place. Carlos had access to all the free cocaine he wanted, either through the government laboratory or received as bribes from the clandestine operators. All free, in unlimited quantities. But why? Why would he want to destroy Ingrid? Carlos knew the dangers of cocaine addition. Ramon hated him for it.

He was brooding at his desk, trying unsuccessfully to control his emotions, when his Adjutant came in.

"We caught him, Sir. We have Juan Lechin."

Ramon glanced up. "How? When?"

The Adjutant looked embarrassed. "Actually, Sir, he came here asking for you. He just walked in the front door. Right now. We searched him and he is unarmed."

Ramon rose, straightening his tie. "Bring me some more coffee and then send him in."

Juan Lechin entered the office confidently, with no sign of fear, walked over to the desk, and took a seat across from Ramon.

"Thank you for seeing me, Captain."

"Your visit is unexpected." Ramon poured a cup of coffee for himself and Juan.

"I presumed you were looking for me and thought I might save you some trouble. Besides, I wanted to see you. I have a proposition for you."

The coffee helped clear Ramon's mind. He leaned forward. "You have a proposition...for me?"

"Captain, I am going to be completely open with you. I assume that you are a sensible man, and that you are a patriot. Or at least an officer who wants to avoid any more unnecessary bloodshed."

"Continue."

"The Catavi massacre is the end of Major Obregon as President. Over eight hundred men, women, and children were slaughtered without mercy. My miners will not stand for it. No civilized people would stand for it. Right now the miners are arming themselves all over Bolivia. They are getting rifles and ammunition from military officers who are fed up with the despot Obregon. Thousands of armed miners will converge on La Paz; they will be joined by other workers and by university students. The outlawed political parties will join in. The garrison at La Paz will do nothing. They will not fight against the people. The masses will march against the Palace and demand the resignation of the President."

"Why tell me this, Mr. Lechin? I am the very man charged with preventing this type of uprising."

"Because there is nothing you can do to stop it, Captain. Never in the history of this country have so many citizens been united in their desire to get rid of a President. I am telling you because I want your help to prevent more deaths."

"How?" asked Ramon, puzzled by the whole conversation.

"In two ways. First, I want you to keep the National Police and your Secret Service men off the streets. The regular Army will do nothing to stop the uprising. I don't want my miners to fight with your men on the streets, even though we will win if it comes to that."

"I see."

"Second, I want you to neutralize the Palace Guard. If they do not intervene, the revolution against Obregon will be brief and bloodless. If fighting breaks out at the Palace, I cannot guarantee the safety of the President."

"I don't command the Palace Guard, Mr. Lechin. Their Commanding Officer reports directly to the President. Since President Obregon personally selected him, I assume his loyalty is very strong."

"But you have access to the Palace. You must neutralize the Guard, Captain. If you don't, there will be a slaughter. My men will not be stopped."

"Why should I help you?" asked Ramon.

"Because if you do, Captain, you can remain in your same position under the new government. Otherwise, you will be put on trial and most certainly go to prison. At best, you will be without a job."

Ramon admired the man's bravado. "Are you threatening me, Mr. Lechin?"

"No, Captain, I am stating the facts. With or without you, this revolution will succeed. Even if I am in prison or killed. The forces against Obregon are too strong to contain. Can I count on your help?"

Ramon leaned back in his chair and reflected. He hated Carlos for addicting Ingrid. And he knew that Juan Lechin was speaking the truth.

"Agreed. Let's talk details."

Chapter 6

The visit was unexpected. Ingrid had not seen Ramon since the day he confronted her about using cocaine. She did not want to see him again because she had made no attempt to quit. She purposely avoided the weekly dinners rather than face the accusation in Ramon's eyes. Now he was here in mid-afternoon, asking to see her.

The idea of meeting him again made her nervous. She checked in the mirror and was relieved that she had washed her hair that morning. She dabbed a little powder on her face, looked around the room hoping to find something to do to delay the moment, and finally went down to greet him in the salon.

Ramon stood by the fireplace with his back to her, deep in thought. Looking at his erect, slender body, and his black, curly hair hanging over his collar, she still felt an attraction for him.

He turned when he heard her footsteps.

"Thank you for receiving me, Ingrid. I would not have come unless it was urgent." He took her hand in his and brushed his lips against the back of it.

"You are always welcome, Ramon. Both Carlos and I value your friendship." She withdrew her hand. "Please sit down."

She sat on a long couch and he sat beside her, which had not been her intention. She felt his eyes examining her, probably checking to see if her pupils were dilated. She hadn't used cocaine since the night before but this didn't make her any more secure. Evidently he was satisfied.

"My visit here today is not pleasant, neither for me, for you, or for Carlos. But it is necessary." He paused. "Are you aware of the massacre at Catavi?"

She nodded her head.

"The whole country is enraged. The miners are going to rise against Carlos, and they will be joined by half of the population of La Paz."

Ingrid adjusted her body on the sofa to face Ramon more squarely. "Why tell me this? Shouldn't you be talking with Carlos?"

"He will never step down unless forced to, Ingrid. If he attempts to hold out at the Palace, there will be bloodshed. Carlos could be hurt, even killed. You and Wilhelm would be in danger. If I can neutralize the Palace Guard, Carlos can be persuaded to resign. To do that, I need access to the Palace on the day of the uprising. You can provide that access."

"This is disgusting, Ramon." She rose and looked down on him. "I thought you were his best friend. You're just as bad as the others."

He caught her hand before she could leave. "Ingrid," he said, standing and forcing her to look at him, "this is the only way."

"I will not betray Carlos," she said firmly.

He dropped her hand and spoke angrily, "What power does he have over you, Ingrid? I don't understand. Why are you loyal to a man who has never asked to marry you, who treats you like a concubine, and who is responsible for your cocaine addiction?"

She avoided his eyes and turned away. "You know I can't marry until I know the situation of my husband," she said defensively. "Carlos is helping me to find out what happened to Manfred. I'm sure he would marry me if I were free," she said with her back toward him.

"Your husband is dead, Ingrid. Since 1933. Carlos knows that very well. You see, Carlos killed him."

Ingrid spun around and stared at him, her mouth half open. "You say that to turn me against him."

Ramon was looking her straight in the eye and she could see that he wasn't lying. He withdrew an object from his coat pocket and held it out to her.

"Do you recognize this?"

252

She took the chain from him and gasped, "It's Manfred's medallion. His family crest. How did you get it?"

"I took it from his body, Ingrid. I helped bury your husband, after Carlos shot him. Carlos killed him to save our company. It was necessary, but Carlos himself pulled the trigger. He has lied to you all this time."

Her knees buckled under her. She collapsed on the sofa and stared at the medallion, wishing it would disappear. "It can't be true! He would have told me."

"It is true, Ingrid," Ramon insisted, sitting down beside her. He told her the whole story: how the troops had deserted their front line position; how Manfred had pinned them down with the machine gun, killing several of his own men; and how Carlos had killed Manfred with a shot to the back of his head.

The whole room seemed to close in upon her.

"But why didn't he tell me? I would never have come to Bolivia, and I certainly would never have stayed. He wouldn't lie to me like that."

"He couldn't tell anybody. You can't kill your Commanding Officer in the Army and go unpunished."

"But now, now that he is President. He could tell me. He wouldn't be punished now, even if I told others."

"I don't know his motives, Ingrid, but he has lied to you from the first, keeping you here in La Paz as his mistress, letting you believe he was trying to help. And he is ruining your life with the cocaine. If you continue using it, you will end up on the street, begging for money or worse. He is destroying you."

Tears flowed down her cheeks. She thought of all the things she had done with Carlos, to Carlos, and for Carlos, all the nights they had spent together. How could I have slept with my husband's killer? How could I have done what I did for him? "Maybe he loves me," she whispered.

Ramon shook his head. "You don't destroy the one you love."

She put her hand on her forehead and closed her eyes. Carlos was the only support she had in life. With the war in progress, it was impossible to return to her family in Germany. And what about Wilhelm? How could either of them survive if Carlos was killed?

Could she betray the man she had lived with for four years? Yet he had betrayed her. "I don't know what to do, Ramon."

"First, you must help me on the day of the uprising. We will try to save Carlos. Then, if you will let me, I will do my best to save you, Ingrid. I will get you a doctor, a man who understands cocaine addiction. Together we can break your habit. You can be the person you were before, the woman I have always loved. And when this is over, Ingrid, no matter what happens, I want you to be my wife. I don't care where we live, I don't care what I do, I just want to spend the rest of my life with you."

She looked up at him with tears in her eyes. "You would leave La Paz and Bolivia to be with me?"

"I just told you I love you, Ingrid."

He took her in his arms and kissed her. She didn't resist.

"Now I need your help to prevent more killings."

Chapter 7

Reports of the insurrection reached Carlos at nine fifteen in the morning when Ramon telephoned the Palace. Trucks had been bringing men into La Paz through the night and early morning, dropping them off at different locations, hoping to escape detection, but it was impossible for the men to remain hidden for long in the city, for they were miners dressed in rough work clothes. Some still had dirt on their hands and faces from their last underground shift. Most of them were armed, although the weapons were wrapped in ponchos. Others brandished picks or clubs or furled banners.

By ten o'clock, as their numbers grew larger, efforts to conceal their presence ceased. The trucks continued to arrive, unloading their human cargos, and going back for more. Weapons emerged from under the ponchos and red banners waved in the air. Some miners took up positions at the major street intersections, directing the others. Groups in the suburbs moved toward the center of the city, growing larger and more angry as they approached. Their numbers appeared to be in the thousands as they converged on the Plaza Murillo, the main square of La Paz, the square where the Presidential Palace was located.

When Carlos first learned of the problem, he placed a call to the main Army garrison on the outskirts of the capital. If the small groups could be prevented from concentrating, they could be dealt with by a show of force. To his surprise, the Commanding Officer was unavailable, and did not return his call. He called again and spoke with the second in command, a young Captain, who said he could take no action without the orders of his C.O. Carlos cursed him thoroughly and told him his career was finished unless he acted as instructed, but the young officer would not budge.

Desperate, Carlos telephoned the Commanding Officer of the Military College. He knew the young military students were unreliable but he needed to stop this uprising before it grew. Again, the Commanding Officer, a man whom Carlos had appointed, was not available, and could not be located. He knew now that there was a conspiracy. He was not going to receive help from the local military. However, there had been no reports that the Army was joining the miners, so perhaps he could stop the gathering with the Palace Guard and the National Police.

Carlos telephoned Ramon to review the situation. Ramon was at his office and had been monitoring the growing crowd.

"I've tried to get troops from the La Paz garrison and from the Military College. The C.O. s won't speak to me. The bastards are obviously backing the miners. What news do you have?"

"All bad," Ramon replied. "Trucks are still pouring into the city with more miners. At least eight hundred students have gathered at the University, and it looks ugly. We've spotted other groups carrying banners of the political parties. This is big, Carlos, it's not just the miners."

"I need some police over here to block the entrances to the plaza. We can't let these groups reach the center and join together."

"I don't have enough men, Carlos. The police are scattered throughout the city on their normal patrols. We didn't have any warning that this would happen."

"What good are your Secret Service men if they don't know when something of this size is planned?" Carlos fumed.

"Carlos, since the massacre at Catavi, I haven't been able to keep up with anything. The whole country is like a barrel of boiling tar. Movement everywhere, but it's all obscure."

"Don't use that word 'massacre'. I didn't order the shooting of any miners, much less women and children. I told the Army to protect the mines and the buildings, not to kill anyone."

"But why did you use troops, Carlos? That was a provocation."

Carlos didn't answer. He had received bad advice from Bruce, but the final decision had been his.

"How many men do you have at Police Headquarters?" he asked.

"About thirty."

"And how many men can you pull together quickly?"

"If I call in all the police off the streets, and get some of those who are at off-duty, I might have five hundred all together, including the Secret Service men."

"Then get your men assembled. I need help here. Give them tear gas and weapons and get them to the plaza as fast as you can."

"Okay, Carlos, but it will take time. We have to advise those who are in the streets and at home."

"How long?" Carlos demanded.

"Two or three hours," replied Ramon.

"That's too damn long!" Carlos shouted into the phone. "Get together as many as you can and call me back in thirty minutes." Then he hung up.

Ramon looked at his watch. It was still too early. His timing had to be perfect. He drummed on his desk with his fingers.

In the meantime, Carlos ordered the Commander of the Palace Guard to withdraw the Ceremonial Guards from the front gate and barricade the entrance with sand bags. All members of the Guard were put on combat alert, dressed in fatigues, and issued weapons. Eight men were stationed in front of the main door of the Palace, where they hastily erected a second wall of sand bags. Other Guards took positions at open windows on the second floor, to give them a clear line of fire onto the plaza. The two side doors were locked and barred, with instructions not to open them under any circumstances. The U formed by the building provided a natural fortress, with automatic weapons trained on the courtyard. If there were to be an attack on the Palace, it would be bloody. Even Carlos armed himself with a rifle. Then he waited for word from Ramon, watching from his office window while the Plaza Murillo filled rapidly.

Miners flowed into the square in an ugly silence, their faces grim and determined. Groups of other men, better dressed, arrived waving banners of their underground political parties. Boisterous students from the University joined the crowd and tried to take a leadership role, shouting slogans, but the sullen miners paid little attention. They were waiting for their own leaders. By noon the rebels had packed the square, but there was still no sign of Ramon's men. Demonstrators crushed against each other in the plaza, and the overflow backed up in the side streets, far from the plaza itself. More than eight thousand protesters had assembled.

Carlos called Ramon again, desperate for his men. "What the devil is going on?" he shouted into the phone. "Why didn't you call back? And where are your men?"

"It's been tougher than I thought, Carlos. Some of the police have disappeared. Simply vanished. They've seen the crowds, and don't want any part of it."

"How many do you have right now?"

"About one hundred and fifty," Ramon answered, "but they don't want to fight this mob."

"*Al diablo*! Get them over here right away. Arrest the leaders, and we can still break the demonstration."

"Carlos, how can I get one hundred and fifty men into a crowd like that? They will never let us near their leaders."

"Use tear gas! Use your weapons! These people understand force," Carlos insisted.

Ramon replied calmly, "Carlos, why don't you try to negotiate?"

"Negotiate? For what? With whom? With a group of armed thugs? Hell no!"

"Carlos, please. Be reasonable. There are thousands in the streets now. You're in danger. If you won't negotiate, use the Palace Guard and escape through one of the side doors while there is still time."

"And leave the Palace to this rabble? How can I remain President if I run every time a crowd assembles? They need to see a strong hand, not a frightened rabbit."

"Carlos, you may have to give up the Presidency. Isn't your life worth more?"

"You *Hijo de Puta*! Are you with me or not? Get your men over here, and quick. Do you understand?" screamed Carlos.

"Yes, Carlos," Ramon replied and set down the telephone. But when he hung up, he did not give the order. He had three hundred men assembled at Police Headquarters, men who had been called off the streets before dawn, armed and awaiting his instructions.

Carlos swore under his breath, then returned to his second-floor office window, overlooking the courtyard and square. The day was overcast, gloomy and foreboding, with a damp chill in the air. He looked down on the mass of people jammed together in the Plaza, an endless sea of heads and rifles and picks. Black and red banners stood out above the crowd, proclaiming "Down with Obregon," "Remember the Martyrs of Catavi," "Down with the Butcher," "Throw out the German whore." Men screamed at the top of their lungs, waving their weapons in the air, echoing the slogans. Others were pinned against the Palace gate, pushed by those behind them. The atmosphere was like inflammable gas building up in an enclosed room, waiting for the spark.

He never saw who fired the first shot. Perhaps an overexcited miner or a nervous soldier inside the Palace. Maybe even an agitator, bent on sowing destruction. The shot galvanized the crowd and turned it into a mob. First there was silence, then a low roar, followed by screams of rage. The men nearest the Palace were flattened against the iron grills from behind. Five were crushed to death before the lock ceded and the gate burst open, still partially blocked by sandbags.

Fire from automatic weapons rained down on those first through the gate. The crowd fell back. Return fire sprang up from the miners; those with weapons moved forward while those unarmed made room. Miners braced their rifles against the metal fence to fire at the soldiers inside the Palace. It was an uneven contest, for the soldiers were protected by the parapets, while the miners were exposed behind the iron grill. Miners fell and their bodies were used as shields by other miners. The shouting increased. Two brave men breached the gate, jumped over the sandbags, and dashed toward the main door, firing as they ran. They died twenty yards inside the courtyard.

Carlos called Ramon again, seeking reinforcements, but was told that Ramon had left and was on his way to the Palace. Carlos threw open the window and looked down on the courtyard, now littered with dead bodies. He knelt, braced his weapon on the window sill, and searched for a target. He spotted a thin, gray-haired miner squeezing through the gate and crawling over the sandbags. Carlos snuggled the stock of the rifle against his cheek, drew back the bolt, then slammed it forward to inject the first bullet. He carefully aligned the sights on the old man's chest, and slowly released his breath, as he had been trained to do in the Chaco.

But he could not pull the trigger. Something about the wiry old miner prevented him from killing the man: the determination in his face, the way he ignored the danger, his willingness to make the ultimate sacrifice. He leaned back from the window in shock. The man could have been his father. These were his people. As he watched, the old miner was struck by a bullet from the Palace, and dropped to one knee. He struggled to rise but was hit again and fell forward onto the cobblestones. He made one final effort to push himself up, then fell dead.

Carlos shook his head slowly from side to side. He withdrew the rifle from the window, and placed it on the floor. He rose and went to his desk, where he took pen and paper and began to write his resignation.

When the shooting began, Franco bolted for the nearest doorway and took cover. Protected by the concrete doorframe, his back pressed against the closed bronze doors of the National Bank building, he had a clear view of the Plaza Murillo and the Palace. He leaned the miner's pick he carried against the door and stuck his cold hands under his dirty poncho. With his knit wool cap and his face smeared with dirt, he looked like any other miner, except for his height. To complete his disguise, Franco had wrapped a dirty, gray wool scarf around the lower half of his face. Miners often covered their noses in this fashion to ward off the cold, and to prevent bad air from entering their lungs.

"Shouldn't we be out there with the crowd?" the shift boss on his left asked.

Franco pulled his scarf down to answer. "No. It's safer here."

"How do we know what the union leaders are doing if we can't see them?" the second shift boss asked. Both were dressed like Franco.

"Who cares? I'm sure as hell not going to get killed just to catch some union leader breaking the law."

"I thought that was why we're here," the first shift boss said.

Franco rolled his shoulders. The door was cold on his back. "That was the original idea. To get some dirt on the leaders. But the owners didn't know that the miners were going to attack the Palace. That's a fucking war out there now. You wanna get killed, that's your business, but me, I'm staying here until the shooting stops."

"Should we split up?"

"Nah. It's safer if the three of us stick together. I'll tell you when it's time to move. Jesus Christ, look at that battle out there. If it continues, we won't have to worry about union leaders any more. They'll all be dead."

Two hundred yards away, on the residential side of the Palace, Ramon watched Ingrid's window. He was worried, seriously worried, for he had planned to reach the Palace before any violence started. Shooting had begun, and it sounded bad. Few people remained in the side street where he was waiting; the action was at the front gate. He had handpicked a group of twenty men he could trust and who were trained in close combat. They were dressed in standard police uniforms and carried automatic weapons. The plan had been to get inside the Palace, capture the Commander of the Guard, and force Carlos to negotiate.

The curtain of Ingrid's third-floor bedroom window was drawn back, and she appeared in full view from the waist up, an easy target for a rifleman. He waved to her and the curtain closed again. Ramon moved his men quickly across the street, stationing them on either side of the secondary door, the door used by the servants and staff.

In her bedroom, Ingrid stepped away from the window and hugged herself to stop her trembling. Since she had learned the truth regarding her husband's death, she had been on the verge of completely losing control. She knew that she should hate the man who had killed her husband, then tricked her into becoming his mistress - the man who had made a prostitute of her to further his political aims. When she thought of the way he had deceived her all these years, she was furious. But at the same time she remembered the nights they had spent together, two perspiring bodies continually exploring for more pleasure, which merged into one, and she blushed thinking of the joy that he had given her. She hated him, but she also loved him.

She was shaking so much that she went to her night table and removed a small tin of white powder. She opened the container and looked at the white substance that had dominated her life since that fateful night with General Bustamante. When she thought about that night, how Carlos had used her, and what the General had done to her, her stomach turned. The tin shook in her hands and some of the precious powder drifted onto the night table.

She stared mesmerized at the white substance. She could take a sniff of the powder right now and forget the world outside. She could forget her pact with Ramon, forget any betrayal of Carlos, forget everything that had happened to her, and float in near ecstasy while events unfolded on their own. It would be so easy.

Or, she could start all over, without cocaine, without Carlos, and make a new life for herself. One look in the mirror made her decide. The dark circles around her eyes, the gaunt cheeks, the dress that hung too loosely on her, all spoke of death. She flung the tin to the floor, sending up a fine cloud of white dust, then ran down the stairs to the ground floor, stopping only to collect her son on the way.

Two soldiers guarded the side door; the main force was protecting the front gate. She recognized one of the Guards.

"The President has instructed me to leave, Sergeant. The situation here has become too dangerous."

"But the streets are even more dangerous, Baroness. Bullets are flying everywhere. The mob has gone mad."

"I know, Sergeant, but Captain Sanchez is meeting me at the door and will escort me to safety. He is outside now. These are the President's orders."

The Sergeant hesitated, and then accepted her story. He could be jailed for disobeying the President, or even offending his German mistress. He and his companion removed the wooden two-by-four which barred the door from the inside. They slipped the lock and peeked through the crack. Sure enough, there was Captain Sanchez standing in front of the door. Just as they relaxed, the door burst inwards, throwing the Sergeant to the floor. Uniformed police swarmed into the Palace, automatic weapons at the ready. Both soldiers threw their hands up in surrender.

Ramon spoke quickly, "Ingrid, take your son and go back to your bedroom. It's too late to try to leave. Lock the door from the inside and don't let anyone in except me. Do you understand?"

Ingrid nodded and grabbed Wilhelm's hand.

"You," said Ramon, pointing to one of his men, "go with the Baroness and stand guard outside her door. Don't let anyone near her."

The policeman followed Ingrid up the stairs. Another man was left behind to guard the two prisoners.

Ramon took his remaining men and set out to find the Commander of the Palace Guard. The first group of Guards they encountered surrendered immediately and was disarmed, for they had been caught from behind. The second group heard Ramon and his men approaching and turned their guns inward. A firefight broke out within the Palace itself.

As the defenders turned their attention to the intruders within the Palace, the miners noticed the slackening of defensive fire and rushed the front gate. This time they managed to push the gate wide open and charged the front door, slaughtering the remaining Guards posted there. A group of miners battered the main door with their rifle butts as a roar of vengeance rose from the crowd. Sensing victory, they spilled through the open gate, filling the courtyard, shouting, "Death to Obregon," "Kill the German whore!" The front door fell to their onslaught, and they poured into the Palace itself.

Carlos heard the mob storming the front door through the broken window of his office. Shattered glass shards lay scattered on the carpet. He heard shooting and angry cries inside the Palace itself, and the pounding of running feet. He lay down his pen.

When the door burst open, he was blotting the ink dry. A group of miners rushed through the door, their picks and rifles fluttering above their black faces and clothes. Carlos stood and held up the paper in his hand to calm them. He spoke with as much authority as he could muster, "You have won. Here is my resignation. I am willing to go into exile."

His words stopped them for an instant. Then one miner shouted, "Exile, never! Remember Catavi!"

They charged forward and fell upon him, overturning his desk in their rage. Carlos raised his arms to shield himself, but the blows came from all directions, enveloping him. He felt a pick pierce his thigh and he fell. On the floor the kicking began. His arms and legs were shattered by rifle butts. He looked up through blood-filled eyes to see a giant blackness hovering over him and the flash of a pick descending like a vengeful silver talon.

The situation had gone from bad to worse for Ramon. The Guards had decided to fight and it was dirty work, going from room to room, trying to dislodge them. When the mob breached the front door, the confusion increased. Despite their Police uniforms, the crowd mistook his men for the Palace Guard and killed several of them. Ramon himself was captured with four of his men. He tried to persuade the miners who held him that he was on their side, pointing to the Police uniforms, but they were mistrustful. After disarming his group, the miners held them in one of the reception rooms of the center section. Ramon demanded to see Juan Lechin.

The shooting died down quickly as resistance disappeared. Only sporadic shots could be heard coming from the Guards' wing. The mob shouted profanities as they ravaged the Palace, destroying antiques. Priceless paintings were dragged from the walls, velvet curtains pulled down. They used their picks to hack at upholstery until chairs fell apart. Fires were started, fueled by the riches of centuries. The noise was worse than the battles in the Chaco. Ramon could do nothing to stop it.

Finally, after what seemed an eternity, Juan Lechin appeared, accompanied by a group of armed miners. He embraced Ramon and thanked him for his help in subduing the Palace Guard. The miners patted Ramon and his men on the back, hugging them as brothers, and returned their weapons.

"What has happened?" Ramon asked Juan as they walked toward the front entrance, now wide open, one door dangling precariously.

"The people have won. As of today there will be no more military dictators telling us what to do. We will elect our own President. Obregon is dead. Look for yourself," he said, pointing through the door toward the front gate.

A body dangled by its feet from the arch of the gate, bound by ropes. A mob surrounded the corpse, jabbing it with their rifles and picks. Others spat on it. Still others cursed the swinging figure.

Carlos' face was unrecognizable, but the torn uniform was his.

A frown crossed Ramon's face. "And the Baroness? Where is the Baroness? You agreed that she wouldn't be hurt."

Juan turned to look at Ramon. "You mean the German whore? I don't know where she is."

Ramon's face turned white. "I need some help. Follow me," he shouted to his four policemen. "Hurry," he cried, running toward the residential wing of the Palace.

When the shooting died down and it was apparent that the danger was over, Franco led his two men into the Palace, mingling with the other miners. Inside, chaos reigned. Through the smoke of small fires, looters rushed past carrying tables, chairs, and paintings. Others hauled off table linen and towels. Still others clutched handfuls of silverware, dropping knifes and forks as they ran for the door. Entering the kitchen, Franco saw that even the pots and pans had been stripped from the walls where they formerly hung.

Satisfied that there was no booty left on the ground floor, but eager to take advantage of the confusion, Franco and his two men climbed the stairs to the second floor, where the pillaging continued. Miners pulled curtains from the windows, paintings from the walls, and ran toward the exits. Four men pushed past carrying a couch. Two miners battled over a silver picture frame in the middle of the hall.

Discouraged at having arrived late, Franco led his men to the third floor. Entering the hall, he saw several open doors, but only a few looters. He started down the corridor and a fallen policeman, lying dead in front of a closed door, caught his attention. Franco tried the handle, but the door was locked. Sensing an opportunity, he swung back his pick and smashed it into the door above the handle. The wood splintered. He swung again and one panel of the door shattered inward. A third blow forced the lock and the door swung open.

Franco entered the room, followed by his men. His eyes opened wide when he found himself inside a bedroom. A blonde woman and her son huddled together against a wardrobe in the corner. While his men searched for anything of value, tearing open drawers, flinging clothes on the floor, Franco walked over to the woman.

"Give me your jewelry," he ordered.

Ingrid stripped the rings from her fingers and unhooked her earrings, handing them to Franco. Then she removed a gold bracelet from her right wrist and passed it to him. She unfastened her watch and offered it. Franco took each item in his large hand and stuffed them in his pocket.

"Where is the rest?" he asked threateningly.

Ingrid pointed to the far side of the room. "In the vanity table. The drawer on the right."

One of Franco's men rushed to the table and flung open the drawer. He lifted out a leather box and opened it, then turned to show the contents to Franco.

Franco smiled and looked at Ingrid once again.

"Your necklace. I want your necklace."

Ingrid winced. "It belonged to my late husband. It's the only thing I have of his."

Franco grabbed the necklace and yanked. Ingrid cried out as the clasp refused to break and the chain cut into her skin.

Wilhelm ducked his head and butted Franco in the stomach, flailing away with thin arms. "Leave my mother alone," he cried.

The blows of the thirteen year old made no impact on the burly Franco. He drew back his right hand and slapped the boy with all his might. Wilhelm flew across the room and landed in a heap against the wall. The three men laughed.

Ingrid leaped forward and clawed at Franco's face. "Don't hurt my son," she screamed.

Franco dropped his pick in pain, using both hands to ward off the crazed woman. Blood ran down his left cheek where her fingernails had dug in. He slapped her hard with the back of his right hand, stunning her. Then he shoved her with all his might.

Ingrid spun in a backward circle and collapsed in a corner, her back against the wall, blood dripping from her nose.

Enraged, Franco approached her. "You bitch!" he shouted, then kicked her in the ribs.

Ingrid screamed in pain.

Franco grabbed her outstretched legs and dragged her from the corner, her head bouncing on the floor. "You filthy whore!"

As he dragged her, Ingrid's skirt bunched above her waist, exposing her thighs and panties. Franco stopped when he reached the center of the room. "Hold her down," he ordered his two men, who rushed to immobilize her arms.

"I'll teach you to mess with me." He sat down on top of her and seized her throat with his massive hands. He leaned forward and squeezed. Her eyes bulged as he tightened his grip, choking the life from her.

He felt a sharp blow on his back and a searing pain burst into his lungs. His eyes widened in disbelief as he turned, his own pick buried deep in his body, to stare at the frightened boy. Wilhelm released the pick handle and stepped back, his mouth open.

Franco rose slowly, every movement an agony. The pick slowly rotated inside his chest, pressing against his exploding heart, as the weight of the handle sought the perpendicular. Standing on wobbly feet, the pick handle extending awkwardly from his back, he turned to the small retreating figure. His arms rose, rigid fingers curled in anger. He took an agonizing step toward Wilhelm. Then another.

The boy moved back into a corner, his body shaking, his face white with fear. Franco came closer, and with each step the steel point of the pick twisted in his back, digging into his heart. He extended his arms in a last effort to reach Wilhelm, and collapsed forward on the floor.

As Franco's two men stared in disbelief, Ramon burst into the room, followed by four armed policemen. The two supervisors threw up their hands.

Ramon fell to his knees alongside Ingrid. He carefully lifted her upper body, pressing her tight against him. She buried her face in his chest and sobbed.

"It's over now, Ingrid. It's all over," he whispered, rocking her gently back and forth. He felt Wilhelm's arms close around both Ingrid and him, pulling all three of them together.

Epilogue

Ocampo, Bolivia

May, 1943

A noise awakened her. It was the middle of the night and she needed her sleep. Maria Obregon had been ill for a long time now, forever it seemed. Always tired, her frail body grew lighter and more fragile each day.

She heard the drunken laugh of a man, followed by that of Segundina. Evidently he had knocked over a table in the darkness. She heard them talking in the next room, trying to keep their voices low without success. Then the bed began to squeak, first slowly, then more quickly. The man was grunting now. Like a pig, Maria thought.

It had been going on for years. After Don Simon died, Segundina had been fired and could not find work. One day she came home with a man, ordered her mother out of the room, and remained with him for thirty minutes. When the man left, Segundina had money. After that other men came frequently as the word spread. At first, when she was young, they were the merchants of the town, even the Police Sergeant, but now they were mainly unwashed farmers and passing truck drivers.

When Carlos began sending money from La Paz, Maria asked Segundina to stop, but she refused. She used her earnings to buy alcohol and cigarettes and lipstick, and a real bed. She didn't even stop when Carlos became President. Her father would have killed her, but he was dead. Maria was afraid to tell Carlos what was happening. Anyway, he had become inaccessible. He never wrote or visited them. Only the money.

After Carlos was killed - Maria made the sign of the cross and asked forgiveness - the money stopped. So Segundina continued her prostitution. Now she was older and fatter, heavily painted and sloppy from drink. And Maria was slowly dying, listening to the squeaks in the darkness.

She thought of the two men in her life. Of Luis, who had given her two children and had provided support until the day he died in the mines. Of Carlos, who had gone to the Chaco so innocent, and who had returned with such high hopes for changing his country. He had gone on to become President, the first Indian President, but she had seen no change in Ocampo. The farmers still rose before dawn, worked for the new landlord without pay three days a week, and chewed coca throughout the day. They were born on dirt floors, lived in poverty, and died in misery.

Maria was ready to die. She wanted to go now. She knew Luis would be waiting for her, they would hold hands again and her problems would cease. She was not sure about Carlos. He had led a different life. She closed her eyes, and the rhythmic squeaking faded away.

THE END

About the Author

Sidney Harris has spent most of his life working overseas, first in Latin America and then in Europe. His love for Latin America began at Princeton University, where he graduated in Latin American Area Studies. After service in the U.S. Army, he lived in Lima, Peru, and Mexico City, Mexico, for over fifteen years, traveling extensively throughout the region. He is fluent in Spanish and Italian.

He now lives in Dallas, Texas, and has written three novels: Eye of the Condor; A Picnic in Eden; and To Lima with Love, all of which have settings in Latin America. He is the winner of the Best Novel Award of the Greater Dallas Writers' Association and the Rose Trilogy Award for Most Publishable Novel. The prologue of Eye of the Condor was previously published in Book Marks, Brown Books, Dallas, Texas.

Printed in the United States
23836LVS00002B/31

9 781418 437541